ULTIMATE DC

Travel ■ Walk ■ Explore

KEN WILCOX

tdp ■ Tired Dogs Press

Ultimate DC
Travel - Walk - Explore

ISBN: 9780996225977
Library of Congress Control Number: 2026910657

Designed by Tired Dogs Press.
Photography by the author, except page 21 by Josh Fitzgerald, and pages 82 and 119 by Kris Wilcox. Maps by Creative Force Maps, OpenStreetMap (p. 6-7), and the author.

Front cover: U.S. Supreme Court
Back cover: M.L. King, Jr. Memorial, Adams Morgan, WWII Memorial, U.S. Capitol Dome, General Nathanael Greene, Marine Corps/Iwo Jima Memorial, C&O Canal barge Charles F. Mercer.

Visit Ken's blog on travel and trails:
www.kenwilcox.com

Disclaimer

<u>Use this guide at your own risk</u>! This guide provides only basic information to help you plan and enjoy your visit to the areas described. It assumes you have the ability to self-navigate, travel and walk safely in an urban environment. The author and publisher assume no responsibility for damages or injuries of any kind that might in any way be associated with the use of this guide. If you do not agree with this disclaimer, then you should not use this guide.

Dedicated to:

The National Park Service staff of the National Capital Region for looking after this fabulous place.

Contents

Tidal Basin sunset, National Mall.

Acknowledgements

I need to express a few thank-yous, first to the friends, associates and total strangers who provided insight and bits of info necessary to fill in the gaps, correct my errors and help shape this guide into what I hope is a useful resource for travelers and newcomers to Washington, D.C., or just "DC" as the locals call it. Thanks to my loving wife, Kris, for fixing my imperfections and tolerating endless detours to collect notes and photos when we were supposed to be headed elsewhere.

Big bear hugs to fellow Northwesterner and long-time mountain buddy, Bud Hardwick, for traveling thousands of miles to DC to join in my madness, manuscript in one hand, red pen a-blazin' in the other. His keen insight and contributions were substantial. Any remaining errors, of course, are entirely Bud's (except those following page 1).

Thanks, too, to my office pal and travel-advisor extraordinaire, Lee E., for often popping by with the scoop on a new place to visit, an experience to be had, outdoors or in, and not to be missed. And thanks to Rob H. for joining in the legwork and offering valuable suggestions for this new edition.

I also want to acknowledge the good work of the park rangers, interpreters and maintenance staff of the National Park Service, about to celebrate in 2026 the agency's 110th birthday. It's so easy to take their work for granted, yet DC would be in a complete shambles without them. Let's also thank the museum staff and volunteers of the Smithsonian Institution—and so many others! They do amazing work and are always generous in pointing the way and sharing information.

For all the anonymous conversations that revealed or confirmed a factoid or historical nugget, and for all the fine coffee shops with Wi-Fi and a comfy stool by the window, I'm grateful.

Summary of Walks

Around the National Mall	Miles	Hours	Kids/ADA*	Page
CENTRAL LOOP	3.7-4.1	2-4	❀❀/☼☼	42
EAST LOOP	4.1-5.2	3-4	❀❀/☼☼	58
WEST LOOP	4.0-6.0	3-4	❀❀/☼☼	76
GRAND LOOP (All 3 Combined)	12-14	6-12	❀/☼	92
More Sights & Walks	**Miles**	**Hours**	**Kids/ADA***	**Page**
River Loop & T. Roosevelt Is.	5.0-6.5	2-4	❀❀/☼	97
Georgetown Loop	1.6-3.8	1-3	❀/☼	105
Embassy Row	1-3-2.7	1-2	❀/☼☼	110
Dupont Circle to Adams Morgan	2.2	1-2	❀	115
Rock Creek Hiker-Biker Trail	2.7	2-3	❀/☼	118
Peirce Mill–Boulder Bridge	4.0-6.0	2-4	❀❀	119
Rapids–Rolling Meadow Loop	2.2-4.2	2-3	❀❀	122
National Zoo to Dupont Circle	3.3-4.8	2-4	❀❀	125
Chinatown to Dupont Circle	1.7	1-2	❀/☼☼	129
Old Downtown–Chinatown	2.0	1-2	❀/☼☼	132
Capitol Hill–Eastern Market	2.8	2-3	❀/☼☼	137
Anacostia Riverwalk	1.0-3.2	1-3	❀❀/☼☼	140
Potomac Heritage Trail	3.6-9.6	2-6	❀❀	144
Four Mile–Bluemont–Lubber Run	4.6-8.0	2-4	❀❀/☼	148
Old Town Alexandria	2.5	2-3	❀/☼☼	152
Old Town & Waterfront	1.6	1-2	❀❀/☼☼	156
MVT: DC–Old Town	3.3-6.7	2-4	❀/☼	161
MVT: Old Town–Dyke Marsh	2.8-7.8	2-4	❀❀/☼☼	165

*Good/very good (❀/❀❀) for kids. Good/very good (☼/☼☼) for wheelchairs and strollers.

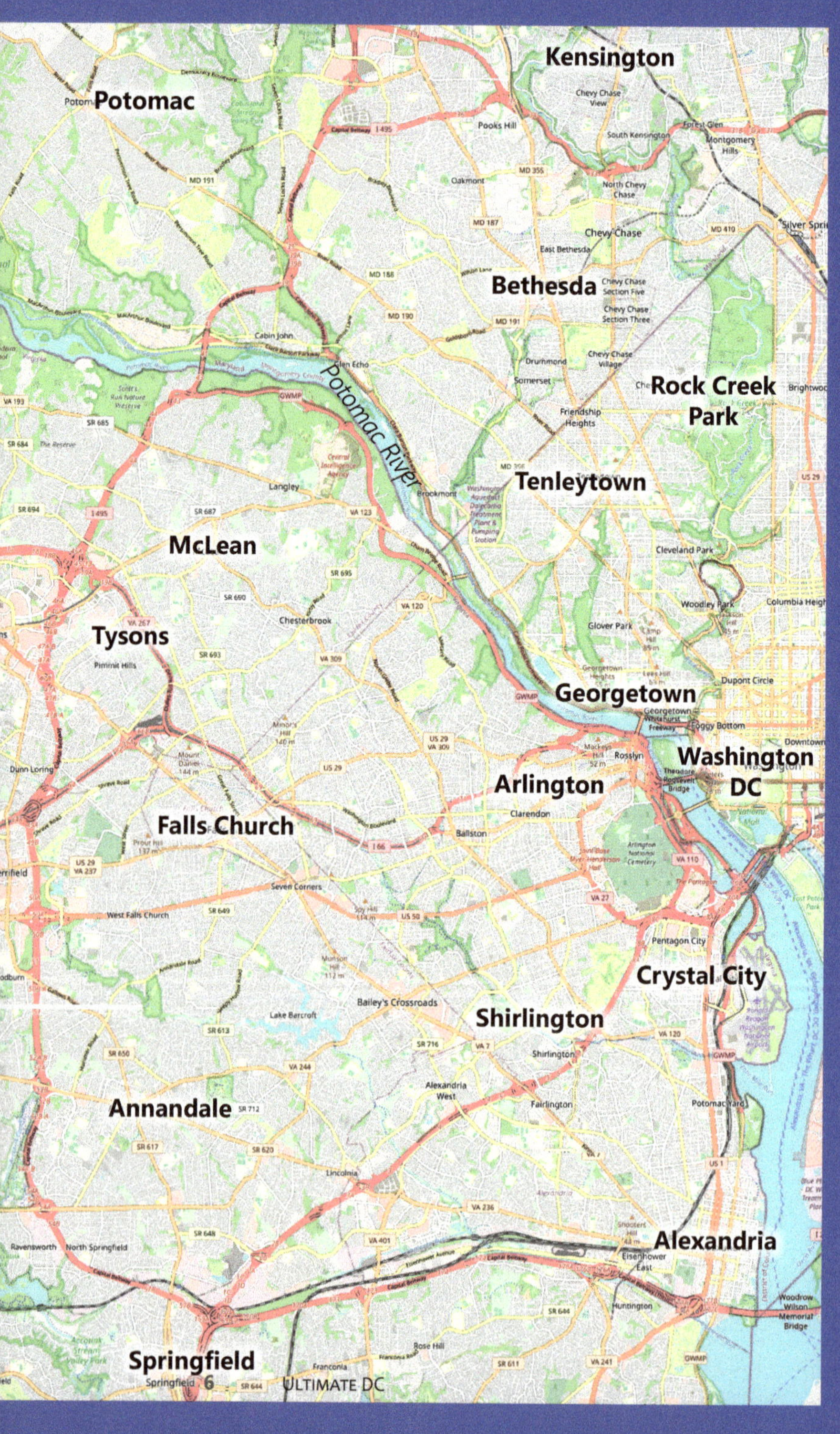
Kensington
Potomac
Bethesda
Rock Creek
Park
Potomac River
Tenleytown
McLean
Tysons
Georgetown
Washington
DC
Arlington
Falls Church
Crystal City
Shirlington
Annandale
Alexandria
Springfield

Map data from OpenStreetMap.org and Tracestrack Maps, May 2026.

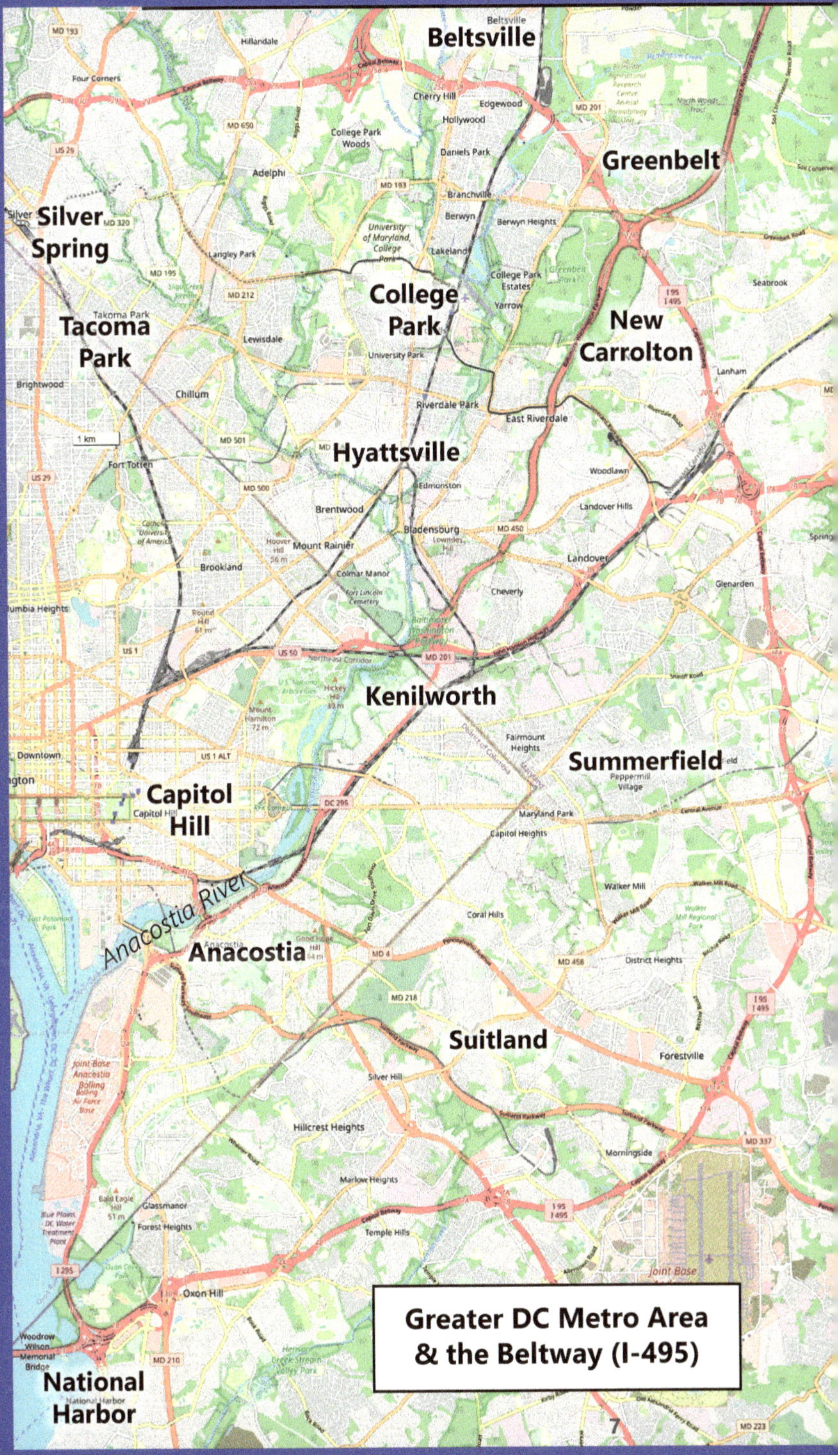

Beltsville

Greenbelt

Silver Spring

College Park

New Carrolton

Tacoma Park

Hyattsville

Kenilworth

Summerfield

Capitol Hill

Anacostia River

Anacostia

Suitland

National Harbor

Greater DC Metro Area & the Beltway (I-495)

Crossing Freedom Plaza.

Introduction

Welcome to Washington, DC! Whether you came here to visit or to make DC your new home, you'll find the American capital to be as rich in beauty, history, culture, diversity, imagination and good fun as any other world-class city.

It's no mystery that DC is a city of stunning monuments and memorials, iconic architecture, expansive parks, trails and gardens, outstanding museums and galleries, countless miles of scenic waterfront, and vignettes of American history seemingly hidden or commemorated under every rock and tree. Much of the grandeur here is spread across the **National Mall** and into the oldest parts of the city.

Somewhat less conspicuous are the countless connections to the people and cultural traditions from around the globe that have contributed immensely to the American story. A stroll around the National Mall, from one amazing landmark to the next, truly is a world-class experience.

Street vendor at Eastern Market, Capitol Hill.

But the good stuff doesn't stop there. Areas that loosely surround the Mall, like Capitol Hill, Chinatown, Dupont Circle, Embassy Row, Rock Creek Park, Georgetown, across the Potomac and Anacostia Rivers and beyond—areas I like to think of as the **National Nearby**—are also rich with sights and surprises that offer easy, fulfilling additions to any itinerary.

Together, the National Mall and "National Nearby" form the core of the American capital—and a perfect stomping ground for urban exploration. Getting around becomes super-efficient and hassle-free when you combine the city's modern Metro system with walking and biking. In fact, more than 90 miles' worth of carless exploration are described and mapped in this guide.

If you're new to DC or just gotta see it all, there's no better place to begin than by completing, in one big push or in bite-sized chunks, a 12-mile "grand loop" centered on downtown and the National Mall—something I've audaciously dubbed as a "National Jaunt."

Seriously, if we can have a National Zoo, National Cathedral, National Arboretum, National Symphony, National Airport, National Christmas Tree and a Nationals baseball team, why not, in this fabulous foot-friendly city, a National Jaunt?

Even if you mainly want to catch the best of the best, including all the major monuments, memorials, museums, iconic architecture, plazas, gardens, quaint neighborhoods and the rest, **Ultimate DC** captures it all, as well as many other lesser-known sights we might otherwise miss.

While the "Grand Loop" is an ambitious trek around the National Mall, it simply combines the three moderate loops so there's no need to knock out a half-marathon in a day. The point is to keep it fun and rewarding, not a chore. If you love to walk, the loops are well linked. And a few shortcuts

Martin Luther King, Jr. Memorial overlooking the Tidal Basin.

are described if you want to move on to the next fun thing. The options are described and mapped beginning on page 40.

This guide also weaves a web of interconnecting walks for exploring historic Georgetown, Capitol Hill or Old Town Alexandria just across the river; scenic saunters around Chinatown, Dupont Circle, Embassy Row, Adams Morgan and across Key Bridge into Arlington, Virginia; along the banks of the Potomac and Anacostia Rivers; on some wilder trails in Rock Creek Park and elsewhere; and several short scurries between Metro stations (the DC subway). The Metro system is almost always the quickest and easiest way to get around the city. (*See* **Getting Around DC** *on p. 25.)*

Given so many choices, the harder part may be deciding where to begin, which is really what this book is about. An "Ideal Scenario" for a 2 or 3-day visit focused on the National Mall is suggested on p. 19. Or just browse all the walks listed, choose one and see where it takes you!

As explained later, the Navy Memorial on Pennsylvania Avenue—"America's Main Street"—offers an optimal starting point for exploring both the National Mall and the heart of downtown DC.

Residents and new arrivals to DC might enjoy walking (or biking) each route over a season or two, to become better acquainted with the geography of this extraordinary city. DC, after all, is about much more than monuments and politics.

First-time visitors, on the other hand, could spend their days aimlessly running around the Mall, arms waving, screaming for joy. Once you catch your breath and ease off on the throttle a little, you can begin to get a better sense of it all, and maybe, by completing one or more of the loops decribed, see what you missed the first time. See also **Tips for First-time Visitors** on p. 32.

If you love the outdoors and go giddy like I do discovering new places, then I hope this guide helps you engineer a footloose frenzy of your own in DC's eminently walkable outdoors.

—Ken Wilcox

The First 100 Years

The American capital of Washington, D.C., truly is an extraordinary city, and the curious traveler who visits for more than a day or two is almost assured of taking home a bucket full of happy memories. Of course, it hasn't always been that way.

In precolonial times, the region surrounding today's DC was the domain of more than a dozen Algonquian tribes who more or less shared a common language. Native villages were known to exist along the Anacostia River (the Anacostans) and along both shores of the Potomac River, including a place that would later be known as George Town.

Like so many other regions across the Americas, native people's lives would be upended, or worse, in every way imaginable. Tribes were decimated by disease, war and even forced removal during the early slave trade, as colonists from Europe began moving into the region in the mid-1600s. The struggle intensified as the first tobacco plantations became established in the Maryland and Virginia British Colonies.

With the new arrivals came a great deal of conflict, not just between natives and settlers, but among the settlers themselves, who also unwittingly delivered the misery of alien diseases to the native population. Some tribes disappeared entirely. Others like the Rappahannock survived these calamities, but were largely forced to seek safer harbors elsewhere. Yet even today, several thousand indigenous Americans live in the greater DC area. Many continue their cultural traditions on their own lands or immersed in society at large.

When Americans declared their independence from Britain in 1776, Georgetown and Alexandria were already bustling tobacco ports reliant on slave labor forcibly imported from West Africa. But there was no Washington, D.C. then. In fact, much of the land that would later become the iconic National Mall was river bottom and swamp or marsh land leading eastward to a rise of dry ground that one day would be called Capitol Hill.

In 1790, Congress granted President George Washington the task of locating a capital city within a new Fed-

A likely river scene before there was any notion of a Washington, DC.

eral District, up to ten miles square, somewhere on the Potomac River. He naturally chose his familiar stomping grounds around Alexandria, Virginia, a little north of his family estate at Mount Vernon.

The site had much going for it. It spanned both sides of the Anacostia and Potomac Rivers and included the two port towns and several other waterways near the Potomac River's limit of navigation (and tidal influence). It was also located well inland from Chesapeake Bay and the Atlantic Ocean, which offered relative protection from sea marauders and British invaders, or so it seemed.

The district's first cornerstone was laid in 1791 at the site of the future Jones Point Lighthouse just south of Old Town Alexandria. The boundary was surveyed in the shape of a diamond and marked with a heavy stone at every mile. The district was called *Columbia*, an early colloquial name for America. The commission assigned to create the new capital decided to name the city itself after the first president.

Washington hired the French-born, New York architect Pierre Charles L'Enfant to lead the design of the city. Thomas Jefferson helped supervise the work, while also seeking to rein in L'Enfant's exuberance for a grand and sprawling capital.

According to L'Enfant's plan, "Congress House" would connect to the "President's House" by way of a broad avenue named for Pennsylvania. A standard street grid would be enhanced with diagonal avenues named for other states, crossing at circles and squares that could host parks, plazas and monuments to remember our heroes.

L'Enfant also envisioned a 400-foot wide, mile-long boulevard lined with trim gardens extending west from Congress House. Someone would later refer to that space as the "Mall."

Only a year into his work, L'Enfant was fired. He'd been too pushy with his big ideas, and though many of them

Pierre L'Enfant's 1791 "Plan of the City."

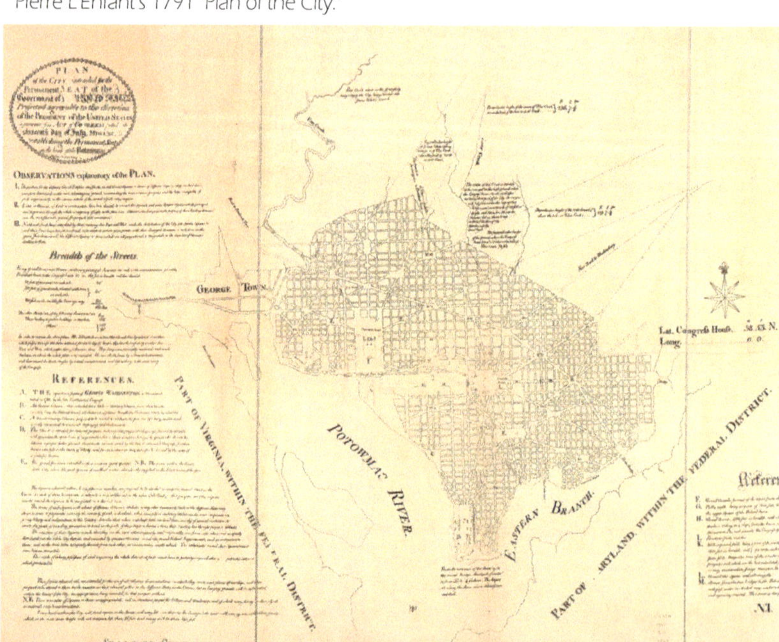

Smithsonian Castle.

stuck, he'd managed to alienate both the commission and the president. It was a messy breakup and Pierre (or Peter, as he might have called himself) struggled for years just to get paid for his work. Congress eventually relented and gave him a meager stipend to get him out of their hair.

George Washington, meanwhile, retired to Mount Vernon, passed the presidential baton to John Adams in 1797, then passed away suddenly in December 1799 after a short illness and dubious medical care. The White House was nearly complete and the Adams family moved in the following autumn. The north wing of the Capitol (Congress House) was finished the same year. The south wing, joined to the other by a wooden structure, would take another decade to complete.

With the White House and Capitol now occupied and standing like lonely outliers on an oil canvas, the British set them afire in 1814. They were soon rebuilt, however, and in the 1820s, a center section and small dome were added to the Capitol. In 1855, nearly a mile to the west, a second highly symbolic structure, the Smithsonian Castle, would add its marvelous footprint to the future of the city.

From a humble and tested beginning, DC grew rapidly during and after the Civil War to end slavery. In 1862, with President Lincoln's support, Congress freed all slaves in DC, nine months ahead of the Emancipation Proclamation. These factors combined led to rapid growth of the city. In 1876, an old cobblestone street named for Pennsylvania was paved in asphalt, as if to solidify DC's road to the future as the nation's center of power, if not the world's. And there would be no turning back.

Inscription at Freedom Plaza.

THE NATIONAL MALL

The National Mall is one of those iconic landscapes that helps define America. It's been called "America's front yard," where we come to honor, celebrate or raise hell about the things we care about. We listen to music and fly our kites here, and pay tribute to our heroes and others who've passed. We mark time and history with our monuments, and enrich ourselves and coming generations with trees, gardens and world-class galleries and museums.

But like the city that surrounds it, ithe National Mall has been a work in progress for over two hundred years, and it remains so today.

In 1835, President Andrew Jackson received word that an English fellow named Smithson, an unmarried scientist, had left his fortune—about $12 million in today's dollars—to the people of the United States. According to the will, the money was to be used for "the increase and diffusion of knowledge." An institution was formed and its members haggled over how to spend the cash.

Other than some limited parks and gardens, little more had been done to implement L'Enfant's vision for the Mall until 1848, when the cornerstone was laid for a ginormous monument to George Washington. Ironically, L'Enfant had suggested only a modest pedestal with a sculpture of George on a horse. The obelisk was barely a third finished when funding ran out in 1854.

The Smithson money, however, had found a lasting purpose. By 1855, the Smithsonian Castle was completed, thanks to the magnanimous generosity of the bachelor scientist. The Castle rekindled some of the L'Enfant enthusiasm for grandeur and set the stage for the veritable parade of palatial buildings lining the Mall today, including 11 of the Smithsonian's 19 museums and galleries.

The Capitol Building was also expanded north and south, and the original dome, which now looked rather puny on such a big building, was replaced by a much larger dome. In December 1863, with much fanfare and in the midst of a Civil War, the 7.5-ton statue of Lady Freedom was hoisted by former slaves to the top of the cast iron dome. Just months earlier, President Lincoln had signed the law ending slavery in the capital. This while thousands of Union soldiers camped on the Mall before the war ended in 1865.

With the ever-popular Castle filled to the brim with exhibits and visitors, the Smithsonian's National Museum (now the Arts and Industries Building) was built to relieve the pressure and was completed in 1881. Seven years later, the Washington Monument was finally finished.

Also in the 1880s, the Potomac River was dredged for improved navigation

Freedom atop the Capitol Dome.

and to fill a vast area of mosquito-laden wetlands adjacent to the city. That ambitious project created more than a square mile of dry land between Washington Monument and the river bank we see today. The Tidal Basin came 20 years later. Up on Capitol Hill, the spectacular Jefferson Building of the Library of Congress opened in 1897.

By 1900, the U.S. had indeed emerged as a major world power, with DC at the center of it all. A great city should also look like one, some insisted, rather than the partly glorious, partly ramshackled place that it was. Many residents and members of Congress were eager to see more rapid progress and renewal, especially around the Mall.

Modern times and a multitude of ideas warranted a fresh assessment of the possibilities. A Senate Park Commission, sponsored by Michigan Senator James McMillan, was assigned the task in 1901. Commission members spent six weeks in European cities gathering ideas before coalescing around a new vision.

Completed in 1902, the McMillan Plan recommended an expanded Mall with more natural landscaping, sprawling lawns, hundreds of trees, major monuments, reflecting pools, prominent museums and stylish government buildings. It called for the removal of rail lines and tackier commercial structures that had cropped up over the years, and relocation of the train station to a proposed new Union Station. The Plan also envisioned new parks elsewhere around the city, plus major parkways along Rock Creek and the Virginia side of the Potomac River, reached by a new Memorial Bridge across the river.

Pierre L'Enfant must have sat up in his grave in awe. His grandiose vision for the city had at last garnered some posthumous respect. The details would be substantially modified and the scope broadened, now that the dry land around the Mall had grown considerably, but the late architect's central concepts remained. In 1908, L'Enfant's body was exhumed from a grave in Chillum, Maryland, so he could be reinterred as a national hero at Arlington National Cemetery.

Despite deep disagreements over the enormous cost to implement the McMillan Plan, the construction of Union Station was the first major project to be authorized. It was completed in 1907. The U.S. Department of Agriculture's regal building on Jefferson Dr. followed in 1908, then the Smithsonian Museum of Natural History in 1911. In 1912, 3,000 cherry trees, a gift from Japan, were planted around the Tidal Basin. The Lincoln Memorial, begun in 1914, was finally finished in 1922.

Smithsonian Museum of Natural History.

Inside the Library of Congress.

The new U.S. Supreme Court building, crafted with marble from Spain, Italy, Georgia, Vermont and Alabama, opened in 1935. In 1938, FDR attended the groundbreaking for the Thomas Jefferson Memorial. In subsequent years, other monuments, sculptures, museums, galleries and government buildings joined the parade, along with the parkways, Memorial Bridge and the greater city that surrounds them.

Over the past century, much of what we see today has blossomed from the vision of those who kept the L'Enfant and McMillan fires burning. Though we may have differed at times on the finer details and squabbled over what to leave natural and what to put where—the statues, fountains, gardens, the newer museums, monuments and memorials—most of the parts do seem to complement the whole quite swimmingly.

That's not to say there aren't challenges. The landscape and many of the monuments and public facilities within the National Mall were not designed to handle such heavy use by millions of visitors, including very large (and wonderful) outdoor events that have been occurring regularly now for years.

To consider ways to preserve what we love about the Mall while accommodating such high use, the National Park Service embarked on a major planning effort in 2006. This work resulted in the *2010 National Mall Plan* (**npshistory.com/publications/nama**). The plan's

Potomac River and Thomas Jefferson Memorial from Washington Monument.

purpose is to allow the Mall to:

> *". . . evolve as the nation's premier civic, symbolic, historic, and commemorative space.... respectfully rehabilitated and refurbished, with improvements to the pedestrian environment.... so that the needs of all visitors can be met in an attractive, high-quality, energy-efficient, and sustainable manner.... while respecting the planned historic character and visions of the L'Enfant and McMillan plans."*

Many improvements have been made since that time, with more ongoing for many years. Some changes will be minor, such as better (and more) restrooms, improved sitting, viewing and exhibit areas, refurbished lawns and gardens, better lighting, separated bike paths and improved surfacing along walkways. But more conspicuous and ambitious changes are also envisioned, including a much smaller reflecting pool below the Capitol Building, with more hard surfacing and restrooms to accommodate larger gatherings without damaging so much turf.

A new indoor/outdoor performance venue is planned near the Washington Monument (where the Sylvan Theater is now), along with a major visitor facility at the east end of Constitution Gardens. A new welcome plaza was proposed near the Smithsonian Metro Station, new horse stables for the U.S. Park Police (completed in 2023), and continuing upgrades to the seawall around the Tidal Basin and along the shore of the Potomac River.

Some of these projects are being carried out in partnership with the **Trust for the National Mall**, a nonprofit entity established in 2007 to help raise the $350 million needed to implement the plan (**nationalmall.org**). The Trust has been a pivotal force in restoring the Reflecting Pool at Lincoln Memorial and the seawall at Jefferson Memorial, as well as repairing earthquake damage to Washington Monument and installing acres of new and improved turf west of the Capitol.

While much has been accomplished already by the Park Service and the Trust, visitors will soon notice other changes as well, not all of them without controversy. Most of the projects seem reasonable and sensitively designed, although opinions on that may vary.

For example, some observers (including the author) are not particularly fond of a proposed design for rehabilitating Constitution Gardens. While it's all well intended, plans have included an oversized, odd-looking rectangular structure that would seem to crowd the east end of the pond, altering a part of the area's unique, natural ambience and what is now a sublime view of Washington Monument (*see p. 88*). A hefty structure would seem to contribute little to surrounding architecture or the American story. On the bright side, today's designers are getting very good at innovative

Constitution Gardens.

solutions for sensitive sites.

Apart from the 2010 National Mall Plan, a striking, African American Museum of History and Culture, adjacent to the American History Museum, opened in the fall of 2016. A spacious new Dwight D. Eisenhower Memorial opened in 2020 behind the Air and Space Museum at 4th St. SW and Independence Ave. Other memorials are also being contemplated, but they are typically spearheaded by separate entities and not the Park Service. They also tend not to be part of a current, overarching vision for the Mall, which, oddly enough, doesn't actually exist.

Taking another view on the challenges facing the Mall is the **National Mall Coalition** (**nationalmallcoalition.org**), which has pointed out not only the absence of a common vision among multiple interests and jurisdictions, but also the lack of a clear definition of where the Mall's boundaries are. They argue that too much of the planning and site improvements around the Mall and nearby areas along the Potomac River are being done piecemeal by the various agencies and institutions, without a holistic vision of the Mall's future.

To develop that more unified vision, the Coalition believes it's time to establish, in the third century of the National Mall, a new independent commission, akin to that of McMillan in 1902. The idea has gained some traction, but requires an act of Congress to get rolling. In the meantime, the Coalition seeks to provide a voice for citizens and advocates for preserving what we love about the Mall and adhering to the L'Enfant and McMillan visions, while also thinking out of the box a little to address evolving needs and concerns.

East Potomac Park. Is it part of the Mall?

The Coalition strongly supports, for example, putting a substantial share of parking (including buses) underground and expanding the Mall outwardly, particularly to the south, to encompass other surrounding greenspaces. A thoughtful expansion of the Mall could, in fact, provide a comparable sense of natural open space, while also includ-

National Museum of African American History and Culture, styled after the three-tiered Yoruban crown of West Africa.

ing suitable sites for future museums, monuments and public events that don't overly stress the limited space we currently regard as the Mall. For example, the broad L'Enfant Promenade, from the Smithsonian Castle to the Benjamin Banneker Overlook (beyond the Spy Museum), would seem to offer a perfect extension of the Mall to the Southwest Waterfront.

A new commission could nurture consensus for these and other initiatives, large and small. It certainly makes sense to this writer that we at least try to understand in a clear way what we really have here and how we can sustain it through the generations.

Regardless of our own personal sentiments about what the Mall should or shouldn't be, it's a good thing that so many are even thinking about it. It's an awesome place. Now, more than two centuries since Pierre L'Enfant thunk up the original idea, the National Mall has not only become integral to our mind's image of the nation's capital, it embodies much of the collective spirit of who we are as Americans, and we wouldn't be the same without it.

The National Mall: Where to Begin?

The major focus of this guide, of course, is the National Mall. It's a big place—over two miles long and up to a half mile wide! And all the great sights are spread around the entire Mall. Happily, there are just a few gentle hills, and virtually the entire Mall is kid-friendly and ADA-accessible.

As noted in the Introduction, the Mall can be enjoyed quite nicely by walking one or all three loops—Central, East and West—as noted below. Or you can easily combine all three into a single 12 to 14-mile Grand Loop, for those with the extra umph to see it all in a day or two.

As described later, a favorite starting point for the Central and East Loops is at the U.S. Navy Memorial on Pennsylvania Ave. at 7th St. NW (*see pp. 43, 59 and 77*). It's centrally located, close to many major sights (and coffee shops), and right next door to a Metro station. For the West Loop, the Smithsonian Metro Station works well to access the Washington Monument, as does Bikeshare. All three loops are uniquely rewarding. Detailed descriptions, directions and maps begin on p. 43.

The ideal 2 or 3-day scenario?

Central Loop- Do this 3.7-mile walk in the morning and visit one or more museums and galleries along the way. If you're an early bird and lucky enough to get a timed entry to the Washington Monument, schedule your walk around that. (*See p. 77.*)

East Loop- Do this 4.1-mile loop in the morning and visit one or more museums or galleries in the afternoon. Schedule a timed-entry to the Air and Space Museum or a tour of the U.S. Capitol (or both), and begin your walk at least an hour beforehand. Enjoy the museum and/or tour of the Capitol, then complete the loop.

West Loop - This 4.0-mile loop is where most of the major memorials are—Jefferson, FDR, King, Lincoln and the veterans memorials. The loop begins and ends at the Washington Monument. It can be done anytime, but early morning or late afternoon and into the evening are pretty special, especially for photography.

Looking East to the U.S. Capitol

THE NATIONAL MALL

Looking West to Lincoln Memorial

FROM WASHINGTON MONUMENT

The National Nearby

With all the jaw-dropping sights and picturesque greenspace that define the National Mall, it might seem a little odd to ask what else there is to see in DC. But zoom out from the Mall and the walking spaces expand exponentially—from bustling Chinatown, Dupont Circle and Georgetown, to the architectural gems of Embassy Row and Old Downtown, and from the artful quarters of Adams Morgan, U Street, Barracks Row and Eastern Market, to the spacious, green corridors at Rock Creek Park and along the Potomac and Anacostia Rivers.

The **National Nearby** really knows no bounds, and much good sauntering awaits, none of which requires a car to access. On the Virginia side of the Potomac River, the Metro will take you from downtown DC to Arlington in ten minutes and historic Old Town Alexandria in 20, or a scenic water-taxi ride a bit longer. Or you can bike or strut across the river to reach the Mount Vernon Trail for more good walking (and cycling), or to explore the native forest and wetlands of **Theodore Roosevelt Island**. Dozens of outstanding monuments and memorials from Arlington to Alexandria can also be easily reached on foot.

Author and editor about to ride the Mount Vernon Trail.

Upriver, the **Chesapeake and Ohio (C&O) Canal Towpath** leads from Georgetown across Maryland almost to Pennsylvania. A stretch through Great Falls (National) Park is among the best, though it's a drive or bike ride to get there. Extensive trails follow tributaries of the Anacostia River and other waterways around the city, while the **Capital Crescent Trail** connects Georgetown to Bethesda and Chevy Chase.

Although **Ultimate DC** is mostly focused on the urban core and more immediate surroundings, there's a wealth of good hiking trails within an hour or two's drive of DC. Shenandoah National Park is a prime example with more than 500 miles of trails, including more than 100 miles of the Appalachian National Scenic Trail, or A.T. as the locals call it. Several great guidebooks by others provide the added details.

Miller Cabin, Rock Creek Park.

On Embassy Row.

Newcomers to DC looking to see the sights will enjoy the biggest bang for the buck by hiking all or part of the **Grand Loop** around the National Mall. But once you've experienced this introduction to the capital city, other jaunts in the National Nearby will, in many ways, leave you with a more genuine sense of what the city is about. Recent arrivals wanting to get better acquainted with this greater metropolitan area can begin by exploring some of the 18 additional routes described on p. 95 through 167. You'll not only begin to make sense of the geography, you might even have a nice time doing it.

"It is sometimes called the City of Magnificent Distance, but it might with greater propriety be termed the City of Magnificent Intentions."
—Charles Dickens, 1842

Destination DC

With a DC population above 700,000 and nearby Maryland and Virginia boosting the total metro area to almost six million, it's good we all aren't driving cars everywhere. Especially during the commute, when several hundred thousand Virginians and Marylanders head into DC each work day. A good share of them are riding the Metro (subway). Amazingly, another 24 million visitors from afar find their way into DC annually.

Counting visitors and residents, the National Mall sees 25-30 million visits a year. An astounding 15 million (including repeat customers), walk through the doors of the Smithsonian museums—fortunately, not all at once.

Thanks to the early work and big ideas of Pierre Charles L'Enfant, the master designer of our spacious U.S. capital, there's plenty of room to roam, both within and around the Mall.

That said, some of the Smithsonian museums and other sights can be quite crowded from spring through early fall. Thus timed entrance passes are required at some locations to help smooth the flow of so many people. **Timed-entry** tickets are either required or recommended at the following.

Smithsonian museums:

Air & Space
African American History & Culture
National Zoo

Government facilities:

U.S. Capitol
Library of Congress
National Archives
Bureau of Engraving & Printing
Washington Monument
Holocaust Memorial Museum

If you visit during the colder months (October through February), you'll likely have all the elbow room you need. Whenever you visit, you can find a trove of travel information at **washington.org**.

DC is an exceptionally diverse and energized international hub for business, education, the arts, government, skilled labor, and of course, tourism. One might presume politics has a role as well. The DC government website (**dc.gov**) is a go-to source for information on the laws, economy, demographics, arts, culture, recreation, schools and more.

While the people of DC may be, for the most part, liberal-leaning and politically astute, everyday life in the District—going to work, school, daycare, a picnic in the park, the movies, a ball game, a walk, a libation on the porch—is really no different than in any other major city.

DCers get their news from the same sources as everyone else. The "crazy politics" we see on TV is the stuff that happens inside the Capitol Building or behind a podium somewhere, not so much in the streets. Unless there's a protest. Then DC is decidely Protest Central. From a small pop-up rally to a half-million-strong national march, DC is no stranger to Americans determined to share their views, whatever the cause.

DC Statehood

Speaking of good causes, you may notice that the license tags on nearly every vehicle in DC includes the phrase, "End Taxation Without Representation." If it sounds familiar, it may be because Americans fought a revolutionary war on similar grounds.

Because DC is not a state, it does not have a voting member of Congress, which means those 700,000 Americans living in DC have no one to vote on their behalf, whether it's taxes or any other federal law or policy enacted by Congress. They are, in a word, disenfranchised, without the same rights that all other Americans enjoy.

Congress could rectify this almost overnight by a simple majority vote to establish DC as the 51st state of the union. And rather than continue referring to DC as the District of Columbia, advocates of statehood propose it be named the **Douglass Commonwealth** (still "**DC**"), in honor of one of its most illustrious citizens, Frederick Douglass. He was not only a statesman, orator, author, abolitionist, former slave and civil rights leader in the 1800s, he lived in DC. His home at Cedar Hill in Anacostia is a National Historic Site you can visit (*see p. 181*).

More info: **dcvote.org**.

Constitution Gardens, National Mall.

Getting Around DC

Once you've landed in DC, there are any number of ways to get your itchy feet into the metropolis, to the Mall, or wherever your travel takes you. If you arrived by air, then buses, shuttles, taxi, rideshare, Metrorail (**wmata.com**), MARC Train or rental car will take you into the city, depending on the airport.

From the Airports

From National Airport (DCA), the Metrorail (subway) Yellow Line offers the quickest service into downtown DC, literally just 10 minutes away. As of 2022, the Metro also now serves Dulles Airport (IAD), although it's farther afield and takes closer to an hour to ride to or from downtown via the Silver Line. It costs just a few bucks. From the Baltimore-Washington Airport (BWI), many rely on the MARC commuter train (**mta.maryland.gov/schedule/marc-penn**) to and from Union Station. It's fast, frequent and also costs just a few dollars. Research their websites for latest fares, schedules and station locations. Airport signs also point the way.

A SmarTrip card is handy for the Metro fare, but you can also just tap a credit or debit card at the turnstyle and the correct fare will be charged automatically. Taxi and rideshare can be arranged on arrival at the airport. These and traditional airport shuttles are pricier, but also convenient.

DC by Car or Public Transit?

If you came to DC by car and plan to see the sights, you'll do well to leave your vehicle at the hotel or at long-term parking or a regional park-and-ride lot (if permissable). Unless you know your way around the city, driving in DC's big-city traffic can be stressful and confusing for newbies, with traffic circles and diagonal avenues going every which way. A few highways can have steep tolls, $20 or more, during busier commute times.

Union Station.

If your game plan is to visit the monuments, museums, galleries and the like, parking anywhere close by can be difficult, since there is often far more demand than spaces to park. Odds are better early and late. To see the sights, you'll need to do a fair bit of walking regardless. All major sites are also ADA-accessible, with some reserved parking for those with a disability tag or placard.

To avoid the traffic snarls and parking

nightmares, think public transit, which in DC is quite excellent overall. Despite a few minor quirks, it's hard to beat the price and convenience of DC's modern **Metrorail** subway system. Stations downtown and near the Mall will get you close to the fun stuff (*more below*).

The National Mall, however, is over two miles long, and all the great places to visit are scattered throughout. While it's a veritable paradise for avid footsters, you can ease things a bit by taking advantage of the many **Capital Bikeshare** stations that surround the area, or by snagging an **e-scooter** if that's your thing. Or consider the **hop-on, hop-off buses** which typically stop at all the right places.

DC by Metro

Fast and frequent Metro trains serve nearly 100 stations around the region, mostly underground in the downtown area, with tracks rising to the surface in the outlying areas. Trains run early and late, especially on Friday and Saturday nights. A typical fare is below $3, with day and multi-day passes also available. There's no schedule to worry about, since the trains run so often. Just enter a station, tap your SmarTrip or credit card at the turnstyle and hop on the next train going your way. Then tap out as you leave.

Gallery Place/Chinatown Metro Station.

The trains are referred to by color: Red Line, Blue Line, Green Line, etc. Direction is indicated by the last station in each direction. Maps are posted around stations and on the trains, as well as online. You can snag a paper map at the station. To get from where you are to where you want to be, just follow the signs for the end stations along your route.

Elevators and escalators, including some of the longest in the world, run from ground level to the platforms. Many will walk up or down the moving escalators. So the general rule is to stand right, walk left. And keep your bags and kids in front of you. Bikes, wheelchairs and strollers should use the elevator.

On the platform, stay back from the edge (*duh*). A fall could be deadly. The "third rail" is high voltage and trains often enter the stations at high speed. Be sure to stand aside so people can exit the train before trying to board. Then board quickly and hang onto your kids. Often the doors will close after just thirty seconds or less. They aren't like elevator doors, so don't try to hold them open (see *If you get separated* on the next page). In case of emergency, look for the intercom button in the car or on the platform.

If you find yourself on a crowded platform downtown during rush hour, there's no need to fret about squeezing onto a full train. Chances are a half-empty one will arrive within a couple of minutes. On the other hand, if it's after 7:00 pm or a sports event has just ended, you might want to join the crowd, due to longer wait times at night. If you happen to get on the wrong train or miss your stop, just get off at the next stop, reverse your direction and discombobulate accordingly. Note also that track and equipment upgrades or repairs often occur evenings and weekends, which can cause brief (or longer) delays.

All listed walks in town can be reached by Metrorail or Metrobus, some more readily than others. Route descriptions and maps are included in this guide to help you find the nearest Metro stations.

For points between Washington Monument and the U.S. Capitol, Metro stations are conveniently located at National Archives/Navy Memorial, Federal Triangle, Smithsonian and L'Enfant Plaza. West of the Washington Monument (toward Lincoln Memorial) and around the Tidal Basin, stations are not so handy.

The Metrobus system (also **wmata.com**) is great for downtown, outlying areas and for shorter rides in areas less convenient to a Metro station. Georgetown, for example, has no Metro station, so many rely on frequent buses along Pennsylvania and Wisconsin Avenues to get around.

At the National Mall, buses stop at just a few locations. Most will simply walk to

If You Get Separated

- When a party of grownups gets separated, common sense usually kicks in and all find a way to reunite. If kids are involved (or someone who depends on your assistance), then it's worth having a plan in place beforehand. Pick a spot, perhaps a prominent nearby landmark or your next or last destination, and agree to meet there. Write down cell phone numbers in case yours dies and you need to borrow one to make a call.

- It's especially important that kids know how to find lost parents in a big, scary city. In case there's any doubt, it's always okay to call **911** to report a lost parent or child or other emergency. If the circumstances are Metro-related, call the Metro Transit Police at **(202) 962-2121**. Cell service is now widely available in Metro stations and on the trains, even in the tunnels.

- On the Metro, there's a pretty simple solution to getting separated. If you got on the train and the door closed before the rest of your party could board (it does happen). Just get off the train at the next stop and stay put. Those who were left behind can board the next train from the same position on the platform. When they arrive at the next station a few minutes after you, voila! You'll be right there waiting for them. Beware, though, that if you stepped off toward the back end of an eight-car train and your friends boarded a six-car train, you may need to hustle up the platform to find them.

- If a kid gets left behind, the same strategy may work for the older ones, but for younger kids, here's where I would immediately use the emergency intercom button to explain the situation to the conductor. If the train hasn't left, they can reopen the door, or work with you and other Metro staff to help get you reunited. Be sure the kids (and adults) know what to do in the event of an unplanned separation.

the Mall from the Metro stations above, which might take 5 or 10 minutes, rather than wait 5 or 10 minutes for a bus to come by. Friendly bus drivers will generally help you find your way.

Scheduled or private tours and hop-on, hop-off buses also offer excellent means of getting introduced to the city and the sights. Look for their kiosks inside Union Station and elsewhere, or search online.

Other than Metro, taxi and ride-share service is prolific downtown and around the Mall. Rates are controlled by the city and many accept bank cards. Pedicabs are fun for short jaunts, while water taxis will shuttle you across the river to or from Georgetown, Old Town Alexandria and National Harbor. Segway tours are also common and easy to learn for most newbies. Guides are knowledgeable and many also lead bike tours. Book online or with a smartphone app.

DC by Bike

Exploring DC by bicycle is an awesome way to see the sights inside or outside the Beltway. A growing web of dedicated bike paths and bikelanes offer hundreds of miles of good riding, including many paths around the Mall, in Rock Creek Park, into Maryland and Northern Virginia and along the major waterways. For in-city routes, look for the free *DC Bike Map* at bike shops and visitor info kiosks, or find it online at **ddot.dc.gov/page/bicycle-maps**.

DC seems to get even more bike-friendly every year. You certainly can't miss all the Capital Bikeshare stations around the city. Called bike docks, there are now more than 800 of them in the metro area hosting thousands of individual step-through bikes, including e-bikes.

You can quickly grab a ride with the super-easy-to-use smartphone app from **capitalbikeshare.com**. The website explains how it works. In 2026, a $10 day pass was good for unlimited 45-minute bike rides (or $0.15 per minute for an ebike).

The bikes may look a little clunky, but they are quite ridable for old pros and beginners alike (age 16 or older). The seat is adjustable, the brakes are solid and shifting gears is a breeze.

The red and black bikes have become seriously popular with DCers for short-hops around the city. But take note that they are really meant for very short-term use, say 45 minutes or less at a time. If you keep a bike for hours, be prepared to pay up the nose. But for quick trips between museums, events, Metro stations, night spots and the like, Capital Bikeshare is a great solution. Helmets are recommended, though you'll need to provide your own.

If you want to cruise for more than a couple of hours, you can rent a quality bike from local bike shops or other rental outfits (seach online).

For longer rides, excellent off-street touring on paved paths can be found on the Mount Vernon Trail (18 miles), Capital Crescent (13 miles), Rock Creek trails (varied lengths), Custis Trail (4 miles and hilly), Washington and Old Dominion (W&OD) Trail (45 miles), Four Mile Run Trail (7 miles), Sligo Creek Trail (10 miles), Anacostia Riverwalk (20+ miles), C&O Canal Towpath (184 miles, mostly unpaved) and others.

If you choose one ride, the family-friendly Mount Vernon Trail, maintained by the National Park Service, is among the best, with easy access from Georgetown's Key Bridge, Lincoln Memorial via Memorial Bridge, Thomas

Lovely day for a ride. Bikeshare dock near Lincoln Memorial.

Jefferson Memorial via the I-395 bridge, or from the riverfront in Old Town Alexandria (*see p. 160*).

You can also reach the trail from the Rosslyn, Arlington Cemetery or Crystal City Metro Stations. Bikes are allowed on Metro trains, but no more than four per car and not inside the middle doors. Expect a few busy, but generally easy, road crossings along most routes.

At Rock Creek Park, portions of Beach Dr. are closed to cars, making the park exceptionally bike-friendly. (*See also* **nps.gov/rocr**.)

Walkable DC

Fortunately, Washington, DC, is also a highly walkable city. In fact, it's consistently rated as one of the most pedestrian-friendly cities in America. More than a third of DC households don't even own a car. It helps that the setting is magnificent and the Metro stations are nicely spaced. Wander a bit, hop on and off the Metro, or snag a bike from one of over 800 Capital Bikeshare stations, and you'll soon notice how easy and enjoyable it is to move around the city with two feet. It doesn't matter much whether you amble, ramble, strut, stroll or gavot, DC is one of those places where it just feels good to be upright and mobile.

In the greater Metro area, you'll generally find comfortably wide sidewalks, pleasant surroundings and a cool city vibe from downtown or uptown to Georgetown and Old Town, with sufficient wads of greenspace, plazas, sculptures, statues, fountains, historical sites, murals, contemporary urban art and stunning architecture scattered throughout. Barrier-free facilities are commonplace and obstructions can be easily avoided in most areas.

Or check out the wilder parts of the city via the extensive trail systems at Rock Creek Park, along the Potomac and Anacostia Rivers, and beyond. Add to that the seasonal foot ferries, or water taxis, leading from DC to Old Town Alexandria just across the Potomac River, or National Harbor located downriver on the Maryland side.

Canine pals out for a morning stroll.

This is not to say that the city planners and engineers have achieved mobility perfection and can all retire now, but we can certainly celebrate the progress that's been made even over the past decade. The city still has its fair share of upturned bricks on quaint, old sidewalks, trails that need work, and a few Walk/Don't Walk signs on timers that defy all logic, but the experts will surely sort it all out in due time.

In a city where the great indoors—the art galleries, Smithsonian museums, the U.S. Capitol, the monuments and the rest—can be downright humbling, there's also a big outside here well worth the rambling. For most of us, the place to begin is on the National Mall.

Where Am I?

Regardless of how you choose to get around, it helps to know a bit about the general layout of the city. As originally conceived by George Washington's hired architect, Pierre L'Enfant, numbered streets run north and south, beginning at the Capitol. Lettered streets run east and west, also from the Capitol.

All are modified by NE, NW, SE or SW, depending on what quadrant of the city you are in. The Capitol Dome is at the center of the grid. Avenues generally run at a diagonal and are named after the states, the most prominent being Pennsylvania Ave. linking the U.S. Capitol to the White House, more or less. (Free DC maps are widely available.)

Zero Milestone (see p 51).

The geography of downtown DC can seem a little mysterious and complicated for first-time visitors and transplants, perhaps due to all the diagonal avenues, discontinuous streets and traffic circles that seem designed to get you lost. But there's a method to the madness and like any other unfamiliar city, navigation gets easier once you've gotten acquainted with a few main thoroughfares and landmarks. If you stood by the Washington Monument and could remember this much, you'll be doing well: U.S. Capitol: east; Lincoln Memorial: west; downtown: north; Potomac River: southwest.

Weather & Seasons

Barring blizzards and hurricanes, DC is good for exploring pretty much anytime of the year. Early spring and fall are awesome under frequent blue skies and colorful foliage. There might be a nip in the air early or late in the day, so dress accordingly. The heights of summer and winter can be poaching hot or crispy cold, but there's nearly always somewhere cool or cozy to duck into.

In summer, most mornings are pleasant, but start early to avoid the mid-day heat. Sudden thunderstorms are common and exciting—and potentially dangerous if you get caught in the middle of one. Duck indoors to be safe. Carry an umbrella (often sold on the street) if storms are in the near-term forecast. Warm nights around sunset and later are a joy for Mall wandering, as our national landscape is artistically transformed by the soft illumination of trees, walkways, pools, old buildings and monuments. At night, the views of Washington Monument and the Capitol from Lincoln Memorial and the WWII Memorial are stunning.

Fall can be especially gorgeous, with generally milder temperatures, bluer skies due to less humidity, fall foliage and waning crowds. But keep an eye on frequently changing weather forecasts and wide temperature swings from one day to the next.

As for winter, the crowds are gone, but snow and ice and occasional frigid temperatures can present some obvious challenges to footsters. Pick a dry, ice-free day, wear suitable shoes and your favorite warm and fuzzy accoutrements and enjoy. Then seek out a lonely museum, gallery or coffee shop for a warm-up.

Restaurants & Lodging

In the past, your favorite travel guide might typically list a ton of places to stay or enjoy a meal at your destination. These days, however, there is so much information online, and with nearly everyone traveling with a smartphone, we'll presume that you can do your own homework to sort out lodging and restaurant options that fit your style. There are literally thousands of places to stay or eat in greater DC

With lodging, unless you're part of a package tour already, you'll find plenty of mid-level and luxury hotels downtown and in the various commercial centers around the region. Larger groups should try to book well in advance.

And there are countless short-stay rentals (and a few hostels) that often

Georgetown's M St., one of many dining hotspots around DC.

appeal to independent travelers. We won't advertise them here, but they are easy to find online. Again check the reviews, compare prices. And perhaps most importantly, look for locations that are convenient to the Metro system.

My wife and I enjoy walking, so if a rental is within a half mile (or 10-minute walk) of a Metro Station, and only requires strolling along quiet neighborhood streets, that's perfect for us. We might stretch it to a mile if we find something special. Failing that, being close to a bus stop can also do the trick. Rideshare services can be a blessing too, especially at night. If you're driving, then almost anywhere can work. Again, we prefer to avoid the hassles of traffic and parking, which means we're mostly getting around by Metro and our own two feet.

As for meals, we are independent travelers ourselves, so we enjoy browsing dinner options while we're moseying around in a new place. Like many others, when we find something that looks intriguing, we might look it up online to check the reviews. We might do the same for a morning coffee or breakfast.

Whatever your style, you can find a ton of choices downtown, along all the main avenues, at the Wharf and in the surrounding communities from

Alexandria to Arlington, Virginia, and from Silver Spring to National Harbor, Maryland. If you like the more quaint, historic vibe, then it's hard to beat places like Eastern Market, Adams Morgan, H Steet NE, Georgetown, Chinatown, Anacostia and Old Town Alexandria, among others.

At the National Mall, your main choices are food trucks and cafeteria dining at some museums. For a step up and far more options, head north to downtown, especially along or near 7th St. NW. You'll also find many great places for a morning coffee throughout the downtown area.

Safe Travels

While due caution is advised in any big city, areas described in this guide are commonly enjoyed by locals and visitors alike with no special worries. From spring through fall, you'll find early-morning joggers, commuting footsters and families at sunset cruising around most areas of the Mall and public spaces all over the District. The winter chill might keep many folks indoors, while you can find thousands of people milling about the National Mall on warm summer nights.

Security might seem higher near

Tips For First-Time Visitors

- Pick up a map of DC, including the National Mall, downtown, Potomac River and some portion of Rock Creek Park. Freebies are easy to come by at information booths, hotels, etc.
- Grab a Metro map and optional SmarTrip card at any Metro station (*see* p. 26).
- Wear comfortable walking shoes. Your feet will thank you later. For most kinds of weather and terrain, we prefer light hikers. If you're prone to blisters, add thin liner socks.
- Bring along sunblock, lip balm, sunhat, possibly an umbrella or light poncho if there's a serious threat of rain.
- Go light, carry only what you need. If you lug a bag or daypack, you'll need to stop at the security bag check as you enter museums, etc. It's nice to stroll right in. Expect tighter security in government buildings (no food, liquids, large bags, sharp objects, etc.).
- Busier times at museums seem to be mid-morning through mid-afternoon (spring/summer), though crowds are highly variable, depending on school and tour groups. Note some museums and galleries are open later than others.
- Most major monuments can be visited after dark and many are great at sunset, especially from Washington Monument to Jefferson, FDR, King, Korea, Lincoln, Vietnam and WWII Memorials.
- Major monuments have restrooms, but museums and galleries often have nicer facilities. Some Metro stations have hidden restrooms. If desperate, ask the station manager.
- Keep a refillable water bottle at your side on hot summer days. Drinking-water fountains are also widely available around the Mall and elsewhere.
- Carry a smartphone, if possible. You can often find an outlet for charging at local eateries and coffee shops while enjoying a break or meal. Museums may have an outlet in a quiet corner somewhere.

the many government buildings downtown and around the Capitol, for obvious reasons. Friendly patrols by park police on horseback are fun to encounter. Some officers ride bikes and occasionally even Segways, which helps keep the petty and not-so-petty offenders at bay.

It also helps just having lots of people around. If the Mall is the first stop on your D.C. visit (as it should be if this is your first time here), you aren't likely to get too lonesome out there.

Decades ago, Washington, D.C. had an unenviable reputation as a crime-ridden city. But that's pretty old news now. It's not quite Shangri-la yet, but violent crime rates have fallen dramatically since the 1980s and 1990s. Well over 400 homicides occurred annually in the early-1990s, falling to 128 in 2025—even as the population was growing at a good clip.

While there is little to fear in the areas covered by this guide, be mindful, of course, that D.C. is a large metro area and crazy things can happen. So trust your instincts, go where the happy people are and avoid wandering into isolated or unpeopled areas, especially at night. Be discreet with your money and your valuables (or leave them in a safe place) and hang onto your stuff on crowded streets and around Metro stations. Beware of scammers preying on your kind heart. If anyone does try to mess with you while you're using Metro, the Metro

- To cool off when it's hot out, galleries are often less crowded than museums.
- Frequent tours are offered at many public buildings, such as the U.S. Capitol, Library of Congress, U.S. Supreme Court, Washington Monument, Bureau of Engraving and Printing, and at museums and galleries. Free tickets may be required, so check their websites or information desks for details.
- Tag along on a free docent or ranger-led tour for good stories and insight.
- Commercial tours are another great option, on foot or by bike, Segway, hop-on/hop-off bus or water taxi. Promotional brochures are easy to find. Watch for coupons and online deals.
- Pets must be leashed at the Mall and are often more restricted near monuments. Watch for signs or ask a ranger.
- Speaking of tips, keep a few dollars handy for tipping street musicians. Stop and listen, enjoy the moment.
- Take a lot of breaks.

The National Park Service would like us all to cut back on the use of disposable water bottles in our parks. The volume of discarded plastic bottles, even when dropped in recycle bins, can be overwhelming in popular areas like the National Mall. So think "refillable" and use the water fountains.

Police welcomes your call at (202) 962-2121. Call **911** for emergencies.

For what it's worth, I've yet to be hassled on a train or bus or sidewalk, trail or in a park, anywhere in DC. But keeping an eye on your surroundings is good practice just the same. For other tips on enjoying your visit hassle-free, check out the DC Metropolitan Police website at **mpdc.dc.gov**.

Perhaps a bigger threat is getting whacked by a vehicle when crossing the street, as in jaywalking against a walk signal. DC footsters are notorious for ignoring those pesky, flashing Don't-Walk signs. Way too many of us dash through traffic with a smartphone stuck to one ear, oblivious to the guy in the sports car who just stomped on it from the alley so he could squeeze in ahead of that bus over there. Doggonit, he just didn't see you in time.

The traffic police seem to rarely enforce the rules around jaywalking (though they can ticket you in a nanosecond if you mis-park your car). I'm not so straight and narrow to suggest that everyone must abide by the almighty traffic light at all hours, but it's a poor habit to routinely ignore the signals, especially with traffic present, not to mention setting a bad example for the wee ones. It only takes one small misstep to ruin a perfect day, and we don't like those odds. So keep your precious body off the one-in-a-thousand probability curve and wait for the light.

Too Much Information?

- This guide is meant to help you map out the more interesting and scenic ways to explore and experience this world-class landscape. While the walking routes described connect all the best sites (and sights), we've tried not to regurgitate the boatloads of information widely available in other books, brochures, interpretive displays, websites and the like. A few tidbits are provided to give you a better idea of what you're looking at. The year of completion of a structure or monument is shown in parentheses for most points of interest identified in the text.
- Still, it's nice to have the deeper scuttlebutt at your fingertips, so carry along a smartphone or tablet for quick internet access. Several online resources deserve mention here. The Smithsonian maintains an excellent, mobile-friendly website at **si.edu**, and wi-fi is available in many of their facilities, including most of the Smithsonian museums and galleries. The National Art Gallery (nga.gov) also has Wi-Fi and an informative app with audio tours.
- Another great source of instant info when you're on-site is the National Park Service's app for the National Mall, which includes a rich supply of background information on monuments, memorials and historic sites around the Mall, as well as maps, directions and schedules for ranger talks and tours. An online search for "NPS mall app" should get you to the download page. See also **nps.gov/nama**.
- For more general travel information about Washington, DC, including lodging options, **washington.org** is a good place to start. You'll find more online sources for walks, hikes, sights to see and just enjoying DC's outdoors on p. 190.

Cherry Blossoms!

In spring, DC's famed cherry blossoms normally peak for about a week in late March or early April, depending a lot on how long and cold the winter was. The blossoms mark the end of the cold season about as reliably as any self-effacing groundhog. DC celebrates the eruption of pink with its annual, weeks-long, multi-event Cherry Blossom Festival (**nationalcherryblossomfestival.org**).

The National Park Service in late winter/early spring predicts) when peak flowering might occur (**nps.gov/cherry**). When it does, sizable crowds begin to fill up the tree-lined walkways around the Tidal Basin each morning before sunrise, ballooning to thousands by lunchtime if the weather's good.

Alternatively, you can avoid crowds and catch the bloom at East Potomac Park or the National Arboretum as well, with the added spectacle of magnolia trees bursting with pink and white flowers. Senate Park along D St., a block south of Union Station, is also good.

Grab your camera and be there at first light—you won't regret it. Or stick around for the late-afternoon and pre-sunset show when the crowds are a little less daunting and lighting can still be perfect for photos.

Late for the cherry blossoms? Not to worry. By the time the delicate petals have blown away in a stiff breeze, all else is on the verge of blooming, as an explosion of green begins to envelop the city. *For more info, see p. 83.*

It's Time to Explore!

Take a look at the overview maps on p. 40-41 illustrating the three loops around the National Mall. Each loop is shown in a bit more detail on the pages that follow. Abundant photos are included to give you an idea of what lies ahead. The directions for each walk are written as sequentially as possible with references to street names and landmarks at every turn. If you drift off-route, the maps should help you get back on track.

Running distances are in bold type. If you haven't walked a lot of miles lately, not to worry. You can walk as little or as much as you like, rest when you like, go where you like. The loops are only suggestions for enjoying the best of the National Mall without too much aimless wandering.

If you're new to the DC area, you might find that it helps to check the maps and reread short sections as you walk them. Look back over your shoulder now and then, not only to confirm your route, but to catch a view you might have otherwise missed.

Construction, special events, presidential motorcades, UFO landings or other temporary closures can blow these route suggestions out of the water. However, there's always a way around and most DC-ers are happy to help with directions.

To help you keep track of the many sights encountered, look to the end of the book where you'll find both an index and a "DC Bucket List" that include all points of interest highlighted in the text. Check them off if you like.

You'll find tips for photography on the next page, along with suggestions on when to shoot (in good weather) to optimize natural lighting.

Cherry blossoms: National Mall and Capitol Grounds

Photography Tips

Washington, DC is quite a photogenic place. Photographers will find a tremendous amount of subject material all along the routes described. Some of the more unusual or interesting photo ops are highlighted in the text.

You don't need to be an expert to go home with a proud portfolio of images. For outdoor photography, the job gets a little easier when you're surrounded by such a diversity of architecture, urban art, changing skies and expansive land and waterscapes, which are almost everywhere you look across much of DC.

Unless you're an expert already, notice when (or before) the lighting looks good and head out with a smartphone or better camera that can at least focus and think for itself, which means about all that's left for you is the composition.

- Early morning, late afternoon or around sunset generally offer the best lighting.
- Cloudy days diffuse the light and tame the contrasts. Stormy skies can be dramatic, often with rainbows.
- Some action shots, like that cool bird above your head, demand being quick on the draw. Don't wait, just shoot it (the photo, not the bird, lol).
- Don't forget to look over your shoulder. Sometimes the best perspectives and lighting are behind you.
- Take lots of shots. Delete the duds later.
- Get creative. Look for odd angles, perspectives, juxtapositions, unusual encounters.
- Experiment with the automatic and manual camera settings.
- Carry a charger or extra battery.
- Power down and enjoy the view.

Sunset over the Tidal Basin.

When to Shoot

To jumpstart your quest for great images, below are some of the more iconic buildings and monuments and desirable times to be there:

- **Lincoln Memorial** (east-facing), morning or after dark
- **Martin Luther King, Jr. Memorial** (southeast-facing), morning, midday or after dark
- **FDR Memorial** (north, west and east-facing), midday or later
- **Thomas Jefferson Memorial** (north- facing), early morning or mid-afternoon to sunset
- **Washington Monument** (every-where-facing), anytime
- **WWII Memorial** (west and east-facing), morning till after dark
- **U.S. Capitol** (east and west-facing), morning or mid-afternoon to sunset
- **Supreme Court** (west-facing), mid-afternoon to sunset
- **Library of Congress** (west facing), late morning to sunset
- **White House** (north and south-facing), mid-morning to sunset
- **National Archives** (north and south-facing), morning or mid-afternoon to sunset
- **Old Post Office** (north and west-facing), morning/mid-afternoon to sunset
- **Smithsonian Castle** (north and south-facing), morning to sunset
- **Smithsonian Arts and Industries** (north, south and west-facing), mid-morning to sunset
- **Union Station** (south-facing), mid-morning to sunset
- **National Cathedral** (west and north-facing), mid-morning to sunset
- **Basilica of the National Shrine of the Immaculate Conception** (south, east and west-facing), morning to sunset

Getting to Know the National Mall

How big is it?

Depending on how you measure, 1.5 - 2.0 square miles.

Washington Monument to Lincoln Memorial - 0.8 mile
Washington Monument to the U.S. Capitol - 1.4 miles
Washington Monument to the White House - 0.6 mile
White House to Thomas Jefferson Memorial - 1.1 miles

This is meant as a fun map for visualizing the National Mall, its many museums, memorials and momuments, and the surrounding downtown area. If you walk all three loops shown on the next two pages, you should be able to identify many of the buildings and features shown. How many can you name? (By the way, that red highway running north-south across the Mall is actually I-395—it's 20 feet underground!)

The National Mall in Three Loops

West Loop

4.0 Miles
Begin & End at Washington Monument

Central Loop

3.7 Miles
Optional Start at Washington Monument

Suggested Starting Locations

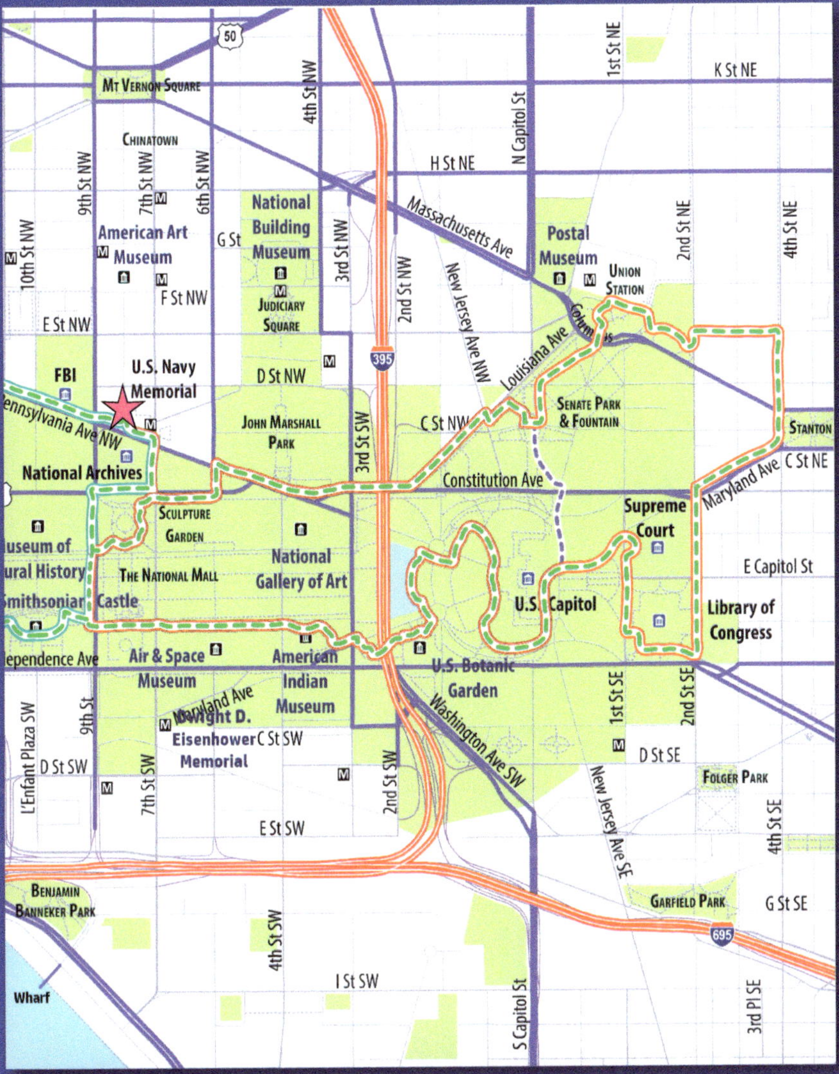

CENTRAL LOOP

Both East & Central Loops Begin & End at U.S. Navy Memorial

EAST LOOP

4.1 Miles

0 0.1 0.2 0.3 0.4 0.5 mile

THE NATIONAL MALL: CENTRAL LOOP

U.S. Navy Memorial - Freedom Plaza
WWI Memorial - White House - Renwick Gallery
Washington Monument - Smithsonian Castle

- *Distance:* 3.7 - 4.1 miles - *Allow 2 - 4 hours*
- *Start:* U.S. Navy Memorial - *Near Pennsylvania Ave & 7th St. NW*
- *Nearest Metro:* Archives–Navy Memorial–Penn Quarter

Points of Interest: U.S. Navy Memorial • National Archives • Old Post Office Freedom Plaza • WWI Memorial • U.S. Treasury • The Extra Mile • Lafayette Square • White House • Andrew Jackson Memorial • Renwick Gallery Ellipse & Pavilion • Washington Monument • Smithsonian Castle Arts & Industries Building • Museum of Natural History • Sculpture Garden

Lone Sailor, U.S. Navy Memorial. To begin the loop at Washington Monument, turn to p. 53.

U.S. Navy Memorial

Spend a few minutes taking stock of the fountains, the intricate bronze bas-reliefs (like miniature sculptures, over two dozen of them), the Lone Sailor and other maritime features. Every spring during the Blessing of the Fleet, a bit of water from the world's seven seas and the Great Lakes is dribbled into the pools of the Navy Memorial. Military bands often perform here in the evening during the warmer months (free).

If you have a Navy vet in the family, maybe peek inside the **Naval Heritage Center** in the big curvy building to the right (9:30-5:00 daily). Browse exhibits and search for, or leave, information about veterans you may know.

Let the Expedition Begin!

The **U.S. Navy Memorial**, dedicated in 1987, is a perfect place to kick off a Washington, D.C. walkabout. The memorial is next to the **Archives–Navy Memorial–Penn Quarter Metro Station**, centrally located at 7th St. NW and Pennsylvania Ave. It's also close to the museums on the National Mall, as well as downtown Washington. If you're walking over from the Mall, 7th St. is about midway between the U.S. Capitol and the Washington Monument.

The Central Loop begins with aneasy ramble from here to the White House in 1.3 miles, which for most mortals requires about an hour of leisurely walking. From the White House to the Washington Monument is another 1.3 miles. From the Monument to the Smithsonian Castle is 0.6 mile, and closing the loop at the Navy Memorial adds another half mile, for a total loop of 3.7 miles. Allow 2 to 4 hours to complete the walk, or more if you plan to visit the museums. Other highlights along the way include great plazas, public squares, gardens, lesser known monuments and outstanding architecture.

To begin, look for the giant map of the globe sprawled across the circular plaza of the Navy Memorial near the top of the Metro escalators. Technically, it's a map of the world's oceans called **The Granite Sea**. Interestingly, the memorial is exactly where Pierre L'Enfant, the 1790s architect of the city, thought it should be—a tangible example of his extraordinary legacy.

Before departing the plaza **[MILE 0.0]**, look south across Pennsylvania Ave. to the **National Archives** (1935). Inside this striking edifice you can view the original Declaration of Independence and U.S. Constitution, among countless other historic documents. It's well worth a visit when you have a chance. (*Open 10:00-5:30; timed-entry tick-*

ets recommended; **visit.archives.gov/visit/tickets**.) Enter from Constitution Ave. on the opposite side. You'll be right there near the end of this loop!)

Put a big toe on the map of the globe somewhere near your home, snap a selfie and start walking. Head west toward 9th St. NW (away from the escalators) along the wide, treed sidewalk of Pennsylvania Ave.

Cross 9th St. NW to a veritable forest of street trees and pass the **FBI's former J. Edgar Hoover Building** (1974) on your right. The building, one of the largest in DC, has been controversial since it was built, mainly for its mundane design. The agency announced in late 2025 it was moving across the street and three blocks west. For now, try to look innocent and keep marching.

Across Pennsylvania Ave. is the more stylish **U.S. Department of Justice** building (1935), named for Robert F. Kennedy in 2001. On the next block (left) is the headquarters of the **Internal Revenue Service** (1936), also controversial, but not for its architecture. You might keep a hand on your wallet as you walk by.

After crossing 10th St. NW [MILE 0.3], crane your neck up and left to admire the century-old clock tower of the **Old Post Office** building (1899), a historic marvel of Romanesque architecture that in 2016 was converted to a controversial luxury hotel. By agreement with the developer, the historic character was preserved, as well as public access to one of DC's more prominent national landmarks.

At 315 feet high, the Old Post Office is the third tallest building in DC, after the Washington Monument (555 feet) and the Basilica of the National Shrine of Immaculate Concep-

An unusual collection of historic American flags flutter above the sidewalk at the old FBI building.

America's Main Street

Also known as **America's Main Street, Pennsylvania Avenue** is a designated National Historic Site. It's been at the center of countless national events for over 200 years, from major parades and festivals to large demonstration marches and the grand presidential procession on Inauguration Day, when hundreds of thousands of onlookers line the street. Even since the good old days when Pennsylvania Ave. was lined with sketchy bars, brothels and makeshift housing, it's remained a major artery in the heart of downtown Washington.

You can look beyond the luxury hotel and still admire the majestic Old Post Office building dominating Pennsylvania Ave. An elevator ride to the observation deck above the giant clock ought to be on your DC bucket list.

Ben Franklin statue near 12th St.

Federal Triangle

The **Federal Triangle** is the cluster of federal office buildings built here in the 1930s and contained within the triangle of 15th St. NW and Pennsylvania and Constitution Avenues. The Old Post Office was included within the redevelopment footprint and was supposed to be demolished way back when to accommodate the architectural symmetry of a Great Circle between the buildings. But citizens loved the Old Post Office and demanded that it be saved. Thankfully, it was.

The upshot? There's only three-quarters of a circle of building facades here, which makes the Old Post Office something like a square peg in a round hole inside a triangle, and all within the big diamond known as DC.

Curving walkway, Federal Triangle.

tion (328 feet). The National Cathedral is just a shade lower at 301 feet. All are spectacular and worth visiting. (The clock tower was temporarily closed in early 2026, its status uncertain; entry is off 12th St. on the south side of the building. See p. 182 for more about the basilica and cathedral.)

Cross Pennsylvania Ave. at 11th St. NW and look straight ahead for a small sign describing some of the history of the area. Continue along Pennsylvania Ave. to a marble statue of **Benjamin Franklin** (1889) relocated here in 1982. Cross 12th St. NW, then turn immediately left and briefly head south along 12th St. to the arched corridor just ahead. Enter and follow the tunnel-like curving walkway to the right for some interesting photo ops.

This building was originally designed to replace the Old Post Office, but is now the headquarters of the **Environmental Protection Agency**. Note the view back at the Old Post Office and surrounding **Federal Triangle**. There may be another sign nearby (if still in place) that offers more nuggets of history.

Amid this near circle of buildings, continue along the curved wall to the **Federal Triangle Metro** escalators. The Loop heads right past the escalators. (Incidentally, if you continued down 12th St. to the next traffic light, you would find the Museums of Natural History on the left and American History on the right.)

At the Metro escalators, the one-quarter circle mark of the curved facade, turn right through more archways and into the great circular space of **Woodrow Wilson Plaza**, a fine place to lunch or linger. Free noontime concerts are common here in summer (nice acoustics). Straight across the plaza from the escalators is an entrance to the **Ronald Reagan Building and International Trade Center** (1998), the largest building in DC. You'll find 3.1 million square feet of floor space here in which to swivel your rocker and ponder your export strategy.

The building also houses a humble, but interesting, **Woodrow Wilson Memorial** to our 28th President (free; **wilsoncenter.org**). Some of his personal effects are on display, along with video and stories of Wilson's progressive efforts to protect workers, reel in financial abuses, help bring an end to WWI, and establish the League of Nations, for which he received a Nobel Prize. Yet his stature was ignobly diminished by his misguided support for racial segregation. To enter you'll need to pass through a quick security check. Once inside the main entrance, a food court and large atrium should be dead ahead. The memorial is to the left.

Woodrow Wilson Plaza.

To exit Woodrow Wilson Plaza, follow the pedestrian corridor north to Pennsylvania Ave. If you're unsure which way is north, stand in the middle of the plaza facing the Metro escalators and turn 90 degrees left.

Inscription at Freedom Plaza.

Cross Pennsylvania Ave. to the north and saunter left across the unexpected expanse of **Freedom Plaza**, fully restored in 2026 [MILE 0.6]. Near the east end, **General Casimir Pulaski** sits on his mighty horse watching over the place. Pulaski was a Revolutionary War hero credited with saving George Washington's life during the Battle of Brandywine near Philadelphia. Then Pulaski himself was killed in another battle at Savannah in 1779.

Looking at your feet as you meander across the plaza, you'll notice that a large map of DC, **Pierre L'Enfant's 1791 plan** for the capital, is inlaid into the granite and marble surface (*see photo on p. 8*). The map is surrounded by notable quotes about the high stature of this fair and worldly city.

General Pulaski was an effective strategist and horseman during the Revolutionary War and is considered to be the "Father of the American cavalry." He was bestowed honorary U.S. citizenship in 2009.

To the right is the **National Theatre** (1923), established in 1835, twice destroyed by fire, and now operating as a nonprofit (**broadwayatthenational.com**). Left across Pennsylvania Ave. is the **Wilson Building** (1904), hosting DC government offices, including the mayor and city council. Be sure to look

General Pershing, prominent at the WWI Memorial.

back down America's Main Street for a good telephoto shot of the Old Post Office and U.S. Capitol (better with afternoon light).

Continuing across Freedom Plaza, angle slightly right to its northwest corner at 14th St. NW. Just ahead on the north side of Pennsylvania Ave. is one of the classier hotels in DC, the historic **Willard** (1901). It's hard to believe that, as recently as the 1970s, it was so forlorn and neglected, it was threatened with demolition. Its lobby is where President Grant applied the term "lobbyist" to those who pestered him. Martin Luther King, Jr. worked on his "I have a Dream Speech" here, and Freedom Plaza was named in his honor. A display in the back of the hotel (near F St.) shares some of its stories.

Bronze Bald Eagle Sculpture.

Cross 14th St. to the **WWI Memorial** completed in 2024 (formerly Pershing Park, 1981). Signs and panels describe the history of the Great War to end all wars—until it didn't. A Peace Fountain remembers those who were lost, and a statue of **General John Pershing**, venerated leader of American forces during WWI, stands to the left. Continue to the northwest corner of the WWI Memorial at 15th St. NW and look for a small, striking **Bald Eagle** sculpture donated by the National Wildlife Federation in 1982, marking 200 years since it became our national symbol.

In the White House Visitor Center, the official seal used by President Lincoln.

If desired, you could cross 15th St. here to the General Sherman Monument, although it's often gated. The Loop, however, jogs left (south) briefly to catch the nearby **White House Visitor Center**. Walk downhill on 15th St. or amble through the WWI Memorial to the next light; cross Pennsylvania Ave. and walk left a few yards to the visitor center entrance. The building also houses the **Department of Commerce** (1932). A recent $12.5 million renovation included new exhibits, artifacts, video, an interactive model of the White House and immaculate restrooms. The White House Visitor Center opens early (*7:30-4:00*), offering a nice morning activity before the museums open. (Tours of the

White House for U.S. residents must be arranged far in advance by contacting your member of Congress.)

Return to the Bald Eagle and continue up 15th St. NW [MILE 0.9], or cross and take a quick spin around the **William Tecumseh Sherman Monument if it's open**. It's a solemn reminder of the brutal end days of the Civil War. Then ramble north (uphill) on 15th St. past the **U.S. Treasury** (1869) on the left. Out front is the prominent statue of the first Treasury Secretary and close advisor to George Washington (and now Broadway star), **Alexander Hamilton**. The Secretary was mortally shot in the famous 1804 duel with his nemesis, Vice-President Aaron Burr. A strange way to settle scores, it would seem.

General Sherman Monument.

Notice the series of large bronze medallions embedded in the sidewalk in what's known as **The Extra Mile**. The markers commemorate many individuals whose work has contributed great things to America and the world—Clara Barton, Rachel Carson, Cesar Chavez, Frederick Douglas, Samuel Gompers, Helen Keller, Juliette Lowe and John Muir, to name a few. (The Extra Mile leads up 15th St., then turns right at G St.)

Alexander Hamilton and the U.S.Treasury, familiar icons on a U.S. $10 bill.

Once past the Treasury, just beyond G St., turn left and stroll west on the broad pedestrian avenue (a closed street) a block to **Lafayette Square** (1824) on the right. A statue of the **Marquis de Lafayette**, a dear friend of George Washington and decisive leader at Yorktown in the American Revolution, greets you at the corner. The two cherubs at Lafayette's back hint at the struggle for America in its infancy in the 1770s.

Along The Extra Mile.

Keep walking to enjoy your best view of the **White House** (1800), front and center, including the **North Lawn and Portico** [MILE 1.3]. When heads of state come knocking, they typically enter from this side. The presidential motorcade also zips through here on occasion, although the police will have chased you off well beforehand. You can credit Frederick Law Olmsted, Jr. for the

Marquis de Lafayette.

landscaping around the White House.

Imagine the good old days of 1829 when President Andrew Jackson, in his brash yet neighborly Tennessee way (he was also a prolific slave owner), simply invited everybody, you and I included, to park the horses, kick the mud off our boots and c'mon into the White House, even to the Inaugural Ball. Fences were for keeping the cows out—or in, as the case may be. How times have changed. These days, you'll have to settle for a selfie outside the fence. So, put your gown and tuxedo away and wish the current president happy thoughts before heading north, away from the fence and into the middle of **Lafayette Square**.

Jackson Memorial and White House.

Aim for the prominent statue of our controversial 7th president, **Andrew Jackson** (1853), a man of the people, or some people anyway, on his rearing horse above the cannons. Keep walking north through the Square, not quite to H St., the street bordering the park, and prepare to hang a left on the curving red-brick path. The small building to the right contains restrooms—hopefully in better shape than they've been historically. (So close to the White House, maybe we could designate it the National Loo?) The big yellow church across H St. is **St. John's Episcopal** (1816), where almost every president has attended a service.

Now follow the red-brick path leftward to the northwest corner of Lafayette Square and a statue of **General Von Steuben** (1910), another devoted friend of General Washington and Revolutionary America. Across

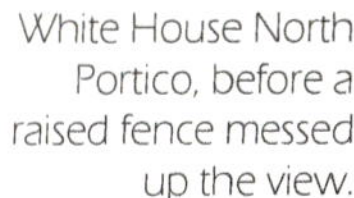

White House North Portico, before a raised fence messed up the view.

Jackson Pl. is the **Decatur House** (1818), sometimes open for free tours and exhibits (see **whitehousehistory.org/plan-your-visit**). The Latrobe-designed house was built for Stephen Decatur, Jr., a Naval war hero of high status. He died here after being shot in the gut in a duel with a fellow officer. Maybe they should have drawn straws instead?

(If it's important, the nearest Metro stations, Farragut West and McPherson Square, are close by on I St., at 17th St. NW or Vermont Ave.)

Head left along Jackson Place back toward the White House to a statue of another Revolutionary War hero and French army commander, **General Jean de Rochambeau** (1902). Turn right at the corner to pass **Blair House** (1826) and the Smithsonian's French-inspired, always intriguing **Renwick Gallery** (1863) at the corner of 17th St. NW and Pennsylvania Ave. (*10:00-5:30 daily*) [MILE 1.6]. The gallery is named for the building's architect, James Renwick, Jr., the same gent who designed the Smithsonian Castle. The Gallery hosts classical and contemporary works of fine American artists.

If you need a break, several coffee shops are nearby along 17th St. (last chance before the Mall). The World Bank, Edward R. Murrow Park and the Mexican Embassy are also close by just off Pennsylvania Ave. (*see p. 177*).

Next, head left down 17th St. to the far end of the imposingly elegant **Eisenhower Executive Office Building** (1888) on your left. Pass a security post just beyond to find a path on the left. Before taking this path (if open), look across the street to the former Corcoran Gallery (1897). Thousands of contemporary works of art from the Corcoran were absorbed into the National Gallery of Art in 2015, while the historic building was remade into George Washington University's **Corcoran School of the Arts and Design**. A new gallery was planned as part of the renovation and is sometimes accessible to the public. Student

St. John's Episcopal Church, attended by all presidents since James Madison, Lincoln especially.

This anti-nuke peace vigil near the White House has been sustained since 1981. Conchita, who was there almost from the beginning, passed away in 2016 at the age of 80. Others now maintain the vigil.

Once the Corcoran Gallery, the Renwick Gallery was called the "American Louvre," despite its modest size.

Eisenhower (a/k/a Old) Executive Office Building. President Nixon liked to hide out in an office here, to escape the business and busyness of the Oval Office.

works may be on display just inside (up the steps from 17th St.).

If you need to make a beeline for the Mall, continue down 17th St. Otherwise, take the curved walkway on the left (noted above). It leads past a tall monolith topped by a golden figure. This is the **First Division Monument** (1924) originally commemorating Army veterans of WWI.

At a sidewalk intersection head left, cross a driveway and continue toward the black iron fence. The **Butt-Millet Fountain** on the right commemorates two well known men from DC who perished with the sinking of the Titanic in 1912.

First Division Monument.

If security hasn't closed it off, you might notice a gathering of onlookers enjoying a good view of the **White House** across the **South Lawn** [MILE 2.0]. In Andrew Jackson's day, you could clippety-clop your buggy right up to the door and say howdy. Today, not so much.

Keep walking along the fence a short distance, then cross the drive rightward at a designated spot between the security fences. As soon as you get to the other side, look to the right for the **National Christmas Tree** (1973), also encircled by a simple fence. During the winter holidays, choo-choo trains chug charmingly around the cheerful tree—fun for the kids, especially after dark. Mosey over for a closer look and to find a small pedestal nearby that marks the **Zero Milestone** (1923). This was the point from which highways and places throughout America could have theoretically been measured, except that they weren't—a cool idea that got a little complicated.

White House, South Lawn.

Now, facing Washington Monument, note the giant circular lawn here called **The Ellipse**. Walk left (clockwise) on the obvious perimeter path, passing the **Ellipse Visitor Pavilion** (1994), a low building with pudgy white columns (also restrooms, refreshments). About 80 yards past the Pavilion, look to the left for a thrifty-brave-and-reverent-looking monument hidden in the trees—an idealized tribute to the **Boy Scouts of America** (1964).

That big government building over there opposite 15th St. is the **Department of Commerce** (1932), later named for Herbert Hoover. There's not too much to see there besides the White House Visitor Center, so keep on ellipsing till you're halfway around.

If you love lawn, the big one here ought to really spin your mower. The Washington Senators played baseball here in 1860. Union troops camped in the area during the Civil War, before it became a dump. Conversion to a park began in 1879. The vast Ellipse is sometimes abuzz as a gathering place, but can also be a bit of a yawner. To jazz it up for everyday use, perhaps we could add a lawn-bowling green. Or since jazz is uniquely American, maybe a giant labyrinth in the shape of a saxophone?

Keep circling till you reach an intersection near the main avenue between The Ellipse and the Washington Monument. The White House should be due north. Turn left and look for two square, low-profile, granite fountains—the **Haupt Fountains** (1969)—adjacent to Constitution Ave. These were donated by Enid Haupt, an avid urban gardener, philanthropist and friend of Lady Bird Johnson. Cross Constitution Ave. to the tidy **German-American Friendship Garden**, dedicated by President Reagan and German Chancellor Helmut Kohl in 1988. Turn right.

From this vantage point, the **Washington Monument** (1888) towers majestically above the sweeping lawn. From the Friendship Garden, head on up to the flags, but keep an eye peeled for the **Jefferson Pier**, a a three-foot-tall granite marker that is due south of the White House and due west of the Capitol.

While the Washington Monument lines

Boy Scouts Memorial. If you're not a boy, take heart that the Extra Mile markers include Girl Scouts' founder Juliette Gordon Low (on G St. near 15th St.; photo, p. 48).

National Christmas Tree.

German-American Friendship Garden.

up perfectly with the U.S. Capitol and Lincoln Memorial, it stands about 100 yards east of the White House-Jefferson Memorial axis, due to once swampy ground at that location. Look for it about 100 yards downhill from the monument. Thomas Jefferson thought it a perfect location for an early survey marker to lay out the city, though it wasn't used much.

At 555 feet in height, **Washington Monument** (1885) [MILE 2.6] is the world's tallest obelisk. The 12-ton cornerstone was set in 1848 and contained a time capsule, though it's now buried about 20 feet underground and encased in concrete. The monument was only 150 feet tall after six years of construction when funding ran out. The Civil War delayed further progress until 1877. Marble was brought in from a different quarry, thus the slight difference in coloration above the 150-foot level. Another factoid: the monument weighs over 40,000 tons.

For a free timed-entry ticket to the top and the eagle-eye view, you'll need to either be lucky enough to snag one online (*see* **nps.gov/wamo**; *easier in winter*), or visit the **Washington Monument Lodge**, early in the morning when a line forms at the window for same-day tickets. The Lodge is the little stone building located downslope and 500 feet to the east of the obelisk. The entire day's tickets can rapidly disappear in the busy season, so plan to arrive early at the ticket window (*opens at 8:30*).

The U.S. Capitol Building is prominent to the east. To the west, the WWII and Lincoln Memorials beckon, almost insisting we go there now. The WEST LOOP begins and ends here, so you could do it now, then finish the CENTRAL LOOP. Otherwise, save it for an early morning or late afternoon/evening trek. You won't regret it. Lighting can be perfect for photos.

Keeping with the CENTRAL LOOP from Washington Monument, circle down to the ticket Lodge, which also contains a bookstore

A cloud-splitting monument.

In August 2011, a rare 5.8 magnitude earthquake, centered 80 miles from DC, seriously damaged the monument. Though mostly cosmetic, the monument was closed for nearly three years while repairs were made. It reopened to the public in May 2014.

African American Museum.

and restrooms. On the way there, you could also cross 15th St. NW to Madison Dr. to access the National Museum of African American History and Culture (2016; *timed entry required; info:* **si.edu/museums/african-american-museum**), or the Museum of American History (1964) next door to the east. Both are on the north side of the Mall, and like all the museums, are highly recommended.

Otherwise, continue south past the ticket lodge and uphill slightly to the next traffic light at Jefferson Dr. Turn left (east) and walk to 14th St. [MILE 2.9]. Look right (south) to the distant red-brick building with the clock tower. It's called the Yates Federal Building (1880) and served as headquarters for the U.S. Forest Service since 1990. However, the agency announced in early 2026 that it was moving its headquarters to Salt Lake City. The cute visitor center inside the building was "temporarily closed."

At Holocaust Memorial Museum looking north to Yates Building.

Also on 14th St., just beyond the Yates Building you'll find the main entrances to the Holocaust Memorial Museum (1993) and the "money factory," aka the Bureau of Engraving and Printing or BEP (1914). Both are free, though BEP requires a timed-entry pass for tours (*Mon-Fri 8:30-5:00 in summer*; **bep.gov**). The Holocaust Museum is open 10:00-5:30 daily (**ushmm.org**). The walk over there and back adds 0.4 mile to the loop.

Department of Agriculture.

It's worth checking for a last-minute tour of the BEP, which prints of billions of dollars in U.S. currency every year. Most is printed in Fort Worth, Texas. If you see a little "FW" on a bill, it's the latter. Otherwise, it was printed right here. Coins are minted elsewhere.

The Loop crosses 14th St. and follows Jefferson Dr. to 12th St. passing the ginormous Department of Agriculture building (1930), longer than two football fields placed end to end. Notice too The People's Garden at the corner (about the size of two end zones).

S. Dilllon Ripley Center's dome provides access to extensive art galleries underground.

Just ahead on the right are the recently renovated Freer (1923) and Arthur M. Sackler (1982) Galleries of Asian Art. You could

Smithsonian's first Secretary, Joseph Henry.

easily spend a couple of hours exploring these free Smithsonian galleries, as well as the adjacent **S. Dillon Ripley Center** (1987) with its varying exhibits and kid-friendly **Discovery Theater**. (Ripley was a former Smithsonian Secretary.) Most of the galleries are underground on several levels and fun to explore. You can access them by entering through the small, green-patina domed structure next to the Smithsonian Castle. Incidentally, the Smithsonian Metro Station is across the street from the Freer Gallery.

Next, of course, is the **Smithsonian Castle** (1855), the first major building to be constructed on the National Mall. Keep left to walk to the main street entrance [MILE 3.2]. Before you enter, notice the tall statue across the street of **Joseph Henry**, the first Secretary of the Smithsonian Institution.

You'll definitely want to do a walk through the Castle for some amazing history of the Smithsonian, its improbable beginning and prime benefactor, the English scientist **James Smithson**. (Note that the Castle may be closed temporarily during renovations; if so, back up a few paces and walk around to the garden in back.)

Inside the entrance is the crypt containing Smithson's remains, shipped here from Genoa, Italy, in 1905. On his death in 1829, he willed his fortune to the people of the United States, for the "increase and diffusion of knowledge." He'd never even visited the U.S.

The Castle was designed and built to house the offices of the Smithsonian Institution. Smithson chose the name. The Castle held the growing collections of plant and animal specimens from around the world. As the collections expanded, so did the work of preserving and displaying them in order to meet Smithson's vision of "diffusing" all this scientific knowledge to the public (*see p. 14 for more*). Thanks to his enormous gift, and that of countless others, the Smithsonian Institution's facilities, most of which line the National Mall, have grown to represent the

The Smithsonian Castle

The Castle was designed by the young, prolific architect, James Renwick, Jr., who also designed St. Patrick's Cathedral in New York and the Renwick Gallery building near the White House. The castle was made of red sandstone from a quarry near the C&O Canal, 30 miles outside DC. The tallest tower is 145 feet high.

largest museum complex in the world.

The Castle is still the Smithsonian Institution's main office, so the upper floors are generally off limits, unless you're able to score a member tour of the building. Be sure to wander down the long hall to the exhibit area in the **West Wing**. Exhibits include a sampling of items from the other museums, plus 3D models and historic photos of the Castle and National Mall in 1863.

Also inside are an information desk, gift shop, deli, restrooms and Wi-Fi. You'll find a wealth of information here and online at **si.edu** regarding museum details, more history, research and education materials, Imax movie showtimes and upcoming events.

The Smithsonian Castle is especially fun to gander at on the outside. So head out the back door to the "back forty," or should we say, four acres comprising the **Enid A. Haupt Garden** (1987). By spring, it's all trimmed out in Victorian style with tidy flower beds, walkways, sculptures, fountains and sitting areas.

Poke around the gardens and mosey left on the red brick walkway around the east end of the Castle to the **Folger Rose Garden** and Jefferson Dr. Next door is the spectacular **Arts and Industries Building** (1881). Though vacant, this was the Smithsonian's first official museum, built after the Castle was bursting at the seams from the thousands of specimens collected and the many thousands of visitors who came to see it all. In other words, Smithson's dream had materialized in a very big way.

Known in its day as the **U.S. National Museum**, the design of the Arts and Industries Building is a delightful exercise in 19th cen-

With a couple of large, romantic buildings rising above the Enid Haupt Garden, photographers will find plenty to point their lenses at here. Ms. Haupt, a New York publishing mogul, donated $3 million to establish the gardens, which also double as the roof of the art galleries below.

If the Smithsonian has a plan for the Arts and Industries Building (currently an events venue), they aren't talking, not yet anyway. Well, how about a National Museum of Merriment, with interactive (non-digital) fun, humor, games, brain teasers, toys of the world, magic and attitude—to match the architecture, of course.

"Graft," the stainless steel tree at the National Sculpture Garden.

Winter ice skating at the Sculpture Garden, National Archives behind.

Tip >> If you walk over to the steps behind the Lone Sailor, you can follow 8th St. north for two blocks to the National Portrait Gallery, plus endless choices for a meal or libation throughout the downtown area.

tury architecture, making it one of the more striking historic buildings in Washington. Extensively restored over a decade ago and glorious on the outside, it still needs much additional work inside and apparently a purpose and a suitor before it can reopen—a crisp $100 million would make a great start.

The National Museum grew almost exponentially in the late 1800s, which drove construction of a separate **Museum of Natural History** (1910). Everything "natural" would go there, and the rest could stay at Arts and Industries (more or less). It's directly across the Mall from the Castle and is now one of the most heavily visited museums in the world.

We're now almost to the end of the CENTRAL LOOP! *If you want to continue to the* EAST LOOP *(to the U.S. Capitol), turn to the next page now.*

But to complete the CENTRAL LOOP, simply cross the Mall toward the **Museum of Natural History** (explore it now or later), then keep right of the building to amble through the National Gallery of Art's **Sculpture Garden** (also a cafe and restrooms) next door (*free, 10:00-5:00 daily*; **nga.gov**). Be sure to look at the curious house as you walk by. The center rink is a popular for ice skating in winter. Free Jazz concerts happen 6:00 pm Friday evenings from mid-May to mid-July. But you'll need a pass, possibly at the gate or online (**nga.gov/calendar/jazz-garden**). (The EAST LOOP also ends here, so you can catch it then too.)

To finish the CENTRAL LOOP, exit the Sculpture Garden past the giant eraser to the corner of 9th St. and Constitution Ave. Cross the latter to the **National Archives** building. As noted earlier, you can find the entrance a few steps to the right for both general and timed-entry access. Otherwise, continue north on 9th St. to Pennsylvania Ave. and the Navy Memorial on the other side [MILE 3.7].

Congrats! You've completed the CENTRAL LOOP on the National Mall!

The National Mall: East Loop

Smithsonian Museums - Botanic Garden - U.S. Capitol Library of Congress - Supreme Court - Capitol Hill Union Station - National Art Galleries

- *Distance:* 4.1 - 5.2 miles - *Allow 3 - 4 hours*
- *Start:* U.S. Navy Memorial - *Near Pennsylvania Ave & 7th St. NW*
- *Nearest Metro:* Archives–Navy Memorial–Penn Quarter

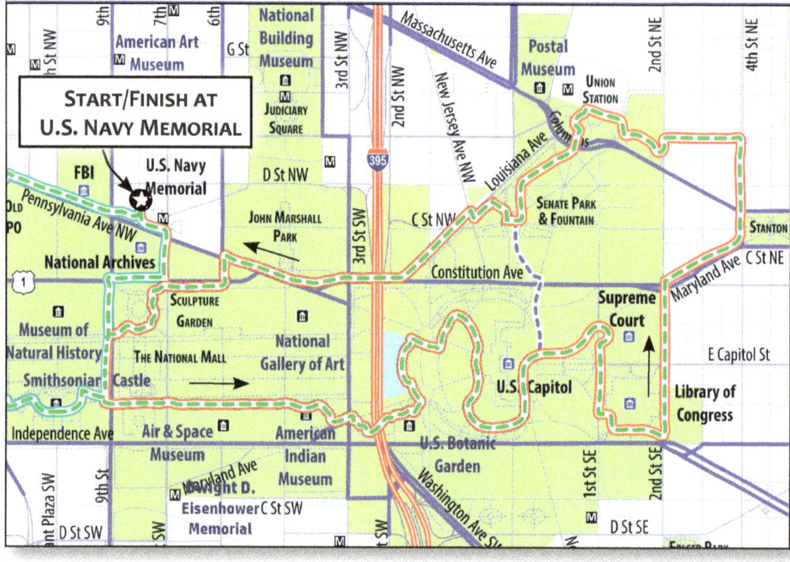

Points of Interest: U.S. Navy Memorial • National Archives • Sculpture Garden Museum of Natural History • Smithsonian Castle • Arts and Industries Building Hirshhorn Museum • National Air & Space Museum • American Indian Museum U.S. Botanic Garden • Bartholdi Park • James Garfield Memorial • U.S. Grant Memorial • Peace Monument • Summerhouse • U.S. Capitol • U.S. Supreme Court Court of Neptune Fountain • Library of Congress • Belmont-Paul Women's Equality Monument • Capitol Hill Neighborhood • Stanton Park • General Nathanael Greene Statue • Union Station • Postal Museum • Christopher Columbus Fountain Senate Park & Fountain • Japanese-American Memorial • U.S Department of Labor John Marshall Park • Canadian Embassy • Federal Trade Commission National Gallery of Art • Andrew W. Mellon Fountain • Grand Army of the Republic Memorial • Temperance Fountain • General Winfield S. Hancock Memorial

Bronze bas reliefs and fountains (below) are highlights at the U.S. Navy Memorial.

On to the U.S. Capitol!

As with the CENTRAL LOOP, a perfect starting point for the East Loop of the National Mall is at the **U.S. Navy Memorial**, near Pennsylvania Ave. and 7th St. NW. From there, we quickly head over toward the Smithsonian Castle, then to the U.S. Capitol and beyond, passing museums, galleries, gardens, the Supreme Court and more.

Note: If you're doing both the CENTRAL and EAST LOOPS back-to-back, you might already be near the Castle and can skip to the first paragraph on p. 61 If not, read on.

The Navy Memorial is next to the **Archives–Navy Memorial–Penn Quarter Metro Station** in downtown Washington. The Metro escalator takes you right there. If you walked over from elsewhere, 7th St. runs midway between the U.S. Capitol and the Washington Monument.

The EAST LOOP begins with an easy ramble over to the Smithsonian's Arts and Industries

Building near the Castle, then aims toward the U.S. Capitol, with a few short meanders to see all the sights. Figure about an hour of leisurely walking in 1.5 miles to the Capitol grounds. You could also spend many hours getting there if you duck into any museums, galleries or gardens along the way.

After the Capitol, the loop makes a minor detour through the historic Capitol Hill Neighborhood to Union Station (at 3.5 miles), before completing the circuit at the Navy Memorial, for a total loop of around five miles. Shortcuts are noted, if desired.

To begin, notice that the middle of the Navy Memorial [MILE 0.0] is a plaza designed as a map of the world's oceans, called the "**Granite Sea.**" Pools, fountains and bronze bas reliefs are all symbolic of the Navy's history and role in the world. (*For more about the Memorial, see p. 43.*)

General Winfield Scott Hancock.

Say farewell to the Lone Sailor and amble toward the Avenue and left to the **General Winfield Scott Hancock Memorial** (1896), with the hero sitting proudly on his horse. Hancock was a decorated Union general during the Civil War, and was prominent in the Battle of Gettysburg. He later ran for president against James Garfield, losing by a whisker.

Cross Pennsylvania Ave. (when safe) to the imposing **National Archives** Building and continue along the left (east) side of the building to reach Constitution Ave. Once there, cross to the obvious gate for the **Sculpture Garden**. East across 7th St. stands the **National Gallery of Art's West Building** (*free, 10:00-5:00 daily*).

National Archives.

Long ago, there was train station on the site of the Gallery, where a disgruntled supporter shot President James Garfield in 1881. He died froman infection 11 weeks later. You'll be very near here again at the end of the loop, in case you want to visit the Galleries of Art or the National Archives then. (*A timed-entry pass is recommended for the Archives; info*: **visit.archives.gov**.)

Amble through the Sculpture Garden, if

African elephant inside the Smithsonian Museum of Natural History

The original National Museum.

Enjoy a short walk at the Ripley Garden amid much floral diversity.

you haven't already, for its abstract structures and critters. Exit past the curious house to Madison Dr. at the southwest corner. (*Read more about the Sculpture Garden on p. 57.*)

The **Museum of Natural History** is to the right (*free, 10:00-5:30 daily*; **naturalhistory.si.edu**). The **Arts and Industries Building** is straight across the Mall. Head there next.

Left of the Castle, the bedazzling Arts and Industries Building was the Smithsonian's first major museum, originally called the **National Museum**. Little did they know how much the Smithsonian Insitution would grow over the next century and a half. (*For more on that story see p. 14.*) Oddly enough, the first event to be held here when it opened in 1881 was the Inaugural Ball for President Garfield.

Before you make your way to the Capitol, scamper back to the near corner of the Castle and look for an interpretive sign for our former ninth planet, **Pluto**. This is the far end of an outdoor exhibit called **Voyage: A Journey through Our Solar System**. Each planet is spaced along Jefferson Dr at a one-to-ten-billion scale, beginning here with poor Pluto, downgraded to a dwarf planet in 2006. You'll pass by the rest of the Voyage exhibit on your way to the Sun near the Air and Space Museum. Do the walk ten billion times and you'd have walked the distance to real Pluto.

Cross the street here to the Smithsonian's **National Carousel** and read the plaque for a surprising tidbit of American history. Grownupss can ride too, by the way. A full restoration was nearly complete in early 2026. At the next crosswalk return to the south side of Jefferson Dr. to visit the **Mary Livingston Ripley Garden** straight ahead. Ripley was an expert gardener and wife of the former Smithsonian Secretary. You can follow this cozy, meandering garden walk (optional) to its end in about 100 yards, and back for a camera-friendly array of flowering plants—like the voodoo lily and Dutchman's pipe. Even the rest benches are eye-catching.

Hirshhorn Museum fountain.

As you exit the Ripley Garden at Jefferson Dr., turn right (east). Close by, look for **Neptune**, the first bonafide planet in the scale model of the solar system and a mere 2.7 billion miles from the sun.

At the Air and Spce Museum, the X-15. The world's fastest rocket plane reached 4,520 mph in 1967. At that speed, one could fly from the U.S. Capitol to the Lincoln Memorial in two seconds.

Continue along the south side of Jefferson Dr. to the steps leading up to the plump, hovering cylinder known as the **Hirshhorn Museum** (1974), a gallery of modern and contemporary art—think Mastisse, Picasso, et al [MILE 0.5]. A wide load of curious objects and art forms are displayed on several levels, so enjoy a look-see now or later. (*Free, 10:00- 5:30*; **hirshhorn.si.edu**.) In the plaza beneath the cylinder, you'll discover the round mass is not solid, but more like a giant donut or spacecraft surrounding a pulsating fountain.

Across Jefferson Dr. and below the street level is the **Hirshhorn Sculpture Garden**. Cross for a short loop among abstract human forms, or view it from above. (A major restoration was wrapping up here in early 2026.)

Return to the south side of Jefferson Dr. and cross 7th St. to find **Uranus** near the corner. **Saturn** comes next near the entrance to the **National Air and Space Museum** (1976). This is the largest and most heavily visited aviation museum in the world.

An author favorite, I hope this survives the museum's restoration! My own dad, Don, was also an airplane mechanic. He called his business "Don's Flying Machines."

This Sun always shines at the Mall. If you walk south on 4th St. a block, you'll find the Dwight D. Eisenhower Memorial. (2020).

A major restoration has been underway for years, and while it's mostly open, final touches may not be complete until summer 2026. (*Free, 10:00-5:30 daily; timed-entry required*; **airandspace.si.edu**.)

Just inside Air and Space is the first plane to break the sound barrier, the Bell X-1 piloted by Chuck Yeager in 1947, and one of only three X-15s ever built. It's still the fastest aircraft ever flown (to Mach 6). Also find John Glenn's legendary capsule, Friendship 7. Glenn was the first American to orbit the Earth (in 1962). Elsewhere in the museum are the Wright Brothers' 1903 Wright Flyer, Charles Lindbergh's famed Spirit of St. Louis, and much more.

Continue east from the museum entrance and look for a small plaque on the wall commemorating the first telegraph dispatched from the air—a **message to President Lincoln** via balloon.

American Indian Museum entrance.

Nearby is **Jupiter**, the fifth marble from the Sun, soon followed by the **Asteroid Belt**, then **Mars**, **Earth**, **Venus** and **Mercury**, all clustered around a grapefruit-sized **Sun**. You are now 3.7 billion miles from Pluto—not bad for a leisurely stroll.

Once the Air and Space restoration is complete, you can hopefully further your celestial pursuits nearby in the **Phoebe Waterman Haas Public Observatory**, although hours may be limited. It once stood at the east end of the Museum near Independence Ave. Inside the smallish, white dome, a telescope was often trained on the moon or solar corona in midday, with occasional viewing of the moon and planets at night, so watch for it.

One of at least 170 tribal flags at the American Indian Museum.

Heading more or less toward the Capitol Building, cross 4th St. SW to the **National Museum of the American Indian** (2004). Follow the walkway along the left (north) side of the museum, passing totems, a waterfall, outdoor sculptures, a natural wetland and **Native American Veterans Memorial** near the main entrance. (*Free, 10:00-5:30 daily*; **americanindian.si.edu**.)

This is another museum you can lose yourself in, so enjoy it now or later. (And check out the Mitsitam Native Foods Café inside—we love the trout and fry bread).

U.S. Capitol and Reflecting Pool.

Past the museum's main entrance overhang is Maryland Ave. Jog left there to cross 3rd St. SW [MILE 1.0]. The **Capitol Reflecting Pool** is just ahead to the left—a good photo op. But come back to this corner to cross Maryland Ave.

After crossing, walk left a few steps and turn right at the gate for a spin around the **Mid-Atlantic Regional Garden**, a mandatory stop if you're of the native plant ilk, or to escape the buzz of traffic on the avenues. Most of the garden is wheelchair-friendly and many plants are labeled. (*Open 7:30 am-7:00 pm daily.*) If you arrive late and the gate is closed, just continue east on the sidewalk, which is also lined with a rich assortment of Mid-Atlantic flora.

Corpse flower bloom at Botanic Garden.

From the garden or the street, aim for the main entrance to the **Conservatory** of the **U.S. Botanic Garden** (1933), originally established in 1820 at another location on the Mall. The entrance off Maryland Ave. is adjacent to a nice plaza and sitting area. (*Free; 10:00-5:00 daily*; **usbg.gov**.) Free concerts sometimes occur at the Conservatory in summer and during the winter holidays, so check the website or information desk for a schedule.

U.S. Botanic Garden.

Mid-Atlantic Garden paths invite a closer look at native trees, shrubs, and flowers found in this part of the U.S., including greater DC.

Bartoldi Park.

The Conservatory offers a good reprieve whether it's muggy or freezing outside, and contains plants from other parts of the globe, from desert to tropical. If you do duck inside, take a stroll through the Jungle, including the canopy catwalk above, accessible by stairs or elevator. From the catwalk windows, you might also notice, across the street to the south, another outdoor garden and a striking fountain within Bartholdi Park.

President James A. Garfield Memorial.

Bartholdi Park (1932) is an extension of the Conservatory, though few tourists seem to wander over to view the flowers and one of the more exotic fountains in D.C. The sculptor was Frederic Bartholdi who incorporated gas lamps in the original design. Bartholdi is better known as the Frenchman who designed the Statue of Liberty in New York. To visit the park, walk around the Conservatory, either along the street on the east side or a path on the west side (when the Mid-Atlantic garden is open).

From the Conservatory's main entrance, return to Maryland Ave. and angle right a little toward the dark statue in the traffic circle. Pause for a moment to acknowledge this **Memorial to President James Garfield** (1887). Four months after his inauguration, a crazed and destitute political minion who had supported Garfield in the election and expected to be awarded a diplomatic job in return, was rebuffed. So he bought a gun and shot the president. Garfield later died from an infection that may have resulted from poor medical care. The assassin was tried and promptly executed.

Ulysses S. Grant Memorial.

Cross Maryland Ave. at the crosswalk (left of the Garfield Memorial) and aim for the nearest corner of the Capitol Reflecting Pool, descending three steps to the waterside walkway. For wheelchair access, keep right on the sidewalk and take the next left.

Follow the water's edge to explore the **Ulysses S. Grant Memorial** (1922), one of the more distinguished monuments on the Mall [MILE 1.3]. Grant, of course, was commander of the Union Army during the Civil War before becoming the 18th U.S. president in 1869. Step up onto the terrace for a closer look at the Cavalry (north) and Artillery (south) and a commanding view of the **U.S. Capitol** (1800).

From Grant, facing the Capitol, cross 1st St. NW. The **Peace Monument** (1877) will be in the traffic circle on your left. Carved in marble in Italy, it commemorates the lives lost at sea during the Civil War. The draped figure facing the Capitol is Peace. The two above are Grief and History.

Rather than bounding up to the Capitol Building from the Peace Monument, continue north along the street past another wide walkway to a right fork leading to the eye-catching, six-sided red-brick structure known as **Summerhouse** (1880), designed by Frederick Law Olmsted. Olmsted also laid out the grounds of the Capitol. Summerhouse is a perfect water stop on a hot day, and little birds seem to agree. Wander inside to see why.

Continue along the same path past a rotund stone pillar nearby which was part of the Capitol's old ventilation system. Follow the curving path toward the **West Steps** of the Capitol Building. This iconic building and glistening dome (fully restored in 2016) are a stunning monument to American democracy. Learn about the building's history and all that it represents during a free and not-to-be-missed docent tour. It begins at the underground visitor center on the opposite (east) side of the building. The Loop will take you there shortly.

Continue to the **Terrace** [MILE 1.7] overlooking the West Lawn and National Mall, as well as the path you took to get here. Washington Monument is 1.3 miles away, Lincoln Memorial is just over two miles. Free concerts by military bands, the National Symphony Orchestra and others are often held here at the West Lawn in the

Peace Monument.

At Summerhouse, enjoy a cool seat and refreshing swig of the Potomac River, DC's main water source.

The ceiling in Statuary Hall, inside the U.S. Capitol.

Full-size model of Freedom inside the Capitol.

U.S. Capitol and East Steps. Below: East Plaza lampposts.

warmer months, with the biggest events during the Memorial Day, 4th of July and Labor Day holidays. (*Search online for dates and details.*) Many of these concerts have been broadcast live on PBS for decades.

Notice the tiered fountain in the central alcove at the Capitol Steps. This is more or less where presidents stand on their really big soapbox to be sworn in and deliver their inaugural speech. Looking up at the building, the **Capitol Dome** and Rotunda are at the center (duh), with the **Senate Chamber** to the left and the **House Chamber** to the right.

Continue south on the walkway to enter a lawn area (water fountain) and pass a small **horse-chestnut tree** on the left, planted in 2014 to honor Anne Frank and the tree she wrote about in her famous diary. Keep left at the pillar and head up the long, gentle hill on a wide path to the East Plaza.

Mosey left into the sprawling **East Plaza**, or what's essentially the Capitol's front yard [MILE 2.0]. Elaborate friezes adorn the gables and two intriguing figures guard the central door, as do the Capitol Police. High above, is the inspiring bronze statue of **Freedom**, nearly 20 feet tall and weighing seven and a half tons. Try to imagine how she was placed there, by freed slaves in 1863, in the midst of a Civil War. The crest of her headdress is 288 feet above the plaza. Wow.

Notice a couple of large glass skylights in the plaza. They allow light into the Visitor Center below. Toward the back of the plaza is a line of six large, ornate **lampposts**. and stairs leading down to the **Capitol Visitor Center**. (*Free, timed-entry required, Mon-Sat 8:30-4:30, closed Sunday and some holidays; info*: **visitthecapitol.gov**.) If you don't see a big crowd lined up outside, ask at the door if last-minute tickets might be available (or check online).

The 45-minute tour of the Capitol begins with an excellent short film, before your group departs with a knowledgeable guide.

You can also browse **Exhibition Hall**, see a full-size model of Freedom, and renditions of the Capitol Building over the past two centuries, plus artifacts and statues of high achievers from the states. Arrive a little early to get through security. Check the website for details and for what not to bring inside, as well as how to get a ticket to the visitor galleries while **Congress** is in session.

Note that if you do head down to the Capitol Visitor Center and go through the security check, you can take an underground pedestrian tunnel to the Library of Congress, and vice-versa. However, you'll need a timed-entry ticket for the place you going to. For the Supreme Court, you'll need to stay above ground.

From the East Plaza, look eastward (away from the Capitol toward 1st St. NE. The Library of Congress is the double-domed building to the right, and the U.S. Supreme Court is to the left. Head to the **Supreme Court** first. (*Free, 9:00-3:00 Mon-Fri; info*: **supremecourt.gov/visiting**.) Curving walkways lead to crosswalks to the Library or the plaza fronting the Court (1935).

From the big doors, you can admire the Supreme Court's 16 marble columns.

Above the columns in the West Pediment are Lady Liberty in the center, Chief Justices Taft (left) and Marshall (right). The sculptor, Robert Aitken, surprised folks by including himself in the work (second from the right).

The U.S. Supreme Court building was sited here within view of the Capitol as a not-too-subtle reminder of the checks and balances in democratic government guaranteed by the Constitution.

Court of Neptune Fountain.

At the Court, seated figures out front are the **Contemplation of Justice** (female) and the **Authority of Law** (male). The gender association could make for some lively conversation.

Although you cannot enter through the giant doors above the plaza—each door weighs over six tons—you can still climb the steps and enjoy mingling among the marble columns. The building really gleams in late afternoon sunlight. The public entrance to the court's **Great Hall** and exhibits, and if your timing is good, a potential tour of the courtroom, is below and right of the great stairs and columns. Wheelchair access is to the left. When the court is in session, long lines can form early to observe the justices in action, amid the legal wranglings of the parties involved.

Thomas Jefferson Building

After the British burned the Capitol Building in 1814, and along with it over 3,000 books, the retired president sold his massive personal collection to Congress for the new national library. The Library of Congress has since become the largest library in the world, with more than 170 million items archived.

A block south on 1st St. is the **Library of Congress** (1897). Keep to the sidewalk long enough to check out the **Court of Neptune Fountain** (1898), a dramatic sculpture of mythical figures in a pool, inspired by the 18th century Trevi Foundatin in Rome. If necessary, hike up the steps, about three flights' worth, to the Library's entrance above an archway; wheelchairs enter below. Or just follow the signs. (*Free, Tue-Sat 10:00-*

5:00, till 8:00 pm Thur; info: **loc.gov/visit**.)

There's much to explore inside the main Library, also known as the **Thomas Jefferson Building**—old books like Gideon's Bible, old maps like the first to say "America," George Gershwin's piano, many exhibits, murals, columns, stairways and a spectacular ceiling. The **Reading Room** is also quite the thing. More than 39 million books are shelved and catalogued here, though you can't exactly check them out. Browse the website for details. Do visit sometime and catch a docent tour, if possible.

Awesome ceiling inside the Library of Congress.

For the 4.1-mile loop, return to the Supreme Court, go north on 1st St. four blocks to Union Station, and skip to the bottom of p. 71. For the 5.2-mile loop and a spin through the historic Capitol Hill Neighborhood, walk around the south side of the Library near Independence Ave. to 2nd St. NE; turn left **[MILE 2.6]**. Across Pennsylvania Ave. are a number of local hotspots over the next several blocks in case you have an urge to chill or chow down.

(To add an hour or two of additional exploring, see p. 137 for a 2.8-mile Capitol Hill Loop from here to Barracks Row and Eastern Market, where there's a Metro Station at Pennsylvania Ave. and 7th St.)

Outside Folger Shakespeare Library.

Otherwise, head left on 2nd St. After passing the back side of the Library of Congress, the next building on the right at the end of the block is the **Folger Shakespeare Library and Theatre** (1932), highly recommended if you're the literary type. *(Free, 11:00-6:00 Tue-Sun, till 9:00 pm Fri; info*: **folger.edu**.). Watch for the statue with

Historic Capitol Hill Neighborhood.

Belmont-Paul National Monument.

At Stanton Park, General Greene's right index finger points down Maryland Ave. to the Capitol.

Inside Union Station.

a catchy quote. Inside the Folger's East Capitol St. entrance is a small, but interesting exhibit hall and a perfect Elizabethan theater for taking in a play.

Next cross East Capitol St. On the left is the highly decorated rear end the Supreme Court building. Notice the immortal words near the gable or East Pediment. Among the figures are Moses, a tortoise and a hare.

In another block, cross 2nd St. and turn right at Maryland Ave., or cross to visit the **Belmont-Paul Women's Equality National Monument**, designated in 2016 to honor women's suffrage. The building dates to 1800 and has been the home of the National Women's Party since 1922. Open for tours only (*Thur-Fri-Sat, 11:00, 1:00, 3:00*). If you stopped in for a look, re-cross 2nd St. NE to walk past the **Veterans of Foreign Wars** (VFW), founded in 1899 after the Spanish-American War.

Follow Maryland Ave. for two blocks, admiring an array of 19th century architectural styles. At 4th St. NE, turn left. Or take the crosswalk over to **Stanton Park** [MILE 3.1] and the statue of Revolutionary War hero, **General Nathanael Greene** (1877). Greene was recognized as a brilliant military strategist, second only to George Washington.

At 4th St., cross Massachusetts Ave. and continue north two blocks before turning left at E St. In two blocks more, cross 2nd St. NE. Jog left and take the short sidewalk angling up the grass, then right on another path at the end of the hedge. Follow this past the **Federal Judicial Center** to a cluster of flagpoles and a walkway leading to **Union Station** dead ahead.

If you haven't already peered inside **Union Station** (1907) [MILE 3.7], by all means do. The beaux-arts building was nearly lost to neglect by 1980, but was carefully restored (a couple of times) to preserve what is truly one of America's grand architectural marvels. The **Main Hall** is 96 feet high and leaved with 70 pounds of gold guarded by

36 Roman legionnaire statues.

The respectable nudes and near-nudes, including six more outside the main entry, are the work of American sculptor Louis Saint-Gaudens. A century ago, political correctness collided with anatomical correctness here, resulting in the artist's begrudging addition of a handheld shield to each male form. Archways, ornate trim and lighting, circular stairs, marble floors and an old Roman clock add to the glamour.

More than 100,000 people can pass through the station in a day, mostly rail, bus and Metro commuters. Besides people, you'll find upscale shops, travel and visitor services, dozens of eateries, including a large food court on the lower level, and sufficiently decent restrooms. Just inside the main entrance, you'll also find ticket counters for hop-on/hop-off D.C. bus tours, and a big reader board for regional train departures. When you've seen enough inside, move to the plaza outside to ogle the exterior décor.

From the main entrance to Union Station, look down the long arched corridor or loggia that leads directly to the Smithsonian's **Postal Museum** just across 1st St NE, a worthy side trip. Then amble over to the big **Freedom Bell** and the gleaming white **Christopher Columbus Fountain**. The Freedom Bell (1981) is an enlarged replica of the Liberty Bell in Philadelphia. Walk around it and the Christopher Columbus Fountain (1912), newly restored in 2026. Wheelchairs can make a wide detour left or right. Notice the figures to either side of Columbus representing the Old and New Worlds. Columbus, of course, is the namesake for the District of Columbia.

Optional: Two other sites are located a block down Massachusetts Ave. at the corner of North Capitol St.: the **National Guard Me-**

Union Station is as awesome as it is large—long enough, in fact, that if you stood it on end it would be taller than the Washington Monument.

Outside Union Station.

Over a century ago, tens of thousands attended the Columbus Fountain dedication and Knights of Columbus parade that followed. Despite the momentous beginning, the fountain had been out of commission for years, until a full restoration in 2026.

At the Senate Fountain, the upthrusting water columns mimic the Capitol Dome.

morial Museum (1991) and the Ukraine Holodomor Memorial (2015) across the street. If you decide to visit them, backtrack to the Columbus Fountain to continue the Loop.

Following Columbus' nose, head south across Columbus Circle (toward the U.S. Capitol) via the extra-wide crosswalk. At the median, drift over to the right-hand crosswalk and past the line of flagpoles, taking a soft right on the diagonal walkway that cuts through a shady corridor of spring-flowering trees and shrubs. Many of the larger and older trees in the surrounding Senate Park were dedicated to former presidents. Some are tagged with little placards noting the common and Latin names for each species.

Japanese American Memorial.

At the far end of this restive corridor, take the obvious crosswalk left and aim for the nearby reflecting pool for a nice mirror-image of the Capitol rising above the Senate Fountain. This is a great place for cherry blossoms in spring, with some varieties blooming later than the more famous trees around the Tidal Basin. Walk around the pool and head up the steps to the main fountain for a look.

Return to Louisiana Ave., cross at D St. and turn left. Walk downhill a few steps to visit the Japanese American Memorial (2000). In this peaceful memorial [MILE 4.1], you'll find the story of the internment camps during WWII, the subsequent Presidential apology, and a list of Japanese Americans who died serving in the U.S. military during WWII. It's a humbling place and a sad reminder of ongoing racism in the U.S.

U.S. Department of Labor (right).

Return to Louisiana Ave. and turn right to cross New Jersey Ave., then C St. and 1st St. NW. If you hear a bell tolling, it's probably the 100-foot belltower visible in the trees to the left, otherwise known as the Robert A. Taft Memorial and Carillon (1959). Taft, a stalwart conservative, was a U.S. Senator from Ohio and son of President Taft.

Continue along Louisiana Ave. another

block to where it merges into Constitution Ave. near a gaggle of white-potted trees. Look right and cross 2nd St. to a red brick walkway. Take this briefly uphill past the **U.S. Department of Labor** (1975) for a slightly better view of the Mall. The building is named for Labor Secretary Frances Perkins, the first woman cabinet member and still longest serving Labor Secretary (1933-1945). She was pivotal in implementing FDR's New Deal.

National Gallery of Art, East Building.

Ahead, the dome and angular buildings to the left across Constitution Ave. are the West and East Buildings of the **National Gallery of Art** (1941 and 1978). While admission is free, they are not part of the Smithsonian, but rather a gift to the American people by banker-collector-philanthropist Andrew Mellon. The curvier buildings on the right at the corner belong to the federal court system.

Now cross 3rd St. NW and follow busy Constitution Ave. to a couple of statues just ahead. **Sir William Blackstone** (1943), a highly influential 18th century English legal scholar is hiding out on the right, followed by a robust monument to **Union General George Meade** of Gettysburg fame.

Union General George Meade.

A short distance beyond the General, reach **John Marshall Park**, dedicated to the longest-serving and supremely influential 4th Chief Justice of the U.S. Supreme Court. He served across six presidential administrations, from 1801 to 1835. (A major park restoration was being completed here in early 2026.)

Cross the busy street at a crosswalk. But first notice the next big building flying maple leaf flags, the **Canadian Embassy** (1989). It's the nearest foreign embassy to the U.S. Capitol. Should you feel like snooping, the steps lead up to the main entrance (wheelchairs stay right), where you'll find an intriguing sculpture from British Columbia. The **Spirit of Haida Gwaii** appears to float in a pool.

Embassy of Canada.

(*Optional*: If you were to walk up through John Marshall Park, paths would lead you to the oldest statue of Abraham Lincoln in the

Civil War Memorial to the Grand Army of the Republic

Organized in 1866 to give veterans of the Civil War a strong voice in the post-war years, the veterans group grew to hundreds of thousands and successfully advocated for pensions and voting rights for Black veterans, while also wielding sway in political campaigns and helping to establish the Memorial Day holiday in 1868. It was originally called Decoration Day, a day to decorate the graves of soldiers killed in the war.

The Temperance Fountain was an ice-cooled drinking-water fountain meant to discourage excessive alcohol consumption in the 1880s.

U.S. Carved by a man (Flannery) who was at the theater the night Lincoln was shot, the statue was dedicated in 1868, three years after Lincoln's death. A good walk through the area is described on p. 175.)

Once across the busy avenue at 4th St., walk south a few more steps and you'll be right between the two buildings of the National Gallery of Art [MILE 4.7]. (*Free, 10:00-5:00 daily*; **nga.gov**.) The angular East Building (1978) is joined with the West Building by a rather joyful underground light tunnel. You have almost completed the East Loop, so you could explore the galleries now or later. Otherwise, continue west along Constitution Ave.

Pass the Andrew Mellon Memorial Fountain (1951) and the Federal Trade Commission (1938) on the right, and the main entrance to the National Art Gallery's West Building. For a quick peek inside, head up to the second floor rotunda.

As you walk past the West Building toward 7th St., notice the 1942 statue next to the Federal Trade Commission depicting a big man (society) struggling to tame a mighty horse (trade). At 7th St., a corner gate leads into the National Sculpture Garden (1999). To the right (north) is the National Archives and its main entrance is up ahead on the right. To complete the Loop, however, turn right on 7th St. and cross Pennsylvania Ave.

Walk up 7th St. (away from the Mall) and cross Pennsylvania Ave. The obelisk on the right is the Civil War Memorial to the Grand Army of the Republic (1909), surrounded by several historic buildings of DC's Old Downtown, now more commonly known as Penn Quarter. The Temperance Fountain (1884), crowned by a heron, is close by.

Finally, mosey over to the Navy Memorial to complete the Loop [MILE 5.2].

You've completed the East Loop!

Tip: >> Wander up 7th St. NW to find many great choices for a beverage or meal.

The National Mall: West Loop

Washington Monument - Thomas Jefferson Memorial FDR Memorial - Martin Luther King, Jr. Memorial Korea & Vietnam War Memorials - Lincoln Memorial WWII Memorial - Constitution Gardens

- *Distance*: 4.0 - 6.0 miles - *Allow 3 - 4 hours*
- *Start*: Washington Monument
- *Nearest Metro*: Smithsonian - *Near the Castle*

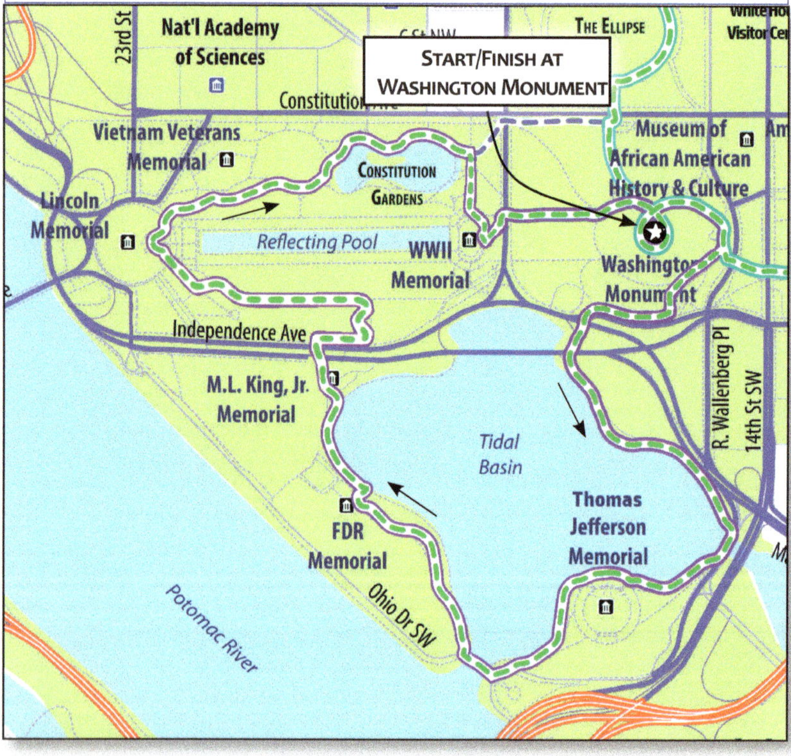

23rd St
Nat'l Academy of Sciences
Constitution Ave
Start/Finish at Washington Monument
The Ellipse
Vietnam Veterans Memorial
Museum of African American History & Culture
Constitution Gardens
Lincoln Memorial
Reflecting Pool
WWII Memorial
Washington Monument
Independence Ave
M.L. King, Jr. Memorial
Tidal Basin
R. Wallenberg Pl
14th St SW
Thomas Jefferson Memorial
FDR Memorial
Ohio Dr SW
Potomac River

Points of Interest: Washington Monument • Tidal Basin • Thomas Jefferson Memorial • George Mason Memorial • Franklin Delano Roosevelt Memorial Martin Luther King, Jr. Memorial • District of Columbia War Memorial U.S. Park Police Horse Stables • Korean War Veterans Memorial • Lincoln Memorial & Reflecting Pool • Vietnam War Veterans Memorial • Vietnam Women's Memorial Constitution Gardens • Signers of the Declaration of Independence Memorial • Lockkeeper's House • WWII Memorial

Washington Monument Lodge, for gifts and tickets.

Superb by Day, Stunning by Night

The WEST LOOP is superb for its iconic memorials and monuments that the National Mall is so well known for. There are many others around the Mall and DC generally, but the biggies—Washington, Jefferson, FDR, King and Lincoln, along with most of the major war veterans memorials—are all experienced up close in this four to six-mile loop. We begin the WEST LOOP at one of the most iconic sites, the **Washington Monument**.

The loop catches many more sites and sights along the way. But if the time or distance seem like too much, you can also just follow your nose from one majestic place to the next. There are a number of Capital Bikeshare docks throughout which can also work great for this loop (*info: p. 28*). The hop-on, hop-off buses typically stop at these locations as well.

But assuming you're up for a great walk, make your way to the base of the **Washington Monument**, the starting and ending point of this National Mall WEST LOOP [MILE 0.0].

There are any number of ways to get here: walk, bike or rideshare from elsewhere, or hope to find parking someplace nearby (can be difficult). The nearest Metro Station is the Smithsonian in front of the Freer Gallery near the Castle, about a 10 or 15-minute walk from the Monument.

Note: If you just completed the CENTRAL or EAST

Need Tickets?

If you plan to snag an elevator ride up the Washington Monument, try to reserve your timed-entry ticket in advance online (nps.gov/wamo). Tickets can be hard to come by, although you might be lucky with same-day timed-entry tickets by lining up at the Lodge ticket window (above) early morning—earlier the better in the busy season (March-October). Lines can form an hour or more before the ticket window opens (*see p. 53*).

The annual Kite Festival on the Mall attracts thousands in late March or early April.

LOOP, it's about a one-mile walk (or bike ride) from the Navy Memorial to the monument. Or you could hop on the Metro to Smithsonian to reduce the distance by half.

Gnarly tree, Survey Lodge behind.

Looking south from the Washington Monument, notice the lawn and stage area below. This is the **Sylvan Theater** (1917) where ranger talks, smaller concerts and other events sometimes occur. Work your way there next and take the path on the right that leads around the stage and toward the street. (Restrooms are tucked in the trees behind the stage.) Turn right at a tee junction and stroll right a couple of minutes to reach a crosswalk for Independence Ave.

Before crossing, notice the gnarly old tree, and behind it the historic **Survey Lodge** (1886) [MILE 0.4]. The stone building is about as old as the Washington Monument. In fact, it was built from the leftover stones. When the monument originally opened in 1888, the elevator was powered by steam, and this was the boiler house.

Floral library.

The elevator switched to electricity in 1901. Since the 555-foot-tall monument offered an excellent reference point for surveying, the building was converted to a facility for surveyors. Park rangers sometimes hang out here to offer info to visitors, but the building is otherwise closed to the public.

Now cross both Independence and Maine Aves. (three crosswalks) to find the path running left along the shore of the **Tidal Basin**. But first look left to see what's blooming at the **Floral Library**, inspired in 1969 by Lady Bird Johnson. The season begins with a modest sea of tulips, then evolves from there year to year.

At the far end of a long parking lot, you can find a kiosk and dock with paddle boat and kayak rentals (*10:00-6:00*). Inquire there or

Thomas Jefferson Memorial and cherry blossoms from across the Tidal Basin.

The "money factory," Bureau of Engraving and Printing.

Pedestrian corridor to 14th St.

At the bridge over the Tidal Basin outlet gate.

search online for details and reservations. Rentals are seasonal and might not be available during poor weather.

At the busy street intersection ahead [MILE 0.7], the loop continues around the Basin, but for an optional side trip, look to the left for the big building with all the columns. This is the **Bureau of Engraving & Printing** (or **BEP**), otherwise known as the "money factory." Much of our U.S. currency is printed here. (*For info on a timed-entry tour, see p. 54.*) The BEP is also adjacent to the **Holocaust Memorial Museum**. Both are free and both entrances can be reached by walking uphill (north) on Raoul Wallenberg Pl. for roughly two blocks and turning right at a narrow pedestrian walkway leading to 14th St. (Expect a quarter-mile walk each way from the Tidal Basin.)

The loop, however, crosses a bridge just ahead at the Tidal Basin's outlet tidal gate. Reconstructed in 1949, much as it appears today, the Basin was designed to use a pair of automatic tide gates and two or three feet of local tidal influence on the Potomac River. (Yes, the Chesapeake Bay tide cycle reaches all the way to DC.) Pressure differentials open and close the gates with no motors required. The flow through the Basin helps flush the extra sediment and goose poop out of the Basin and the Washington Channel boat harbor downriver.

Just pass the bridge is another optional side trip to **East Potomac Park** and **Hains Point**. A crosswalk over Ohio Dr. and the underpass lead to the nearly two-mile-long peninsula, mostly occupied by a golf course, but with good walking or biking all around the perimeter (*see p. 174.*).

From the bridge over the Tidal Basin's tidal gate, saunter around the basin a few minutes more to the gleaming **Thomas Jefferson Memorial** [MILE 1.1]. The Memorial was completed in 1943 and dedicated by FDR, although the bronze statue inside wasn't finished and installed until after WWII.

The design of the building was borrowed in part from the ancient Pantheon in Rome, which was also the model for the University of Virginia's Rotunda, designed by none other than Thomas Jefferson, founder of the university (after his term as U.S. President). You might say our third prez was a versatile fellow.

The high steps at Jefferson Memorial make good bleachers for occasional summer music events.

Climb the steps and savor the view. An elevator is available for those who might like an upward assist. The elevator, along with a gift shop, exhibit area and restrooms are hidden in a tunnel below the memorial, accessed at the near and far ends of the steps.

Behind the columns is the 19-foot tall bronze statue of the third U.S. president. Yet he wished not to be remembered as president, but as the principal author of the Declaration of Independence, which he holds in his left hand, as well as founder of the university. Surrounding the statue you'll find a selection of his more profound exaltations etched in marble walls.

Inside the Jefferson Memorial.

Once you've fist-bumped Mr. Jefferson and thanked him for all his help creating an actual country, continue left along the Tidal Basin. A massive project to reconstruct the seawall is quite evident, especially if you'd walked the old paths in the past. The work was largely completed in late 2025 (ahead of schedule and under budget).

The former seawall was over a century old and had sunk more than five feet in some areas, leading to flooded walkways and damage to facilities and the famed cherry trees that line much of the seawall. The design also takes into account a rising sea level due to climate change.

George Mason Memorial.

Pause at an elevated bridge over the second tidal gate. Before crossing, a brief detour to the left may be in order. Almost hidden among trees behind a small pool is the relaxed bronze figure of another founding father seated on a bench. This time it's the **George Mason Memorial**, Mason being the principal author of what

At sunset, the columns at Jefferson Memorial come alive.

would later become the Bill or Rights in the U.S. Constitution.

You can thank this Virginia statesman for some things we often take for granted, like freedom of speech, press and religion. Mason insisted these ideas be made part of the Constitution—or dadgummit, he wasn't signing. Although he was a wealthy and prolific slaveholder (as were Washington and Jefferson), he also empathized with the abolition of slavery, arguing paradoxically (or hypocritically) that the Constitution should forbid slavery outright.

Cross over the tidal gate and follow the path along the water. The open space to the left is **West Potomac Park,** a local favorite for ball games. The path slips past restrooms and an unassuming entrance to the **Franklin Delano Roosevelt Memorial** (1997) [MILE 1.6]. But the grand scale of the memorial quickly becomes evident, even moreso as you ramble from one "room" to the next.

Technically, you're walking back in time, as you might notice by the various themes within each room. Among the elaborate walls,

The Roosevelts' Fala.

Recalling the Great Depression, at the FDR Memorial.

alcoves, pools, waterfalls and sculptures are the 32nd president's immortal words carved into heavy granite blocks. You'll also pass Eleanor, another American icon, and Fala, the First Family's Scottish terrier.

At the northwest end of the memorial, pass a building that contains restrooms and a bookstore. Nearby is FDR seated in his self-designed wheelchair.

Back on the path rounding the Tidal Basin, the next stop is 300 yards ahead, the **Martin Luther King, Jr. Memorial**. As always, watch your step: the walkway is adjacent to deep water with no guardrail. (It seems odd that there is no subtle railing or black chains here (like in other areas of the Mall) to help keep our collective keisters out of the drink.)

This stretch is also a favorite place to take in the blossoming cherry trees in spring, typically between late March and early April.

Eleanor and Fraklin Roosevelt.

Cherry blossoms near their peak at the Tidal Basin, MLK Jr. Memorial.

Photo: Kris Wilcox

Design of the Martin Luther King, Jr. Memorial was inspired by a line from King's "I Have a Dream" speech:

"Out of a mountain of despair, a stone of hope."

Cherry Blossoms

During the spring bloom, expect the Tidal Basin to be swarmed, with many experiencing the spring spectacle for the first time. For best lighting and more manageable crowds, be there with your camera before sunrise. Anywhere around the basin will do (areas near the M.L. King and FDR Memorials are local favorites).

You can thank Eliza Scidmore for needling officials for two decades (a century ago) to plant these trees. Having traveled to Japan, she thought cherry trees offered a perfect spiffer-upper for what was a messy, recently reconstructed waterfront. Finally in 1912, over 3,000 cherry trees and a stout Japanese lantern were shipped to the U.S., a gift from Japan. The first two trees were planted by First Lady Helen Taft and Viscountess Chinda, wife of Japan's Ambassador. To see the lantern and first trees, detour left along the basin from the Martin Luther King, Jr. Memorial, then retrace your steps to continue.

Enter the Martin Luther King, Jr. Memorial [MILE 2.0]. The bookstore and restrooms are to the left. Though it was a long time coming, the Memorial finally opened in August 2011. A selection of King's best tenets on justice and civil rights are preserved in the surrounding stoneworks. Browse the panels as you walk through this fitting tribute to a great American leader, one whose own monumental work changed a nation.

Exit the Memorial through "The Mountain" and out toward the traffic light to make the wide crossing of Independence Ave. Either continue straight on the path through **Ash Woods**, the closest thing to a forest anywhere on the Mall, or sidle to the right 100

yards to the domed marble structure: the **District of Columbia War Memorial** (1931). Completed in 1931, it honors those from the U.S. capital who made the ultimate sacrifice during The Great War (WWI). The memorial was sized to accommodate concerts by the U.S. Marine Band.

WWI Memorial, dedicated to D.C. residents lost in the war.

Along the east margin of Ash Woods, head west on the wide path toward Lincoln Memorial. You'll immediately pass the new **U.S. Park Police Horse Stables** (2023). Designed to be more accessible to the public than the old stables, the facility allows for a much improved interaction between man and beast.

Privately funded, the new education center and ability to get somewhat acquainted with the animals are inspiring, even if the bland white parts of the building lack the charm of the former stables. (*Open Thur-Sun 9:00-3:00.*)

Ash Woods in winter.

Somewhere along your journey, you might even see the steeds at work. In fair weather, there's a reasonable chance you'll encounter at least a pair of amicable park officers and their mounts on patrol.

For now, journey another couple of minutes west to visit the **Korean War Veterans Memorial** (1995) on the left. Nineteen larger-than-life soldiers appear to be moving quietly over uncertain terrain. The scene gives an almost eerie feeling, especially at night. Each stainless steel figure is over seven feet tall and realistically equipped. Actual photos are etched into the adjacent reflecting wall. Above is a Pool of Remembrance. A major restoration here was completed in 2022.

Say howdy to the U.S. Park Police.

Optional: Also in the vicinity is the **John Ericsson Memorial** (1926) that honors the Swedish engineer who designed the Navy's first ironclad warship, the mighty USS Monitor. Launched in January 1862, the ship was lost at sea in a storm eleven months later. The memorial is not as easy to access as the

Korean War Memorial.

John Ericsson Memorial.

From the Gettysburg Address.

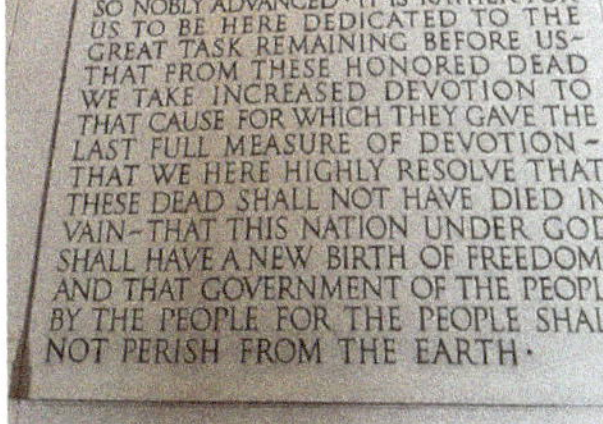

others, but can be found by walking due south of the Lincoln Memorial and crossing Independence Ave. to the traffic circle.

Otherwise, enjoy the final few steps to the **Lincoln Memorial** (1922) above a wide plaza and the grand steps (four score and seven steps to be exact) leading up to the big man above [MILE 2.7]. The numbers are hard to fathom, but millions of visitors climb these steps each year—a mandatory ascent when you're this close to our 16th president.

On the way up, look for the engraved words where Martin Luther King, Jr. stood in the summer of 1963 to deliver his "**I have a dream**" speech. Above sits the president's realistic portrayal, carved from marble and immersed in stunning Roman architecture.

At the terrace, seeing the noble man's steady gaze and 19-foot-tall likeness so close for the first time can be awe-inspiring. On the surrounding walls, many of his most ponderable words, including the Gettysburg Address, are etched in stone. Interpretive rangers and information kiosks are available to further enhance your visit.

A major new exhibit space beneath the Memorial was nearing completion in early 2026 and scheduled to open in time for the

summer celebration of 250 years of American independence. Called the "**undercroft**," the cavernous space is rife with columns and other hidden structures supporting the massive memorial above. Creative use of the space results in a 15,000 square foot area for exhibits, multi-media elements, gift shop, elevator, new restrooms and more. If the weather's nice, expect a ton of company. As with most open-air memorials, the grounds and terrace are open 24/7. On a warm summer evening, it's not unusual to find hundreds of people at midnight still exploring the Mall between Lincoln Memorial and Washington Monument.

View across Lincoln Reflecting Pool.

One can also walk around the outside terrace among the columns for a good look at the Potomac River and the glassy skyline of downtown Rosslyn, Virginia—part of Arlington. Not a bad place for a shady respite from the crowds. From the right spot, Memorial Bridge is also conspicuous, with Arlington National Cemetery at its far end.

(For a scenic two or three hour trek over the bridge, along the Mount Vernon Trail, and back across Key Bridge to Georgetown, see the five-mile RIVER LOOP on p. 97.)

Descending the **Lincoln Steps**, many will pause or sit to gaze out at this iconic and familiar scene: the **Lincoln Memorial Reflecting Pool**, 50 yards wide and over 2,000 feet long (and at most, 30 inches

Lincoln Memorial, stunning by day and by night.

The Three Servicemen at the Vietnam Memorial.

A Vietnam veteran (the author's older brother) remembers a Marine Corps chopper pilot and crew lost in the war. The Wall is an elegantly simple design inscribed with a heavy dose of wartime reality.

Women's Vietnam Memorial.

deep). Lined up perfectly beyond are the WWII Memorial, Washington Monument and U.S. Capitol just over two miles away. You can catch their reflections best closer to the pool.

Once you've admired the man inside and hoisted your jaw back into place, descend to the plaza below the steps and angle a little left toward the corner of the Reflecting Pool. Keep left to visit the **Vietnam War Veterans Memorial**, completed in 1982. The memorial was privately funded in a campaign organized by veterans.

Binders with indexes are available for those wishing to look up a name of someone who perished in the war. The listing gives the panel location where the name is inscribed on the black granite walls close by.

Look back to the right for the statue of the **Three Servicemen** gazing toward their comrades, then walk to the wall.

Together, the two adjoining walls are nearly 500 feet long, tapered to gently sink into the landscape before rising up again. More than 58,000 names are inscribed. The effect can be an emotional experience for many, especially for those close to anyone who served. Name rubbing with paper and charcoal is common means of remembrance.

Many have left mementos here for the fallen, from dog tags and letters to beer and cigarettes, and thousands more items that are respectfully collected and stored by the National Park Service.

At the end of the wall, turn right to reach an intersection in 60 yards. The Loop heads left, but first jog right briefly to visit the Vietnam **Women's Memorial** dedicated in 1993. It depicts three nurses tending to a wounded soldier. More than 11,000 women served in the war, not just as nurses, but in a wide variety of roles. Eight of the names on the Vietnam Wall are women.

Return the to the junction, but continue straight (east) to pass a circular restroom building and **Constitution Gardens** [MILE 3.1].

Keep left to walk clockwise around the pond (undergoing a major restoration in early 2026). In another 200 yards, a path and footbridge lead right to the little island that hosts a **Memorial to the Signers of the Declaration of Independence** (1984). Their signatures, including John Hancock's very own "John Hancock" are inscribed in stone here.

John Hancock's famous signature appeared with that of our second president, John Adams, both willing to dedicate, as the Declaration states, "our Lives, our Fortunes and our Sacred Honor" to the idea of American democracy.

Along the water's edge, take a moment to look back and reflect on the beauty of the National Mall. From Washington Monument to Lincoln Memorial, the landscape's softer edges here, the gentle slopes, open water and scattered trees give the west end of the Mall a more peaceful, natural ambience compared to the eastern parts of the Mall.

Continue around the pond and straight up the short hill to a four-way junction [MILE 3.4]. The Loop goes right, but look a little left for the old stone **Lockkeeper's House** (1833) at the corner of Constitution Ave. and 17th St. It's worth a quick visit (100 yards) before moving on to the WWII Memorial.

The Lockkeeper's House once fronted the Washington City Canal, with the Potomac River lapping at the shore right outside the building. In the 1830s, the canal linked the Potomac with the Anacostia River to improve transport, but like the C&O Canal, the emergence of the railroads in the mid-1800s would ensure their demise. (*See p. 102 for more on the C&O Canal.*)

The stone Lockkeepers House served barge and boat traffic on the Washington Canal, originally envisioned by Pierre L'Enfant in his plan for the city. The old canal is now buried under Constitution Ave.

Constitution Gardens.

Also, in the 1880s, a massive dredging and landfill project pushed the river away by creating a full square mile of new upland, including nearly all the land you just walked from the Jefferson, King and Lincoln Memorials to Constitution Gardens. A sign near the building illustrates where the river's edge used to be. The flow of the Potomac was replaced with the flow of traffic on Constitution Ave. just steps away.

In 2017, the building was carefully moved about 50 feet to give it more breathing room. It was also fully restored and enhanced with a new plaza and pathways.

WWII Memorial, also great by day or by night.

Retrace your steps and carry on to the **WWII Memorial** another 150 yards to the south. Look for the tall archway at the north end of the memorial labeled "Atlantic." This gives a nice overview of the impressive grounds and fountain. The far end reads "Pacific," reminding us of the two major theaters of the war. Wander at will to check out the 56 granite columns--one for each of the 48 states, seven territories and the District of Columbia that existed during the time of WWII.

Many inscriptions, bas reliefs, gold stars and other details recall the solemn history of those years. You might stumble on a bit of authorized graffiti ("Kilroy was here") engraved in the stone. The fountain creates endless photo ops as well, day or night.

WWII Memorial.

The WWII Memorial was dedicated with much fanfare in 2004, after a decade of controversy about where to put it and what it should look like. Some were concerned that the memorial would interrupt the cherished visual corridor between the Washington Monument and Lincoln Memorial.

However, the broad, open design of the memorial seems to have mitigated that concern well enough. It was paid for by a major fundraising campaign and truly is stunning site to behold, especially when lit up at night. Millions visit the memorial every year.

From here, it's an easy shot back up the center of the National Mall to complete the Loop at the Washington Monument [MILE 4.0]. However, if it's in your DNA to see every last thing, head right (south) a short distance along the walkway near 17th St.

Notice the statue in the traffic circle somewhat hidden in the trees. This is the John Paul Jones Memorial (1912). Born in Scotland, Jones became an American naval war hero during the Revolution and is considered the patriarch of the U.S. Navy. Thousands, including President Taft, attended the dedication.

As you stroll the final leg up to Washington Monument [MILE 4.0], watch for the Jefferson Pier about 100 yards below the obelisk and a little to the left. It marks the point on the U.S. Capitol-Lincoln Memorial axis that's due south of the White House (*see also p. 52*).

This completes the West Loop of the National Mall! Congratulations!

And double congrats if you've completed all three loops! Bragging rights are officially secured.

Tip: >> If you're looking for a new part of greater DC to relax or explore with little effort, hop on the Metro and head to any of these local favorites: Eastern Market, Dupont Circle, Gallery Place-Chinatown, Brookland, Waterfront/Wharf, or King Street/Old Town Alexandria.

The Grand Loop

To complete the Grand Loop around the National Mall, you can either walk the Central, East and West loops as described, one after the other, or link them together as noted in the text. Depending on whether you complete the few extra sidetrips described, the total distance will vary between 12 and 14 miles.

You can give your feet a break by including several hop-on, hop-off bus rides, or a few short bike rides (with a Bikeshare day pass). A bike works especially well along the East and West Loops. Snag a bike, ride a little, park it at a dock and repeat. It's a fun to way to cover a lot of ground around the Mall.

The Central Loop, however, follows sidewalks along a few busy streets, so it's not as much fun on a bike.

If your grand plan is to also visit museums, galleries and federal buldings like the U.S. Capitol, Library of Congress, National Archives and others, it makes sense to tour the Mall early and late in the day, saving the hours between for exploring all the indoor wonders. Also a great strategy if the weather's hot.

While the expedition alone can be quite enjoyable, do take time to browse the information provided at virtually every site mentioned in this guide. The National Parks app is another great resource that can add some real value to the experience.

Mini-Loop of the Americas

From the **Lockkeeper's House**, cross Constitution Ave. for a 0.6-mile walk focused on the Americas. Walk north on 17th St. NW, passing the ornate headquarters of the **Organization of American States** (1910) to your left. The OAS comprises all 35 nations of North, Central and South America and the Caribbean, and seeks to promote peace, justice and collaboration.

At C St., you'll find the columned edifice of the **Daughters of the American Revolution** or DAR, a/k/a Memorial Continental Hall (1905), and the adjacent **Constitution Hall** (1929). The DAR, run entirely by women, has a museum, extensive library and exceptional period rooms depicting early American life. (*Open Mon-Sat, hours vary—see* **dar.org**.) Constitution Hall hosts conferences, galas and performances throughout the year.

DAR Continental Hall.

Continue north on 17th St. to the next corner for a glance at the striking bright marble edifice, headquarters of the **American Red Cross** (1917). Retrace your steps to C St. and turn right to pass by the Continental Hall's semicircle of columns. Across the street on the OAS lawn look for a bronze bust of the Italian merchant, navigator, mapmaker and man of big hair (or hat), **Amerigo Vespucci** (2012), for whom the Americas were named. Now imagine what we'd be called if they'd used his last name instead.

Continue on C St. to 18th St. The blocky fortress ahead and right is the **U.S. Department of Interior** (1936).

The author's mom loved the newspaper. We thought she was going to read them all during a visit from Utah, when she made her way along the display at the old Newseum on Pennsylvania Ave. The Newseum is long gone, but it was a wonderful display that we all miss. (Mom too.)

Amerigo Vespucci

Turn left here, or continue straight a half block to visit the **Interior Museum** on the right. Exhibits and tours are available. (Open *Mon-Fri 9:00-5:00; photo ID required; info:* **doi.gov/interiormuseum.**) A major collection of American art and artifacts are stored, with a portion on display. Also find historic murals and a gift shop.

Back on 18th St., walk south to the end of the long hedge on your left to the **Art Museum of the Americas** (1976), a part of the OAS (*Tue-Sun 9:30-5:00*). You'll find a gorgeous Mayan loggia (like an atrium) inside, plus a small, but outstanding collection of works by Latin American artists. New works cycle through every few months.

Across 18th St. from the art museum stands heroic **Simón Bolívar** (1959), the Liberator, on his fearless horse victorious in the fight for Latin America's independence from Spain in the 1820s. Wander over for a look, then follow Virginia Ave. back to 17th St. (*see also p. 177*).

Pass a monument to **José Artigas** (1950), Uruguay's revered liberator, and an array of sculptures outside the OAS.

Cross Constitution Ave. at the light to return to the Lockkeeper's House.

American Red Cross

More to Explore: The National Nearby

To experience more of Washington, D.C. and the surrounding metro area, here are 18 additional walkabouts to choose from. Suggested routes range from easy sauntering to light hiking in varied settings. Each listing includes a map, directions and details for the many sights encountered. Starting locations are marked on the maps with a red star ★, and some mileages in the text are marked with a white dot ○.

Senate Park near the Capitol in spring.

18 More to Explore

P St NW
O St NW
N St NW
37th St NW
35th St NW
Wisconsin Ave
O St NW
Dumbarton St
29th St NW
27th St NW
Rose Park
Rock Cr
Francis Park
24th St NW
23rd St NW
22nd St NW
Prospect St
Old Stone House
Olive St NW
25th St NW
MI 2.7
M St NW
C&O Canal
Pennsylvania Ave
L St NW
31st St
Whitehurst Frwy
K St NW
Georgetown Waterfront Park
MI 3.6
F. Scott Key Br
Boardwalk
I St NW
New Hampshire Ave
G.W. Univ
H St NW
Rock Cr-Potomac Pkwy
Virginia Ave NW
Moore St
19th St
Lynn
Rosslyn
T. Roosevelt Is. & Memorial
MI 1.9
E St
Kennedy Center
23rd St
C St NW
N Meade St
T. Roosevelt Mem'l Br
G. W. Mem Pkwy
MI 4.8
Ohio
Lincoln Memorial
Potomac
Iwo Jima
Arlington Mem'l Bridge
MI 0.0
Boundary Channel
River
Arlington National Cemetery
MI 0.7
Mem'l Dr
J. Davis Hwy
Lady Bird Johnson Park
Columbia Island

1. River Loop & T. Roosevelt Island

- *Distance*: 5-mile loop + 1.5-mile island loop (optional) - *Allow 2 to 4 hours*
- *Start*: Lincoln Memorial, Arlington Cemetery, Rosslyn or Georgetown
- *Nearest Metro*: Arlington National Cemetery, Rosslyn

Points of Interest: **Lincoln Memorial • Memorial Bridge • Potomac River Arlington National Cemetery • George Washington Memorial Parkway Mount Vernon Trail • Theodore Roosevelt Island • Potomac Heritage Trail Key Bridge • Georgetown • Francis Scott Key Park • Old Stone House C&O Canal & Towpath • Justice William O. Douglas Memorial Foreign Embassies • Rock Creek Trail • Kennedy Center**

Mount Vernon Trail at Lady Bird Johnson Park.

*If biking the loop, road crossings require extra caution with kids. On Memorial Bridge and M St. families may want to walk their bikes on the sidewalk. Caution is also advised at the C&O Canal (there's no railing). However, most of the ride is along easy paved paths. Browse local cycling guides and websites for more family rides. See also pp. 160-167.

This scenic five-mile loop sidles up close to the **Potomac River**, including two historic bridge crossings, the ever-popular **Mount Vernon Trail**, an island preserve, the **C&O Canal National Historical Park**, **Georgetown**, and if your timing is right, an optional free performance at the **Kennedy Center** (*6:00 pm nightly*). The **River Loop** intersects with several other walks, including the **National Mall West Loop**, **Georgetown Loop, Mount Vernon Trail** and **Potomac Heritage Trail**.

The loop starts and ends at **Lincoln Memorial** or the **Arlington Cemetery** Metro Station and mostly follows paved paths through nicely maintained landscapes and boardwalks among wetlands. The return includes a quaintly, if not lively, stroll along historic Georgetown's main drag, **M St.**, with links to other nearby walks. One could also break this into shorter walks to or from Lincoln Memorial, Arlington Cemetery, Theodore Roosevelt Island, Rosslyn Metro Station or Georgetown. The entire loop is wheelchair-accessible despite a couple of steep spots. It also makes a great bike tour,* except for the Roosevelt Island side trip which is closed to bikes. To begin at Arlington Cemetery, see the note on p. 98.

From **Lincoln Memorial** [MILE 0.0] and the center of the plaza below the steps, walk left to the Bikeshare dock. Follow the walkway across 23rd St. and up onto **Memorial Bridge** (1932) beyond the trees. The abutments are adorned with golden horsemen from Italy. A wide sidewalk leads across the bridge. Don't forget to look back at the Lincoln Memorial.

The obvious island upriver is **Theodore Roosevelt Island**. We'll dally there soon enough. Straight ahead on the Virginia side of the river is **Arlington National Cemetery** (1864), established during the Civil War. The cemetery's 400,000+ burials include countless American heroes, explorers, astronauts and national leaders, notably the Kennedys (John, Jackie, Robert and Ted).

Traffic noise detracts, but it's a scenic stroll across Memorial Bridge above the mighty Potomac, the second largest river feeding Chesapeake Bay.

The **Changing of the Guard** at the **Tomb of the Unknown Soldier** often draws a crowd. (*On the half-hour April-September, hourly October-March; see also p. 180 and* **arlingtoncemetery.mil**.)

The columned edifice on the hill above Arlington Cemetery is **Arlington House** (1817), a former Lee mansion and now memorial to Confederate General Robert E. Lee. After the Civil War, he stayed in the area, but it's said he would walk by the old house without looking up. In a roundabout way, Arlington, Virginia, got its name from this house. Memorial Bridge symbolically joins Arlington House to Lincoln Memorial as reaffirmation of a unified North and South after the war. Located above the **Kennedy Gravesite**, the House is open to viewing most days of the year.

A little to the left of Arlington House, look for the tall, sweeping arms of the Air Force Memorial (at a distance), rising like a Thunderbirds jet formation (*see p. 181*). At the far end of Memorial Bridge, the path curves left and passes a junction [MILE 0.7]. For the Mount Vernon Trail, continue straight. (Or head right if you first want to visit Arlington National Cemetery, or to locate the adjacent Metro station, a five-minute walk from this junction*.)

From the junction, the trail curves left to a crosswalk for crossing a busy, one-lane ramp to **George Washington**

The Hiker.

*If starting your hike at the Arlington Cemetery Metro Station, exit the station via the south side escalator, swing right (toward the river) to pass "The Hiker" (a memorial to Spanish American War veterans) and follow the sidewalk to the far end of a big traffic circle. Cross two lanes of traffic at a crosswalk (generally not difficult) to the signed junction for the Mount Vernon Trail.

MVT and G.W. Pkwy from Memorial Bridge in winter. The MVT was completed in 1972 and is co-managed with the George Washington Memorial Parkway. In 1983, the trail was also designated as part of the Potomac Heritage National Scenic Trail, which could eventually extend from Chesapeake Bay to southwestern Pennsylvania.

Memorial Parkway. The Parkway is part of the National Park system and locally referred to as the "G.W." or "G. Dubya" Parkway. Cross when safe.

The artful path now meanders southward through **Lady Bird Johnson Park** to a fork. Stay left and cross the Parkway's two northbound lanes at a crosswalk. It's a short crossing and generally quick and easy. If it's busy, be patient, a gap will soon appear. Courteous drivers often stop to let folks cross. Many drivers don't seem to realize they're motoring through a national park. Don't fret too much over these various road crossings—they're just a little annoying.

Once across the Parkway, you'll reach the well used **Mount Vernon Trail** [MILE 0.9]; scurry left for the River Loop. Right would take you three miles south to Crystal City via Reagan National Airport, or six miles to Old Town Alexandria (*see p. 160*). But head upriver to pass beneath Memorial Bridge.

The Mount Vernon Trail (or **MVT**) is a paved, 18-mile bicycle-pedestrian trail linking Rosslyn, Virginia, to George Washington's historic estate at Mount Vernon, south of Alexandria. The next mile of walking will give you a pretty good sense of what the other 17 miles are like—an excellent, family-friendly bike ride.

Another little known fun fact is that this stretch of the MVT is actually on a mile-long island called **Columbia Island**. About 0.4 mile after passing under Memorial Bridge, you'll leave the island when you cross the trail bridge over **Boundary Channel**. The channel marks the boundary between Washington, D.C. and the Old Dominion of Virginia, placing Columbia Island and nearby Theodore Roosevelt Island squarely within DC.

The next series of highway bridges are for I-66 and U.S. 50, which cross over the south end of **Theodore Roosevelt Island**. At an underpass, the trail meets an elevated boardwalk for a quarter-mile. Pass a junction on the left (goes to DC via the I-66 bridge), then reach a parking area and footbridge to T.R.'s island [MILE 1.9]. A trail map should be posted at the far end of the footbridge to help you locate the actual **Theodore Roosevelt Memorial** (1932) hidden in the woods above the bridge, though it's easy to find (go right at the end of the footbridge, then make the next two lefts). It's under a

Boardwalk section of the MVT near Theodore Roosevelt Island.

half-mile round trip from the parking lot to the memorial. Or hike there via the **Island Loop** (*see below*).

The memorial plaza and captivating sculpture of the 26th American president are nicely secluded and well maintained, comparable to sites on the National Mall. Notable quotes are etched in stone, while the protected forest is also a peaceful and fitting tribute.

In the 1700s, the 88-acre island was occupied by a large farm with extensive produce gardens. It was reforested with native trees in the 1930s as a natural memorial to T.R., the old Bull Moose-hunter-conservationist and fifth cousin to FDR. The statue of T.R. was dedicated in 1967. A small herd of deer and other furry things roam the woods, while copious feathered, scaly and sticky things hang out around the wetlands.

If you hiked the island loop to get to the memorial, exit the plaza in the same direction T.R. is facing, then follow the curving path down and right to reach the footbridge. You might notice a few kayakers enjoying a popular circumnavigation of the island. Many rent their boats in Georgetown near Key Bridge.

After dawdling (or doddering) around the island, return to the Mount Vernon Trail and continue past the parking lot and briefly upriver. Just before the trail ramps up, notice the unpaved path on

Kayakers and Key Bridge from T.R. Island.

Theodore Roosevelt.

T.R.'s Island Loop

You can burn an hour or more exploring the web of trails around T. R.'s island. For a 1.5-mile loop, cross the footbridge from the parking area, head right 30 yards to a junction and stay right (left goes up the hill to the T.R. Memorial). Follow this path to where it meets a parallel trail above (MILE 0.3); jog left and right to continue on that (the trail you departed goes to a Roosevelt Bridge overpass). Reach a restroom and water fountain just ahead, then choose the wide right fork.

The trail then circles around to the left past an overpass to begin a half-mile section of elevated boardwalk (or "Swamp Trail") through extensive wetlands. Watch for cypress knees (wood stubs) hidden in the brush. At the far end of the boardwalk climb a short hill and stay left at the next three forks immediately ahead (short spurs on the right lead to the river). The third left (MILE 1.1) heads up slightly to an easy stretch to the memorial (MILE 1.3).

the right—the **Potomac Heritage Trail**. It leads about 10 miles up the river, and while it isn't heavily used, it's scenic enough and is gradually being improved (*see p. 144*). For now, ascend the long ramp, almost a corkscrew, where the climbing path spans the G.W. Parkway. Just beyond, you'll arrive at **Rosslyn**, Virginia, and the north terminus of the Mount Vernon Trail at the Lynn St. traffic light [MILE 2.3]. (If you need to skedaddle to the nearest Metro Station, walk two blocks left, one block right, then briefly left again to reach the Rosslyn Station*.

To continue the River Loop across Key Bridge from the MVT, turn right at the Lynn St. traffic light, follow the sidewalk to a one-lane ramp and cross when safe. Then head across **Key Bridge** (1923) to Georgetown. This is DC's oldest bridge over the Potomac. Named for Georgetown's star-spangled poet-lawyer, Francis Scott Key, it affords broad views up and down the river. The expansive white building way down yonder and hiding behind T.R.'s Island is the **Kennedy Center**; the closer greenspace on the left bank is **Georgetown Waterfront Park**.

Dead ahead is **Georgetown**, settled in 1751. It may have been named for a king, but not a president, or possibly for a couple of colonial Georges who were neither kings nor presidents (the record isn't clear). The dark spires left of the bridge are part of Georgetown University (1879). (*See p. 105 for a closer look.*) Near the north end of Key Bridge, cross one more off-ramp (when safe), this one accessing the Whitehurst Freeway. Near the end of the bridge, notice the **C&O Canal** and **Towpath** below.

As you reach the traffic light at **M St.** [MILE 2.7], amble right through little **Key Park** to find a bust of Mr. Key (1993) near the white columns. Continue along M St. for several blocks admiring the well preserved architecture, some of it dating to the late-1700s and now home to modern shops, eateries and imbiberies. There's a whole lot of history here, so watch for a couple of historical signs and plaques, and walk in the famed footsteps of nation-founders, civic leaders, assorted dignitaries and celebrities, not to mention mere commonfolk like us out for a stroll.

Bust of Francis Scott Key.

When you reach **Wisconsin Ave.**, cross M St. near the golden dome of the former Riggs National Bank (1922). If time allows, wander up the hill a couple of blocks to enjoy a bit more of the G-town hubbub (*see also p. 105*). Otherwise, cross Wisconsin Ave. and keep heading east on M St. another block and a half to the **Old Stone House** (1765), DC's oldest building. Find exhibits, period furnishings and a bookstore/gift shop inside, gardens outside.

** If starting the walk at Rosslyn Metro, exit to Moore St. and turn left. At the end of the block go right, then left on Lynn St. Cross to the east side of Lynn St. and continue across Key Bridge.*

Old Stone House.

Continue to the next corner, go right to recross M St. and head south down 30th St. one block to the **C&O** (Chesapeake & Ohio) **Canal** and **Towpath** [MILE 3.2]. (Restoration work was underway in 2026.) Venezuela's embassy is close by. The suggested route for the River Loop turns right to follow the canal path (if open) three blocks west to Wisconsin Ave. (again) before heading down to the riverfront. To shorten your journey by a third of a mile, you can skip the walk on the Towpath by continuing down 30th St. to a large sundial next to the river, then see the continuation on the next page.

From the 30th St. bridge over the C&O Canal and Towpath, catch a good view of the locks, then head right (upstream) along the canal. Thirty yards from the bridge, look for a bust of **Supreme Court Justice William O. Douglas** (1977) near the canal. Douglas, an avid hiker and conservationist, is credited with preserving the canal and adjoining greenway from development over 60 years ago. His likeness now gazes up the canal at **Lock Number 3** (of 74).

Justice William O. Douglas.

Cross the next street, Thomas Jefferson St., to **Lock 4**. Watch for a canal barge that might be available for tours once the canal restoration is

C&O Canal

In its heyday in the mid-1800s, the C&O Canal was grand infrastruture, a principal transportation corridor that operated for nearly a century. From trade and travel to coal shipments and mail delivery from mills, mines and farms, the C&O served the growing city inside the Capital Beltway, long before there was any notion of a Beltway. Canals were much more efficient than buggies and horses on lumpy, muddy trails—that is, until canal transport was ultimately snuffed out by the big ol' bootheel of steam trains.

Canal construction, begun in 1828, never did make it to the Ohio River at Pittsburgh as originally envisioned, but few would complain. Trains were way cool, and hugely faster. Today, the C&O Canal and Towpath are part of a national historical park that extends 184.5 miles from Washington, D.C., to Cumberland, Maryland, all of it walkable and bikable (*see p. 172*).

C&O Canal in Georgetown.

done. (*For a possible canal barge tour at Great Falls, see p. 183.*)

Cross 31st St. To avoid some stairs up ahead, wheelchair hikers or others may want to turn left here and head down to the riverfront via 31st St. After crossing 31st St., continue along the Canal Towpath—mules walked these paths for decades towing boats and barges up and down the canal. Pass under an attractive, arched **stone bridge**, then a few paces beyond, watch for the stone steps hidden on the right and follow them up to Wisconsin Ave. Turn right and head down to the riverfront.

Strutting down Wisconsin Ave toward the Potomac River, you'll pass an old stone church (Grace Episcopal) and the Thailand Embassy before crossing K St. beneath the Whitehurst Freeway. Enter

Towpath and stone arch bridge.

Georgetown Waterfront Park, a veritable national park, near a large fountain and water play area [MILE 3.6]. Kids young and not so young love running through the spray on a warm day, so expect plenty of company if it's hot out.

Head left along the river with views across the Potomac to Rosslyn's well funded skyline and the big white Kennedy Center downriver. Rowing teams often kick up wake offshore. The park ends at the end of 31st St. and the boardwalk and boat dock, where you can catch a **foot ferry** over to Old Town Alexandria—highly recommended in good weather (*see p. 151*). Continue walking along the **boardwalk** adjacent to a local hotspot, perhaps with a

Riverfront boardwalk.

spring break atmosphere if you happen to catch it at the right (or wrong) time. A large oval **plaza** and **fountain** to the left convert to a winter ice-skating rink.

At the end of the boardwalk (30th St.) you'll find the **sundial** mentioned earlier. The Swedish Embassy (2006) is close by and is sometimes open for exhibits on weekends. It shares a bit of space with Iceland's Embassy. From the sundial, walk between the river and the embassy. Note the **boathouse** to the right; rentals available.

Angle left to cross the bridge over **Rock Creek** and stay right on the paved

Potomac River and Kennedy Center.

path as it swings away from the traffic light. At the light, another paved path heads left along Rock Creek Pkwy.; this is the **Rock Creek Hiker-Biker Trail**, which can be followed 2.5 miles to the National Zoo, or beyond (*see p. 118*.

The River Loop parallels the river toward the sprawling white rectangle, the **Kennedy Center for the Performing Arts** (1971). Just before it on the left is the distinctive curlicue architecture

Hall of Nations, Kennedy Center.

of the Watergate Hotel (also 1971) made famous in the Nixon years. The actual water gate was a flow-control structure at the mouth of Rock Creek. Remnants still exist.

For a quick tour of the Kennedy Center, turn left to cross Rock Creek Pkwy. at the traffic light [MILE 4.1]. Take the sidewalk up the hill to access the entrance on the upper side of the building. Kennedy is worth a visit, especially if you catch it by 6:00 pm (*Wed-Sat, all year long*). An endless variety of performers from around the world appear at the **Millennium Stage**, tickets are free, first-come, first-served. Check the website (**kennedy-center.org**) for upcoming shows or to stream the ones you missed. A free and frequent red shuttle runs between Kennedy and the Foggy Bottom Metro Station (stops at the escalators).

Back at the traffic light, finish your last mile of the River Loop by continuing along the wide path next to the river, passing under the steel and stone bridges of I-66. Jog around a curvaceously angular plaza at **Peter's Point**, once a welcoming area for DC visitors arriving by boat. Across the street are several beach volleyball courts, heavily used on nice weekends.

The path becomes a sidewalk here and climbs a long, easy grade to a pair of **golden-winged horses** near Memorial Bridge [MILE 4.8]. Cross left at the horses and follow the walkway through a couple of intersections to the north end of the **Lincoln Memorial plaza** [MILE 5.0]. If returning to the Arlington Cemetery Metro Station, walk across the entire plaza, then refer back to the beginning of the River Loop for your final easy leg across the bridge to the Metro.

Memorial Bridge from near the golden horses and Lincoln Memorial.

2. Georgetown Loop

- *Distance*: 1.6 to 3.8-mile loop - *Allow 1 to 2.5 hours*
- *Start*: Northeast corner at M St. and Wisconsin Ave. (*Map next page*)
- *Nearest Metro*: Rosslyn, Foggy Bottom (20-minute walk)

Points of Interest: **M Street • C&O Canal & Towpath • Key Bridge • Car Barn Exorcist Stairs • Georgetown University • Volta Laboratory • Volta Park • Book Hill • Georgetown Library • Duke Ellington School of the Arts • Dumbarton Oaks • Montrose Park • Dumbarton Gardens & Museum • Oak Hill Cemetery • Evermay • Dumbarton House • Rose Park • Old Stone House**

Georgetown, M St. at Wisconsin Ave. Many buildings predate the Civil War.

Golden dome and starting point.

When someone says "Georgetown," one of the first things to come to mind is M St. Of course, if you live there, your view is probably more encompassing and maybe all but excludes M St. To be sure, it can get a little crazy sometimes with restaurant goers, tourists and the college crowd. Nevertheless, it's a wonderful old part of DC and warrants much aimless exploring any old time.

You can get to **Georgetown** by Metrobus, which runs frequent schedules. Or easily walk there from the Rosslyn Metro Station across scenic Key Bridge, or from Foggy Bottom via 23rd St. and Pennsylvania Ave. (Consult a city map or ask a fellow pedestrian.)

To extend your experience beyond a lazy stroll on M St., here's a four-mile loop to get you better acquainted with the neighborhood. Hills and stairs will get your pulse up (not wheelchair friendly), though most of the walk qualifies as easy-breezy. It can also be split into two shorter loops, as noted below. Either choice will give you a good introduction to the **Georgetown National Historic District**, designated in 1950.

Begin at the old bank with the golden dome at the corner of M St. and Wisconsin Ave., the approximate centroid of the Georgetown universe [MILE 0.0]. **Wisconsin Ave**. offers an intermediate connector to

split up the walk if desired. To bypass the lower section, head up the hill on Wisconsin Ave. about five blocks to Volta Pl. and skip the next six paragraphs. Otherwise, ignore that last sentence, cross Wisconsin and saunter west on the south side of **M Street**.

The first red-brick building up from the corner was known as the **City Tavern** (now private), built in 1796. It was a favored Georgetown hangout for George Washington and Thomas Jefferson, among others.

Continue up the block to Potomac St. where a cobblestone alley leads left to a **C&O Canal** overlook. (*See p. 172 for more about the canal.*) Either cross the footbridge here and head right on the **Towpath**, or pass behind the building to a narrow alley that leads west to the next footbridge at 33rd St. You could cross the canal there, again heading right or upstream.

Follow the C&O Canal Towpath another couple of hundred yards to the next bridge. Cross here and follow the path up and left to a gazebo and bust honoring Francis Scott Key, namesake for the nearby **Key Bridge** (1923).

Cross M St. at the light and head left

to pass the old **Car Barn** (1895) now used in part by Georgetown University [MILE 0.5]. This large building was a depot for the streetcar trolley system way back when. At the far corner of the buillding, turn right to climb the famed **Exorcist Stairs**, the location of a pivotal scene in the 1970s classic, *The Exorcist*. A marker near the top of the stairs highlights films shot in Georgetown over the years.

Turn left on Prospect St. then right onto 37th St. At the next corner, head left up the stone-lined stairs for a good look at **Georgetown University**'s historic **Healy Hall** (1879), named for Patrick Healy, a once-enslaved early president of the university. Stroll past this old stone edifice (also featured in the same scary movie) to a sculpture of the founder, Bishop Carroll. The striking White-Gravenor Hall is nearby. Amble right to the main entrance gate at 37th St. Turn left, then take P St. to 35th St.

Turn left at 35th St. and walk a block north to Volta Pl. NW; turn right. At the corner, note the **Volta Laboratory**, established by Alexander Graham Bell in 1893. On the next block, pass **Volta Park**, a good place to catch a kids' baseball game in season.

Giant staircase off Prospect St.

Georgetown's White-Gravenor Hall.

Upon reaching Wisconsin Ave. [MILE 1.3] you'll find an attractive, old **stone church** (Georgetown Lutheran, 1914). Note that your starting point is five blocks down the hill, in case you only wanted to walk the 1.6-mile lower Georgetown Loop. For the longer (or upper) loop, head north on Wisconsin Ave.

Thirteen-year-old Helen Keller broke ground for the construction of the Volta Laboratory building. It still houses a nonprofit serving the needs of the deaf.

a block to Q St., before crossing both Q St. and Wisconsin Ave. at the light.

Continue uphill on the east side of Wisconsin Ave. to Reservoir Rd. and a curving stairway just ahead. The stairs, nicely landscaped, lead up **Book Hill**, which by some accounts actually begins at P St. Atop the hill is the **Georgetown Library** (1935), a true neighborhood gem [MILE 1.6]. Pass around the right side of the library to reach R St. and turn left. (To cut the walk short by about 0.7 mile, you could turn right on R St., bypassing the scenic hike through Dumbarton Oaks Park. If you skip Dumbarton, walk only to 32nd St. and jump ahead five paragraphs for the continuation.)

For the more interesting route, follow R St. west (left) across Wisconsin Ave. and keep walking two blocks to 35th St.; turn right. Notice the **Duke Ellington School of the Arts** (1897) perched on a rise. It serves as a high school for high performers and is a joint effort of DC Public Schools, Georgetown University and the Kennedy Center. A locally-famous, giant Adirondack chair sits at the far left end—a fun photo opp.

Follow 35th St. north past the old **Fillmore School** (1893). Formerly the Corcoran School of the Arts and Design, the building was sold to another nonprofit supporting the arts. At Whitehaven Pkwy. two blocks ahead, turn right to return to Wisconsin Ave. Down the hill a smidgeon on the right is the **Georgetown Flea Market**, where artists, collectors and other vendors hawk their goods almost every Sunday since 1972 (*8:00-4:00*), unless the weather's horrid. For the loop, however, cross Wisconsin Ave., jog left, then right on Whitehaven St. In a block, the street curves left. Look for a trail on the right here, signed for **Dumbarton Oaks** and turn right on the unpaved path [MILE 2.2].

Though the trail is well used, it might be somewhat primitive depending on maintenance, but should be quite walkable. Things quickly open up as you descend into a lush valley of meadows and forest. Stay straight at a junction (some steps go left) and before long you'll cross a small tributary of Rock Creek on a skinny footbridge. Just stay on the main path right of the creek. Restoration work is ongoing. Today's Dumbarton Gardens are somewhat visible on the hillside above (more on that below).

In Dumbarton Oaks Park, traces of extensive gardens and landscaping done long ago are apparent, especially in the surviving rock work along the path, several small bridge crossings and the banks and pools of the stream.

Duke Ellington School of the Arts.

The trail appears to end at an open gate and something of a four-way intersection. Of the two trails on the left, the leftmost one climbs to Massachusetts Ave. The other leads down to the **Rock Creek Hiker-Biker Trail** at a bridge in under a half-mile and Connecticut Ave. 0.2 mile farther. (*See p. 118 for a continuation from there to the National Zoo.*) But for the Georgetown Loop, head right up the hill on the narrow paved road known as **Lovers' Lane**. Trudge up the hill on Lovers' Lane to R St. **Montrose Park** (1911), is adjacent to the left and also fronts on R St. This is essentially the top of Georgetown [MILE 2.6]. The park's restrooms are near the street in a small brick building to the left.

The Georgetown Loop turns left (east) at R St., but to first explore the **Dumbarton Oaks Museum** and **Gardens**, turn right on the R St. sidewalk to find the garden entrance opposite 31st St. The museum entrance is around the corner at 32nd St. Nearly 10 acres of gardens are generally open to the public (*2:00-6:00, Tue-Sun, modest fee; 2:00-5:00 in winter, free; see* **doaks.org**).

Then regardless of where you find yourself on R St., head east to 28th St. to continue the loop. You'll pass the securely fenced **Oak Hill Cemetery** (1848) and **stone chapel** on a picturesque hillside with pretty trees and winding paths among hundreds of tilting micro-monuments to the macro personalities of greater Georgetown—a kind of a quintessential cemetery if ever there was one (*open 9:00-4:30 most days*).

As you round the bend to 28th St., you'll pass the well preserved **Evermay** mansion (1801), which now houses a foundation and frequent classical music performances. Turn left at Q St., pass the historic **Dumbarton House** (1800), which hosts tours and special events (not to be confused with Dumbarton Oaks noted earlier). Turn right at 27th St. [MILE 3.0], then make an immediate left and quick right to 26th St., lined with unassuming yet classy old townhomes. Follow this a block to P St. and turn right, then head left on 27th St.

A quiet street in Georgetown.

Much of the surrounding area was once the heart of **Georgetown's African American community**. In 1800, when George Town was a thriving tobacco port, a quarter of its 5,000 residents were still enslaved. The Black population increased rapidly following emancipation, despite persistent racism. Gentrification picked up steam around 1950 and the community remains predominantly white today. Imagine the horsedrawn hustle-bustle on these streets before there were cars.

Glide south on 27th St. for three blocks. Go right on N St. (near Rose Park), left on 29th, right on Olive St. and left on 30th. Walk a block to M St.; turn right. Pass the **Old Stone House** (1765) to end the loop at Wisconsin Ave. [MILE 3.8].

When you reach M St., you could also go left to find the nearest Metro station at Foggy Bottom, a 0.8-mile hike. If you're heading that way, follow Pennsylvania Ave. across the bridge and walk several more blocks to Washington Circle. Circle right to 23rd St. and turn right to find the Metro a block down. This is also where the free shuttle departs for Kennedy Center.

The chapel at Oak Hill Cemetery, designed by James Renwick using stone from the same quarry as the Smithsonian Castle.

3. Embassy Row

- *Distance*: 1.3 to 2.7-mile loop - *Allow 1 to 2 hours*
- *Start/Finish*: Central fountain at Dupont Circle
- *Nearest Metro*: Dupont Circle

Points of Interest: **Dupont Circle • Embassy Row • Gandhi Statue Anderson House • Cosmos Club • Sheridan Circle • General Philip Sheridan Dumbarton Bridge • Massachusetts Avenue Bridge • Winston Churchill Nelson Mandela • Woodrow Wilson House • Mitchell Park Spanish Steps • Phillips Collection Gallery**

As one might expect, countless nations have located their foreign embassies in Washington, D.C., with a good number of them lining Massachusetts Ave. and nearby streets, especially to the north and west of Dupont Circle. Prior to the Great Depression, most of these classy buildings were private mansions. This one to two-hour loop swings by more than 30 of them, some charming and relatively spartan, others palatial and among the more architecturally exquisite old buildings found in the District.

Rather than point out every embassy here, we'll leave it to the reader to seek out the national flags, heroic sculptures and small bronze plaques identifying their respective homelands. Note that attachés (embassy support staff), consulates (often serving travelers and their own citizens), and official residences may also be in the mix. Things do change, so the embassies listed here can vary a bit.

The Embassy Row Loop begins at the fountain in the center of **Dupont Circle** (where the Chinatown-Dupont Circle walk ends; *see p. 129*) [MILE 0.0]. Check out the verse emblazoned around the pool and find the words "in recognition" beneath one of the female forms. Now, with your back to those two words, aim for the walkway leading away from the fountain toward the

Embassy Row

In May, many embassies open their doors to the roving public as part of *Passport DC* and the *European Union Open House*. Saturday events are attended by thousands—a veritable lovefest of cultural togetherness. Wouldn't it be nice if all the neighboring countries of the world got along as well as they seem to here at Embassy Row. You can catch lectures, films, cultural performances and tours at various embassies throughout the year (*see* **eventsdc.com/passport-dc**). To visit an embassy at other times, check their website to see if and when they accept visitors.

circular drive and a crosswalk. Cross to the tiny traffic island amid Massachusetts Ave. The traffic pattern is a little odd here, so wait for the walk sign and watch for cars on the right. Jog left on another crosswalk, then right to follow the left side of **Massachusetts Ave**.

You'll pass a small, brick building and plaza on your left before crossing 20th St. A substantial **farmers' market** bustles here every Sunday morning year-round (*8:30-1:30*). Following Massachusetts Ave., the **embassies** for Portugal and Indonesia are just ahead. After 21st St. there's a humbling statue of **Gandhi** (2000) on the right with the Indian Embassy behind it.

Next is the **Anderson House** (1905) on the left, which hosts the *Society of the Cincinnati*, established after the Revolutionary War. A museum is open most days except Monday (*10:00-4:00, modest admission fee. Info:* **societyofthecincinnati.org**.)

Opposite that is the historic **Cosmos Club** (1901), founded in 1878 by the famed explorer/geographer John Wesley Powell (*members and guests only*). Cross Q St. to stay on Massachusetts Ave. Estonia's Embassy is prominent on a skinny corner to the north.

After 22nd St., you'll pass the embassies to Luxembourg, Togo, Sudan, The Bahamas, Turkmenistan and Greece,

Mahatma Gandhi.

Cosmos Club.

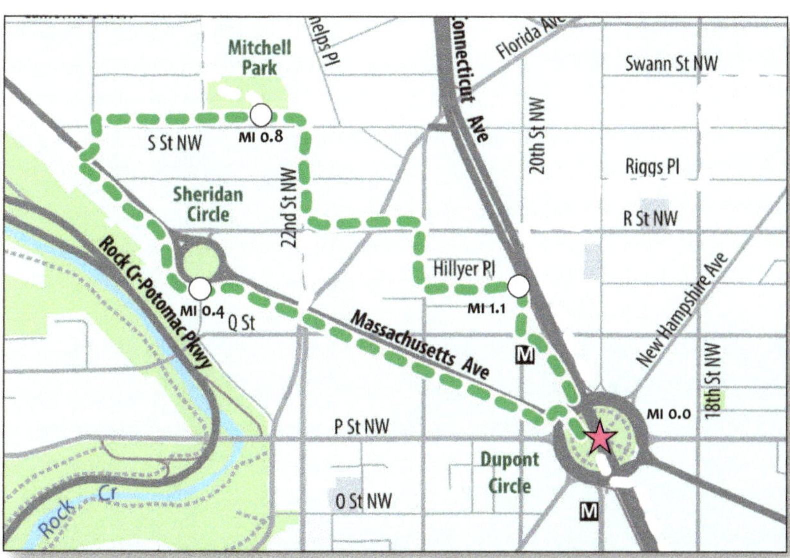

then Ireland and Romania at the corner of 23rd St., opposite **Sheridan Circle** [MILE 0.4]. The statue at the center memorializes **Union General Philip Sheridan** (1908). An inconspicuous marker near the Romanian Embassy commemorates the place where Chilean diplomat Orlando Letelier and associate Ronni Moffitt were murdered in 1976.

The Embassy Row Loop continues around Sheridan Circle (clockwise) passing embassies for Latvia and the Republic of (South) Korea. The Kenya and Vietnam embassies are north of the Circle (several others are a little farther east along R St.).

Stay on Massachusetts Ave. to pass the embassies to Burkina Fasso, the Kyrgyz Republic, Croatia, Madagascar, Paraguay, United Arab Emirates, Malawi and the Ivory Coast, across from the intersection of S St. The loop now turns sharply right on S St. [MILE 0.6] and up a longish hill (not wheelchair friendly). For an easier outing, just return to Dupont Circle via Massachusetts Ave. To see more embassies along Massachusetts Ave., read on. Or to continue the loop, start up S St.

To Georgetown:

If desired, one could hike to Georgetown from Sheridan Circle by heading left on 23rd St. to Q St., then turning right to cross the Dumbarton Bridge (1915) spanning Rock Creek and the namesake trail and parkway below. Bison guard the abutments. From the bridge, another 0.2 mile stroll to 27th St. would intercept the Georgetown Loop (*see p. 117*).

Bison at Dumbarton Bridge.

Embassy Row, Massachusetts Ave.

Optional: One could extend the walk up Massachusetts Ave. another 0.7 mile to see at least a dozen more embassies (Zambia, Marshall Islands, Venezuela, Lesotho, Japan, India, Turkey, Belize, Iran, Brazil, Bolivia, South Africa and Great Britain), as well as statues of **Winston Churchill** (1966) and **Nelson Mandela** (2013) in front of the British and South African embassies. The Massachusetts Ave. bridge crosses over Rock Creek, offering good views along the way.

Just past the British Embassy is the **U.S. Naval Observatory** (1893), the official keeper of the clock in America. Once based on the stars, the timekeeping is now done with lasers and atomic radiation frequencies to provide the accuracy needed to guide Navy ships and keep the GPS apps working on our smartphones.

A digital display for the mother of all clocks ticks off the seconds near the main gate, though maybe not quite worth the extra hike unless you're a true clockster. The clock is accurate to within ten billionths of a second.

Infrequent evening tours were once available and hopefully will become available again.

Now back to the loop. Walking east up S St., pass the Chad Embassy and cross 24th St. to find the **Woodrow Wilson House** (1915) on the next block. This was the former president's home after he left office in 1921. Guided tours are available for a modest fee, but reserve in advance. The neighborhood here is known as **Kalorama**, Greek for "nice view."

Next, pass the Netherlands, Pakistan and Mauritania Embassies (left) and Myanmar (Burma) and Laos (right), as well as **Mitchell Park** on the left [MILE 0.8]. The park offers a perfect greenspace for a snack break or some lazin' in the sun or shade. If you like, take the steps up from mid-block and turn right for a cozy sitting area. Outdoor movies are shown on the lawn Thursday nights in summer. You might catch a music jam on Sunday mornings at 11:00. (Note

Spanish Steps.

that the hike to Adams Morgan splits off near this park; *see p. 115*.)

Continuing along S St. to the far end of Mitchell Park, turn right onto 22nd St. and descend the ornate **Spanish Steps** (1911). Watch for the commerative plaque, then a local history sign on the left near the Dominican Republic Embassy. Continue to R St. and the embassies to Bulgaria and Tanzania,

Woodrow Wilson House.

and hang a left. Keep an eye peeled for a small sign denoting the former home of **Franklin and Eleanor Roosevelt** across R St. from the Mali Embassy.

Cross Florida Ave. and make a right at 21st St. [MILE 1.1]. Then mosey left on Hillyer Pl. across from the **Philips Collection** gallery (bigger than it looks), where you can view the work of the masters (*Tues-Sun 10:00-5:00 most days, modest admission fee*; see **phillipscollection.org**). The Morrocan Embassy, incidentally, is at the next corner.

Follow Hillyer Pl. to Connecticut Ave. and head right on 20th St. to pass some inviting eateries. Just ahead at Q St. is an escalator for the Dupont Circle Metro. Or continue south on Connecticut Ave. to reach your start at the fountain [MILE 1.3]. If you walked the extra 0.7 mile out Massachusetts Ave, the total walk would be about 2.7 miles.

20th St. NW near Hillyer Pl.

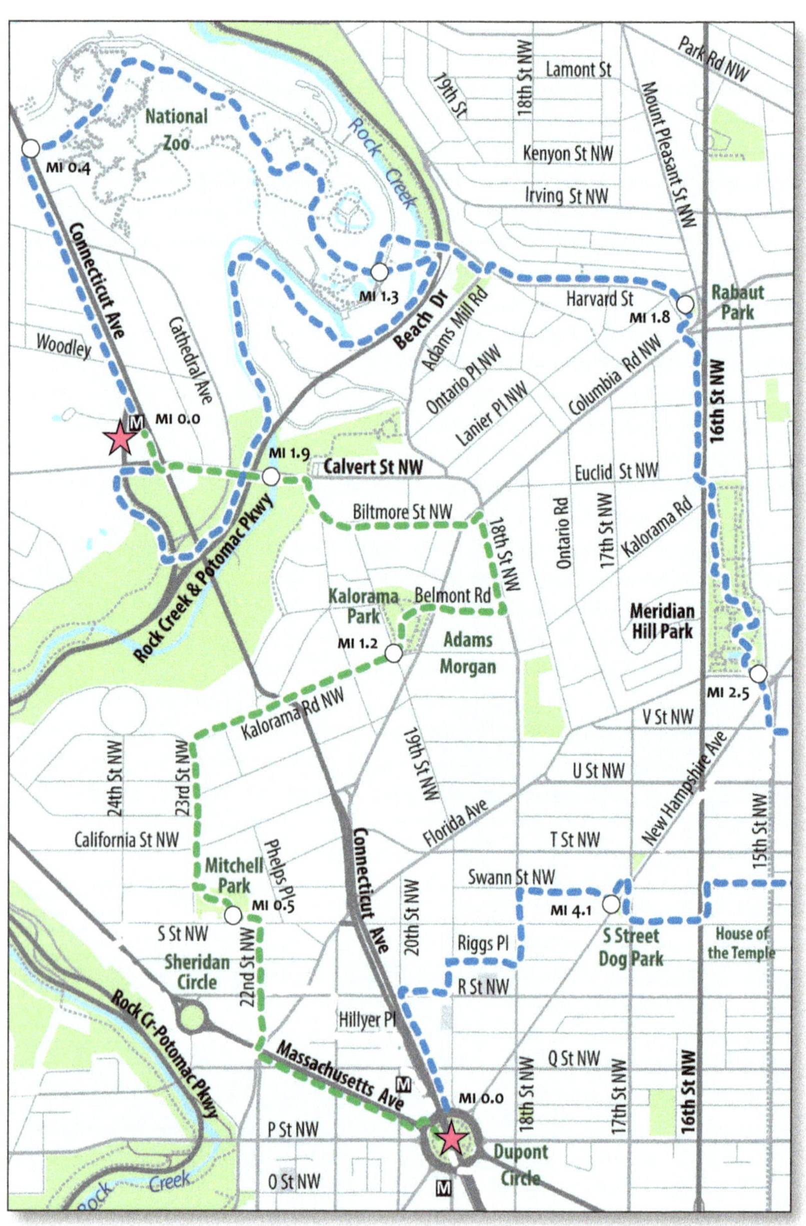
National Zoo
MI 0.4
Connecticut Ave
Rock Creek
Lamont St
19th St
18th St NW
Park Rd NW
Mount Pleasant St NW
Kenyon St NW
Irving St NW
MI 1.3
Beach Dr
Adams Mill Rd
Harvard St
Rabaut Park
MI 1.8
Woodley
Cathedral Ave
Ontario Pl NW
Lanier Pl NW
Columbia Rd NW
16th St NW
MI 0.0
MI 1.9
Calvert St NW
Euclid St NW
Biltmore St NW
Rock Creek & Potomac Pkwy
18th St NW
Ontario Rd
17th St NW
Kalorama Rd
Kalorama Park
Belmont Rd
MI 1.2
Adams Morgan
Meridian Hill Park
MI 2.5
Kalorama Rd NW
V St NW
24th St NW
23rd St NW
19th St NW
U St NW
New Hampshire Ave
California St NW
Florida Ave
T St NW
15th St NW
Mitchell Park
Phelps Pl
Connecticut Ave
Swann St NW
MI 0.5
MI 4.1
S St NW
22nd St NW
20th St NW
Riggs Pl
S Street Dog Park
House of the Temple
Sheridan Circle
R St NW
Rock Cr-Potomac Pkwy
Hillyer Pl
Q St NW
Massachusetts Ave
MI 0.0
18th St NW
17th St NW
16th St NW
P St NW
Dupont Circle
O St NW
Rock Creek

4. Dupont Circle to Adams Morgan

- *Distance*: 2.2 miles - *Allow 1.5 to 2 hours*
- *Start*: Central fountain at Dupont Circle (*Green route on map*)
- *Nearest Metro*: Dupont Circle

Points of Interest: **Dupont Circle • Embassy Row • Spanish Steps Mitchell Park • Kalorama Park • Adams Morgan Duke Ellington Memorial Bridge**

Fountain at Dupont Circle.

Here's another cool jaunt that traverses several historic neighborhoods, including a chunk of Embassy Row, Kalorama Heights and, of course, Adams Morgan. It features architectural styles that span the gamut, from stately and elegant to quotidian and artsy-funky. A lunch stop or refresher beckons at numerous sidewalk cafes along the way.

The walk climbs a few hills, but is a good way to extend the Embassy Row Loop (*p. 110*) or the Chinatown-Dupont Circle hike (*p. 129*). The finish takes you briefly beyond Adams Morgan to the Woodley Park Metro Station. For a more ambitious circuit, follow it up with the National Zoo-Dupont Circle trek (*p. 125*) to form a seven-mile loop.

From near the central fountain (1921) at **Dupont Circle** [MILE 0.0] head northwest on **Massachusetts Ave.** to 22nd St.—see Embassy Row on p. 110 for specific directions to this point, if needed. You'll pass a number of **foreign embassies** and other historic sites of interest, as described in the Embassy Row walk. Turn right at 22nd St., which leads uphill just left of Florida Ave. Walk three blocks north to reach, and ascend, the **Spanish Steps** (1911). Just beyond, at S St., turn left. (Wheelchair hikers would face a tough hill climb up Florida Ave. and Phelps St. to reach S St.)

Mitchell Park.

Saunter past **Mitchell Park** [MILE 0.5] and

turn right on 23rd St., or walk through this attractive park and make your way past the cute, yellow community building to 23rd St. Follow 23rd St. north through **Kalorama Heights** for several blocks to Kalorama Rd. and turn right. Or meander left a little to explore a quiet niche of elegant old homes.

Follow Kalorama Rd. to Connecticut Ave., which, by the way, provides a direct return route to Dupont Circle. The big bridge over Rock Creek, a/k/a the **William Howard Taft Bridge** (1907), is just around the bend to the left.

Kalorama Park

You can catch it later from the other end. Next, cross Connecticut Ave. and continue two more blocks on Kalorama Rd. to 19th St. **Kalorama Park** is on the left, good for a nap in the grass on a warm day [MILE 1.2]. Walk the obvious path up through the park and exit right of the patio and recreation center to cross Columbia Rd. to Belmont Rd.

Follow Belmont to 18th St. in the heart of **Adams Morgan** and turn left. Adams Morgan was once two highly segregated, black and white neighborhoods, intentionally brought together as one over 60 years ago. Blocks of proud and playful, 1800s Victorian buildings suggest some extra inspiration on the part of the architects back in the day. Today, an eclectic amalgamation of shops, ethnic diners and hopping imbiberies line the busier streets, luring unwitting customers to (gasp!) abandon their treks.

As you reach the north end of 18th St. at Columbia Rd., cross left at the light to a small **plaza**. Jog left again to the crosswalk leading to Biltmore St. Follow Biltmore St. west about three blocks and round a curve to Calvert St. This puts you at the east end of the **Duke Ellington Memorial Bridge** (1935) [MILE 1.9]. Note the **presidential mural** across the street. Head left across the scenic bridge, with Rock Creek Pkwy. abuzz below.

Continue to the traffic light at Connecticut Ave. The 900-foot-long Taft Bridge you might have seen earlier is now to the left (south). Via Connecticut Ave., it's a 1.1-mile glide back to Dupont Circle. Or to reach the Woodley Park Metro Station [MILE 2.2], cross both streets here and head north (right) a half block on Connecticut Ave. Or keep on truckin' a few blocks more to reach the main entrance to the zoo (*free, but timed entry required; info:* **nationalzoo.si.edu**).

18th St. in Adams Morgan.

Rock Creek Park

Rock Creek Park (1890) is DC's largest, a nearly 3,000-acre national park and urban wilderness of forested hills, glens, the stony creek, picnic areas, a nature center, well preserved historic features and 30+ miles of trails. A paved hiker-biker path runs through much of the park, often near the creek. The oft-hiked West Ridge Trail passes near the **Rock Creek Nature Center** and links the historic **Peirce Mill** to the north end at **Boundary Bridge**. Closer to the creek is the unpaved Valley Trail. Both run the length of the park. *See map p. 120.*

Other trails link to Silver Spring (*p. 179*), Capital Crescent Trail (*p. 171*), Glover Archbold Park (*p. 172*, C&O Canal Towpath (*p. 172*), Dumbarton Oaks (*p. 105*), National Zoo's Olmsted Walk (*p. 125*), National Mall, tributary greenways and surrounding neighborhoods. Find a trail map at the nature center near Military Rd, on the park's website (**nps.gov/rocr**); or posted at many access points.

The park is a popular place almost year-round, although you can nearly always find a few miles of lonely trails away from the hubbub. Rock Creek Park and its connecting trails span the entire District from the Potomac River to Chevy Chase, Maryland, although the bulk of the park lies north of the zoo.

It's even possible to pick up the Rock Creek Hiker-Biker Trail outside Rockville, Maryland, and follow it all the way to the National Mall—quite a haul more efficiently done on a bike. A big plus is much of Beach Dr. is closed to cars on weekends, making this scenic stretch popular with cyclists all year. To get off the beaten track, lash your bike to a hitching post along the way and wander up a trail—with your trusty map, of course. Most of the unpaved trails, by the way, are closed to bikes. If you choose to drive, a number of trailheads with parking are shown on the park map.

Rock Creek Park is also easily reached on foot from any number of bus stops in all directions and from a few Metro stations, including Woodley Park and Cleveland Park on the west (recommended) and Silver Spring to the north. If you're new to the park, several short to moderate loop options are described in the following pages to help get you acquainted with the layout and better known features.

The main entrance to the zoo is on Connecticut Ave. midway between those first two Metro stations and makes an easy add-on to your walk. Begin at Woodley Park to hike paved paths to the Rock Creek Trail (next page) and lower east entrance of the zoo, returning via the zoo's Olmsted Walk. Note the zoo opens at 8:00 and closes at 6:00 pm (4:00 pm, mid-September to mid-March).

For a more ambitious outing on more primitive trails in wilder terrain, consider the next two loops. Note that the creek is closed to swimming due to water quality issues. If you step off the trail, also beware that poison ivy is very common in the woods. Both the leaves and hairy vines can be toxic. ("Leaves of three, let it be!")

5. Rock Creek Hiker-Biker Trail

- *Distance*: 2.7-mile loop - *Allow 1.5 to 2 hours*
- *Start*: Woodley Park Metro Station
- *Nearest Metro*: Woodley Park

Points of Interest: **Duke Ellington Bridge • Taft Bridge • National Zoo**

It's an easy stroll to the Rock Creek Hiker-Biker Trail through the zoo, but reserve a timed entry. Exit the Woodley Park Metro [MILE 0.0] and walk south on **Connecticut Ave.** to Calvert St. The walk heads right; or detour left to a good view from the **Duke Ellington Bridge** (1935) or straight from the **Taft Bridge** (1907). Both bridges stand 125 feet above Rock Creek.

Connecticut Ave. (or Taft) Bridge. Both Rock Creek Pkwy. and the trail go under the arches.

Back at Calvert St. go a block west to 24th St. Cross and turn left on the path leading down to a crosswalk on the left above Rock Creek Pkwy. This is loosely referred to as the Rock Creek Trail. Cross the road with caution! (Right goes to the National Mall.) Pass under the Taft and Duke Ellington Bridges nearby.

Near a parkway **tunnel** [MILE 0.6], go left along Rock Creek around a horseshoe bend in the creek. This section is gated and closed at night, as is the zoo. If it's closed during the day (rarely the case), it's possible, but not much fun, to walk the skinny sidewalk through the tunnel and pick up the trail at the other gate, bypassing the big bend.

Near the tip of the horseshoe bend, cross a zoo service road. Stay on the Rock Creek Trail to the far end of the tunnel, and soon reach a road bridge. Cross to find the lower entrance to the **zoo** and the lower end of Olmsted Walk [MILE 1.4]. You might be able to walk up through the zoo for a mile to Connecticut Ave. and left there to return to the Metro Station [MILE 2.7]. Or continue past the zoo 1.2 miles, turn left on the Melvin Hazen Trail and left at Connecticutt to return to the Metro.

Marine mammal habitat along the zoo's American Trail.

6. Peirce Mill–Boulder Bridge Loop

- *Distance*: 4.0 to 6.0-mile loop - *Allow 2 to 4 hours*
- *Start*: Mel C. Hazen Trail at Connecticut Ave. (*Map next page*)
- *Nearest Metro*: Cleveland Park

Points of Interest: **Melvin C. Hazen Trail • Western Ridge Trail • Peirce Mill T. Roosevelt Trail • Pulpit Rock • Boulder Bridge • Valley Trail • Rapids Bridge**

Peirce Mill. Park rangers somerimes crank up the gristmill for demonstrations, April-October (try 2nd and 4th Saturdays, 10:00-2:00).

Unlike the other, more civilized urban walks included in this guide, the hike described here takes you into some of the wilder parts of Rock Creek Park. It's not so wild you need to worry about lions and tigers and bears (oh my), though all those critters do happen to be hanging out at the zoo nearby. Instead, you're more likely be met by fearsome deer, squirrels, birds and the occasional red fox, not to mention lots of other folks out enjoying a hike in the park.

The Peirce Mill-Boulder Bridge Loop offers hikers a nice introduction to **Rock Creek Park**, staying mostly near the creek, while taking in a few historical features and scenic bridges. Trails can be rough and rocky in places and trail signing isn't perfect, so carry a map or GPS trails app and keep track of your progress. The route described here is straight-forward, but if you get turned around, a fellow trailster can help get you back on track.

The Cleveland Park Metro Station is a good starting point [MILE 0.0]. Exit the station to the east side of **Connecticut Ave.** and walk north 0.2 mile to the Melvin C. Hazen Trail on the right. Descend several switchbacks to the creek. The trail crosses the creek bed a few times, normally an easy rock-hop.

Follow the yellow-blazed trail through quiet forest to a big lawn and picnic area near **Rock Creek** [MILE 0.5]. A trail on the right crosses the smaller creek on a footbridge, but ignore that and walk across the lawn to the

Boulder Bridge in Rock Creek Park.

Photo: Kris Wilcox

Western Ave
Pinehurst Branch
Beach Dr
Alaska Ave NW
Oregon Ave NW
Utah Ave NW
Rock Creek
Aspen St NW
Fort Stevens
Nebraska Ave NW
Rolling Meadow Bridge
16th St NW
Georgia Ave
Horse Stables
14th St NW
Miller Cabin
Fort DeRussy
Fort Stevens Park
Military Rd NW
Nature Center
Hike #7 Start
Colorado Ave NW
Broad Branch
Rapids Bridge
Beach Dr
13th St NW
Forest Hills
Boulder Bridge
Blagden Ave NW
Connecticut Ave
Soapstone Valley
Pulpit Rock
Peirce Mill
16th St NW
Arkansas Ave
Tilden St NW
Melvin Colvin Hazen Park
Hike #6 Start
Piney Branch
Porter St NW
14th St NW

paved hiker-biker trail close by; turn left. This is actually part of the Western Ridge Trail. Right leads 1.3 miles to the zoo and the bottom end of Olmsted Walk.

Following the paved path leftward, pass beneath Tilden St. to find the old **Peirce Mill** (1829) just beyond. The carriage barn is up the hill and a matching **stone distillery** is across the street (no public access). A 1903 **dam** on Rock Creek looks like a relic from the milling days, but was apparently built to create a scenic waterfall. A fish ladder ascends the opposite side.

Continue along the right-hand path to an intersection with Broad Branch Rd. You'll return to this point later. Cross and turn right to also cross Beach Dr. Then follow the sidewalk over the bridge above Rock Creek. At the far end of the bridge, turn left on the Theodore Roosevelt Trail, a favorite saunter of the late president [MILE 1.0]. The hillside trail is narrow and rough, but not too difficult. In 0.2 mile, reach the Valley Trail and turn left. **Pulpit Rock** is on the left near the junction.

Follow the blue-blazed Valley Trail past a few places where you could access the creek for a break among tons of sitting rocks. Be cautious in stormy weather, due to the risk of flash flooding. At a fork keep right and soon round a big bend in the creek to spot the graceful arch of **Boulder Bridge**—a great photo op [MILE 1.6]. Just ahead, a spur on the left leads to the bridge, although the hike continues straight along the Valley Trail.

The path climbs briefly before easing off again for the next scenic stretch along the creek. Noisy rapids form here during times of high runoff. Take the next spur on the left leading to **Rapids Bridge** [MILE 2.0]. This is roughly the mid-point of the hike. If a restroom stop is calling, you could feasibly stay on the Valley Trail for another 0.2 mile and turn right to tennis courts with restrooms, then return to Rapids Bridge (a half mile round trip). Note that the next hike also passes this footbridge on the hike down from the Rock Creek Nature Center.

Rock Creek. To help improve and protect the park, visit **rockcreekconservancy.org**.

Cross to a wide, unpaved trail on the other side and turn left for the downstream return hike to Peirce Mill. Below Rapids Bridge, two paths ascend the hillside to the right. The second climbs to Ross Drive and the nature center; the Peirce-Boulder Loop continues straight ahead. The trail soon leaves the creek, rounds a bend and climbs a hill to a junction [MILE 2.4]; stay left. After cresting a ridge, the path descends to Broad Branch Dr. and the crosswalk you negotiated earlier [MILE 3.0].

Continue straight to pass the low dam near the mill. From the Peirce Mill walk up to Tilden St. and turn right to reach the first street on left, below the old distillery. Take this access road into a **picnic area** with a small restroom building (decent enough). Skirt the right side and continue across the grass to the Melvin C. Hazen Trail you hiked at the start [MILE 3.5]. Take it back up to Connecticut Ave. for the finish [MILE 4.0].

7. Rapids Bridge–Rolling Meadow

- *Distance*: 2.2 to 4.2-mile loop - *Allow 1.5 to 2.5 hours*
- *Start*: Rock Creek Park Nature Center (*Map p. 128*)
- *Nearest Metro*: None; convenient bus access from Friendship Heights Metro

Points of Interest: **Rock Creek Nature Center • Rapids Bridge Miller Cabin • Milkhouse Ford • Valley Trail • Rolling Meadow Bridge Western Ridge Trail • Fort DeRussy**

This scenic, 4.2-mile hike covers some interesting ground with a few surprises, including a beauteous stretch of boulder-strewn Rock Creek. It offers a tad more of a workout with more ups and downs than the previous loop, but nothing too grueling. We are, after all, still in the big city, though you'd hardly know it once you're two minutes down the trail. The hike catches a good bit of the Western Ridge Trail, Valley Trail, other connecting trails near Rock Creek and several historic sites and bridges. Or knock off two miles with a shortcut option. *See map, p. 120.*

Rolling Meadow Bridge in winter.

Begin at the **Rock Creek Nature Center**, reached by car or via a nearby bus stop on Military Rd. If bussing over from the west (Friendship Heights or Chevy Chase), hop off at the first stop inside **Rock Creek Park** at Glover Rd. Tell the driver you're headed for the nature center and s/he will likely know the stop. An obvious paved path leads south from the corner at Glover Rd. and climbs into the woods to reach the nature center in about 250 yards.

Valley Trail near Boulder Bridge.

The center provides an excellent introduction to local wildlife and common plants in Rock Creek Park. Exhibits inside include preserved creatures behind glass, habitat info and other displays. There's also a small planetarium and creative space for kids, plus ranger-led activities. The info desk has trail maps, while a small gift shop and restrooms round out the amenities inside. Nature trails and interpretive signs await some exploring outside.

For the loop hike, walk left as you exit the center's main entrance. Go to the far end of the upper parking lot, then left down the hill past the horse center. Take the obvious trail at the end of the lot [MILE 0.0]. In under a hundred yards, stay right at a fork. This winding path descends into a little valley before reaching a T-intersection; turn left [MILE 0.2].

Enjoy a downslope glide to Ross Dr. Pass beneath the bridge and soon reach a junction at Rock Creek; turn left [MILE 0.7]. **Rapids Bridge** is just a short hop upstream. (The footbridge marks the north end of the previous hike up from Peirce Mill.) But don't cross yet. Instead, continue up the creek on the prettier west (left) side. For about a mile, above and below the Rapids Bridge, impressive whitewater forms here during periods of high runoff. Countless **large boulders** hint at the watery chaos grinding away at the creek bed.

When you reach the end of a road bridge [MILE 1.3], cross the road (but not the bridge) to a paved path that continues left along the creek. Pass beneath Military Rd. just ahead, then

Site of Fort DeRussy.

after the path rounds a bend to the left, turn right on an unpaved trail [MILE 1.5] and go right again in a few yards more. (To shorten the loop by two miles, you could stay left here to reach **Fort DeRussy** in 0.4 mile and the Western Ridge Trail just beyond that, then skip to the last paragraph for the finish.)

From the junction (saving DeRussy for later), the loop heads right for a pleasant stretch traversing steeper slopes above the creek. The historic **Miller Cabin** is visible across the creek. Not far beyond is **Milkhouse Ford**. An interpretive sign explains the old crossing.

At the next road bridge, cross over Rock Creek [MILE 1.9]. At the end of the bridge, hang a sharp left on a good trail that continues upstream, now on the east side of the creek. Or check out the Miller Cabin first, if desired, with restrooms close by. Back on the

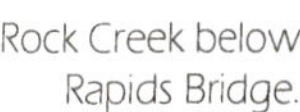

Rock Creek below Rapids Bridge.

Western Ridge Trail junction.

trail, you'll soon intercept the Valley Trail. Stay left and continue upstream to the next footbridge, a slender concrete arch over the creek. This is the **Rolling Meadow Bridge** [MILE 2.3].

Cross the footbridge, briefly head right along Beach Dr., taking the next left on the Pinehurst Branch Trail. Leaving Rock Creek behind, stay right at the first major fork, ignore any narrow offshoots, then continue straight at a signed four-way junction. Ascend the meandering valley to the green-blazed **Western Ridge Trail** [MILE 2.8]. Turn left and follow this all the way back to the nature center, though perhaps easier said than done. Signing is not always clear and the green blazes may not be entirely consistent with the park map.

Ignore a couple of trails left and right before meeting a paved path near Bingham Dr. [MILE 3.2]. Turn left here, stay right at a nearby fork (also paved) and follow this around the bend to cross Bingham Dr. and head back up into the woods. When you reach another road, walk left 40 yards, cross the road and walk toward the woods. The trail seems to disappear briefly, but just head across the grass outside the horse corral—the **Park Police horse stables**. You should easily spot the trail sign and green markers near the fence.

The unpaved path leads around the fence and into the woods again. Ignore the next left and reach a T-intersection [MILE 3.9]. The loop goes right briefly, then left on the paved trail that leads down to the traffic light on Military Rd. However, it's worth making a quick side trip left from the T-intersection.

Barely 100 yards up the trail is the earthen remains of Fort DeRussy, an important Civil War site (0.4 mile via the shortcut before Miller Cabin). Head back to the traffic light to cross Military Rd. to the bus stop noted earlier and the paved path leading up to the nature center [MILE 4.2].

Gravity won this one in Rock Creek Park.

8. Nat'l Zoo to U St. & Dupont Circle

- *Distance*: 3.3 to 4.8 miles - *Allow 1.5 to 3.0 hours*
- *Start*: Connecticut Ave. zoo entrance
- *Nearest Metro*: Woodley Park or Cleveland Park

Points of Interest: **National Zoo • Olmsted Walk • Rock Creek • Meridian Hill/Malcolm X Park • Joan of Arc • Dante & James Buchanan Statues U Street Neighborhood • African American Civil War Memorial & Museum Rabaut Park • House of the Temple • Dupont Circle**

Uncle Beazley.

Doddering around the Smithsonian's National Zoo, of course, makes a great daytrip by itself. But it can also serve as a unique first leg of a longer trek through some other interesting parts of the city. Even if you've already toured the zoo, a relaxed two-hour stroll over to Dupont Circle—with an admission-free zoological send-off—is all the more enjoyable. There are some longer hills and stairs on the route, so this is not the best choice for wheelchair hikers.

For this hike, start at the zoo's main gate on the east side of Connecticut Ave, roughly midway between the Woodley Park and Cleveland Park Metro Stations. It's about a ten-minute walk from either station to the zoo gate [MILE 0.4]. (*Open at 8:00 am, timed entry required.*) If you need to bypass the zoo for some reason, start at Woodley Park and follow the directions for the Rock Creek Hiker-Biker Trail (*p. 118*) to the bottom end of the zoo's Olmsted Walk, where you can intercept the balance of the route to Dupont Circle.

Nice kitties.

As you enter the **National Zoo** (1889) from Connecticut Ave., you are at the top of Olmsted Walk, the broad pedestrian thoroughfare to which all the habitat sidepaths connect. Indeed, it was named for Frederick Law Olmsted, the renowned landscape architect and principal designer of the zoo grounds (and the U.S. Capitol grounds). Keep an eye out for Uncle Beasley, a big, burly, realistic triceratops.

A fun route to consider if you're only passing through the zoo is to take Olmsted Walk past the elephants and turn right to reach the **American Trail**. Follow it to its end near the red barn and farm animals at the bottom end of Olmsted Walk.

Exit the zoo's east gate [MILE 1.3], then walk left to the Harvard St. bridge—not the lower bridge near the gate. Cross **Rock Creek** to the traffic light and continue ahead to cross Adams Mill Rd. (*see map p. 114, blue route*). Follow Harvard St. up the hill to **Mount Pleasant** and **Rabaut Park**, a half-mile trudge from the bottom of Olmsted Walk [MILE 1.8].

Walk through Rabaut Park to where you can see **three old churches**, one tall and cylindrical, and the others with high steeples. The intersection here is rather convoluted, but the plan is to head right (south) on 16th St. by walking left of the church on the right (less confusing than it sounds). A couple of crosswalks will get you there. Look for the street signs to confirm you're on 16th St.

Church at Mount Pleasant.

Joan of Arc, Malcolm X Park.

Follow 16th St. past several **foreign embassies** (Poland, Cuba and Lithuania) to Euclid St. Cross both streets at the light. Continue a few more steps down 16th St., then hang a left into **Meridian Hill Park** (1940), also known locally as **Malcolm X Park**. Take a quick right on the curvy paved path or climb a few steps and turn right to walk south along the central lawn. Note that the park is managed by the National Park Service and is closed overnight. Elaborate paths, stairs and memorials make it an interesting place to explore. A major renovation was underway in Spring 2026.

Make your way to the south end of the central lawn area and a nice overlook of North America's largest **cascading fountain** (except in winter when the water is off). A memorial to **Joan of Arc**, astride a horse and waving her sword, is close by. A legendary **drum circle** has gathered here nearly every Sunday afternoon for the last 60 years, since the death of Malcolm X. Newbies are welcome, if you can muster the vibe.

The game plan is to work your way down to the far southeast corner of the park at W St. and 15th St. NW. The suggested route is to head left at the overlook, descending stairs and paths to the fountain. (Or you can backtrack a little to find a steepish, stairless path leading down to the same area.) When you reach the base of the long staircase, follow the curvy path ahead with a few steps downward to a bold statue of 13th century master poet, **Dante** (1921). Either continue down the curvy way to a modest monument to **James Buchanan** (1930), our 15th president, or wander right for a closer look at the cascade. Descend to the walkway above W St. and head left to 15th St. NW [MILE 2.5].

Cross W St. and New Hampshire Ave. and walk a block down 15th St. to the ornate **stone church**, St. Augustine (1893), on the left. Here, at V St., the route turns left to take a wide swing through the popular **U Street Neighborhood**. (If you need to speed things up, you can save a mile of walking by continuing down 15th St. to U St. directly. From there, you would turn right on U St., then go left on New

13th century Italian poet, Dante.

Stone church.

Hampshire Ave. a couple of blocks to Swann St. to intercept the route in the last paragraph below.)

For the longer, more interesting route, turn left at the stone church onto V St., continue to 14th St. NW and turn right. In a block, turn left on happenin' **U Street** and stroll eastward to 10th St. You'll pass the U Street Metro and a herd of eateries, imbiberies and coffee shops. The evening music scene is a big draw at many area venues.

At 10th St., cross a plaza leading to a second U Street Metro entrance and the inspiring **African American Civil War Memorial** (1998) [MILE 3.2]. Across Vermont Ave. is the associated **museum** honoring the service of more than 200,000 African Americans who served in defense of the Union (*open Tues-Sun 10:00-5:00*; *info*: **afroamcivilwar.org**).

African American Civil War Memorial.

Continue south along Vermont Ave. to the next corner and turn right on T St. Walk this back to 14th St., admiring the old architecture of endless brick townhouses. Cross 14th St., turn left and walk a short block to Swann St. [MILE 3.6]. Turn right and follow Swann to 16th St. Turn left and walk a block south on 16th to find the rather monumental **Masonic House of the Temple** (1915) on the left. The Temple was designed by John Russel Pope, the same architect behind both the National Archives building and Thomas Jefferson Memorial.

Turn right on S St. and take this to 17th St. Cross to the wag-happy **S Street Dog Park**, then go right (north) along 17th St. to the next corner. Cross New Hampshire Ave., turn left, then right to get back on Swann St. [MILE 4.1]. (The shortcut from V St. leads to this point.)

Follow Swann St.. a long block to 18th and turn left there to pass several restaurants with outside seating. In two blocks more, turn right on quiet Riggs St. with the artful gables, then go left on 19th St. and right on R St. near the Sierra Leone Embassy. Connecticut Ave. is just ahead; walk left two blocks to reach **Dupont Circle** [MILE 4.8] and the Metro.

Architectural eye candy, U St. area.

9. Chinatown to Dupont Circle

- *Distance*: 1.7 miles - *Allow 1 to 1.5 hours*
- *Start*: Friendship Archway, H St. at 7th St. NW (*Map next page*)
- *Nearest Metro*: Gallery Place-Chinatown

Points of Interest: **Friendship Archway • Mount Vernon Square • Carnegie Library • Washington Convention Center • Samuel Gompers Memorial Park • Thomas Circle • Mary McLeod Bethune Museum Logan Circle • General George Henry Thomas • Scott Circle • General Winfield Scott Memorial • Embassies • Daniel Webster • Dupont Circle**

8th St. NW, looking north.

Inside the old Carnegie Library are the Historical Society's Kiplinger Gallery (early maps and images of Washington), various collections and a research library (12:00-6:00 Thursday-Sunday; **dchistory.org**).

This little foray through downtown DC samples a collection of lesser known memorials and architectural gems that add to the tangible richness of the national city. The walk also traverses a few urban circles and squares—European-inspired intersections of streets and avenues envisioned as major focal points and memorial sites in Pierre L'Enfant's original design for the city.

Start at the iconic **Friendship Archway** (1986) at 7th and H Sts., outside the Gallery Place-Chinatown Metro Station [MILE 0.0]. Cross 7th St. and keep walking west on H St. to the Calvary Baptist Church at 8th St. NW; turn right. Head north past the conspicuous, **stone bell towers** of another Baptist church and original home of the Washington Hebrew Congregation (1898). President McKinley helped lay the cornerstone.

Keep walking up 8th St. beneath a glassed-in skybridge to K St. across from **Mount Vernon Square**, then amble left to cross K St. at the light. The stately old **Carnegie Library** (1902) looming in the Square once served as DC's main public library. It now houses the **Historical Society of DC.** If desired, mosey right to visit the Historical Society. The signed public entrance is via the ramp below and right of the main steps.

Continue north on 9th St. to the next

corner at Mount Vernon Pl. [MILE 0.3]. The sprawling **Walter E. Washington Convention Center** is just ahead. Go left across 9th St. to begin a 0.8-mile trek along **Massachusetts Ave**. Close by is an unusual architectural contrast of a restored United Methodist Church (1917) next to a modern office building.

At 10th St., cross Massachusetts Ave. and continue west to **Samuel Gompers Memorial Park** (1933), a substantial tribute to the founder of the American Federation of Labor. At the next corner, jog right and left on crosswalks to keep following Massachusetts Ave. After 12th St., dally past the sky-tickling Church of the Ascension and St. Agnes (1874).

Walk two blocks more to **Thomas Circle** [MILE 0.8], staying to the right side. Across the Circle, towering skyward, is another classic church building, the National City Christian Church (1930). President Lyndon Johnson's state funeral was held here in 1973. A little to the north between 14th St. and Vermont Ave. is the Luther Place Memorial Church (1873), another tall and eye-catching stone edifice.

(For extra credit, you could follow Vermont Ave. past Luther Place and the **Mary McLeod Bethune Museum**

Samuel Gompers Memorial.

St. Agnes Church, designed like it came from a storybook.

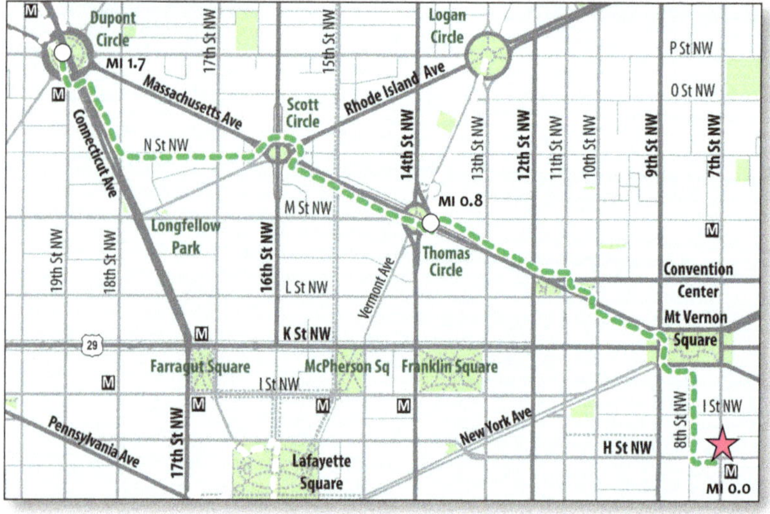

Fifty thousand people attended the Gen. Thomas Memorial dedication in 1879.

on the next block to **Logan Circle** for another generous helping of Victorian architecture, several historical markers and, at the center of the Circle, the mustachioed Civil War general, and later Illinois senator, John Logan, on his fine horse. Then retrace your steps to Massachusetts Ave. Allow 20 minutes or so for this half-mile side trip.)

Now head toward the center of Thomas Circle and the memorial to **Union General George Henry Thomas** astride his stately steed. Leave the Circle to the General's right, aiming for the left side of Massachusetts Ave, across from National City Church. In a nearby pocket park, left of the bike rental station, a **bronze elk** is browsing in the trees.

At 15th St., recross Massachusetts Ave. and continue past the Tunisian Embassy, then a robust monument to the founder of homeopathy, **Samuel Hahnemann** (1900). Short sidewalks and crosswalks lead counterclockwise around **Scott Circle** and the memorial to **General Winfield Scott** (1874). Early critics complained the artist made him look too old and fat, his horse too meek, given his long, illustrious Army career.

Stay left of the Australian Embassy and circle the Circle till you reach the statue of Massachusetts **Senator Daniel Webster** (1900) donning a caped overcoat [MILE 1.2]. Webster's DC home was nearby. Walk around the statue till you're back-to-back with Mr. Webster, looking straight down **N St.** Follow N St., which becomes a restive nook of a street, occupied by foreign embassies, nongovernmental organizations, boutique hotels and a few cozy professional offices. (At 17th St. you could wander two blocks left to the **National Geographic Museum**; *modest admission fee*; **moe.nationalgeographic.org**.)

At Connecticut Ave., note the statue of New Jersey statesman and signer of the Declaration of Independence, **John Witherspoon**. Turn right on Connecticut

Daniel Webster.

(the White House is left). Follow this major thoroughfare and hopping night strip a long block to **Dupont Circle**. The Metro station is semi-hidden on the left near the Circle. The **marble fountain** (1921) in the center of the Circle [MILE 1.7] is dedicated to Civil War Admiral Samuel Dupont. (For more sauntering, try the Embassy Row Loop (*p. 110*) or a trek to Adams-Morgan; *p. 115*).

10. Old Downtown–Chinatown Loop

- *Distance*: 2.0-mile loop - *Allow 1 to 2 hours*
- *Start*: Navy Memorial (*Map p. 36*)
- *Nearest Metro*: Archives–Navy Memorial

Points of Interest: **U.S. Navy Memorial • General Hancock Memorial Temperance Fountain • Grand Army of the Republic • Canadian Embassy John Marshall Park • Abraham Lincoln Statue • National Law Enforcement Memorial • National Building Museum • Chinatown • Friendship Archway Smithsonian American Art Museum & National Portrait Gallery • Martin Luther King, Jr. Library • Ford's Theater • Petersen House • Penn Quarter**

This little spin around downtown Washington ranks right up there with the rest and is one of the more interesting urban treks you'll find near the National Mall. It's a nice reprieve from the Mall if the museums are crowded, and a good stroll among the old architecture, public spaces and urban art that help define downtown Washington. It's also a good excursion for newcomers looking to get better acquainted with the city's complex geography and historic urban core.

The main focus is what's vaguely known as Old Downtown, more commonly regarded as Penn Quarter and Chinatown. There are fine places to linger and copious cool things to see along the way, including a peek inside the National Building Museum, American Art Museum and Portrait Gallery, and Ford's Theatre.

As with the National Mall circuit, begin this downtown loop at the Archives–Navy Memorial Metro Station (*see also p. 43*). But this time we'll head east along **Pennsylvania Ave** (toward the Capitol). From the **Navy Memorial** [MILE 0.0], pass behind the **General Winfield Scott Hancock Memorial** (1896) near the top of the escalators, then cross 7th St. NW at the crosswalk. Notice the **Temperance Fountain** (1884) with the heron on top,

Penn Quarter plaza on 7th St. NW.

Heron atop Temperance Fountain.

inspired to favor water over whiskey as a more proper thirst quencher. To the right is a larger **memorial to the Grand Army of the Republic** (1909), honoring Civil War Veterans of the Union Army. The plaza here is photogenic, surrounded by unique, historic buildings.

Heading up Pennsylvania, cross 6th St. NW and continue to the robust and beflagged **Canadian embassy** with an interesting native sculpture atop the steps. Immediately past that is **John Marshall Park**. The recommended route makes a swing through the park. But you have a choice to consider here also, so read on before leaving Pennsylvania Ave.

If you don't mind stairs and it's daytime, head left through John Marshall Park (two blocks long). If it's late, or if you're a wheelchair hiker, you can backtrack a little and head up 6th St. NW. This avoids the flight of stairs (two dozen steps) at the upper end of John Marshall Park. John Marshall Park can be deserted in the evening, so 6th St. offers a good alternate. If you do choose 6th St., head up to Indiana Ave. and turn right to ascend a short, steep block to 5th St. NW. Cross Indiana Ave. and aim for the red brick pathway at the opposite corner that leads to a bright, golden statue. You'll intersect the John Marshall route here.

Otherwise, you can skip the 6th St. alternate and amble through Chief Justice John Marshall's pretty big park. If you walk up the right side, you'll pass a couple of studious fellows who became so engrossed in their **chess game**, somebody had them bronzed. (Apparently, some bonehead made off with the bronze chessboard, a serious federal crime). Seated above is a statue of **Justice Marshall** (1884) [MILE 0.4], pretending not to notice the little chess game going on in his court. Marshall, in fact, was an avid chess fan.

Justice John Marshall; a chess game.

Beyond Justice Marshall, cross C St. and continue ahead to reach a broad set of steps. Climb these and cross D St., followed by another set of steps to a marble pose of **Abraham Lincoln** (1868) in front of the **DC Court of Appeals** (former City Hall). Turn left and follow the walkway near the building to the brilliant, golden girl and deer statue known as the **Darlington Memorial** (1923). (Intercept the 6th St. alternate route here.)

From the delicate golden girl, angle

Abraham Lincoln, The sculptor, Lot Flannery, happened to be at the play at Ford's Theatre the night Lincoln was shot. About 20,000 people attended the dedication.

toward 5th St. and continue north a half-block to E St.; turn right. The stately, red brick **National Building Museum** (1887) soon comes into view. Also find the **National Law Enforcement Officers Memorial** (1991) honoring the many thousands of officers in the U.S. who have died in the line of duty. The lion figures at either end of the memorial evoke courage and strength. Directly across E St. from the memorial is the mostly underground **National Law Enforcement Museum** (*Thur-Sat 10:00-5:00, modest admission fee*, **nleomf.org**). The museum opened in 2018 and contains many exhibits and thousands of artifacts, including items associated with some of the most notorious crimes, criminals and investgations known in the U.S.

Walk through the memorial to find the Judiciary Square Metro escalator and crosswalk leading to the entrance to the National Building Museum [MILE 0.8]. (*For another good walking route to this point from Union Station, see p. 175.*)

The loop leads around the left (west) end of the building, but you might take a closer look first, both inside and out. (*Thur-Mon 10:00-5:00, nominal admission fee; info*: **nbm.org**.) The National Building Museum occupies an impressive building itself. Built in the 1880s, the 15-million brick structure is famous for an elaborate Civil War frieze that extends for nearly a quarter-mile around the exterior of the building. Widows of Civil War veterans came here to collect

Exterior frieze, Building Museum.

Darlington Memorial.

National Building Museum

Inside the National Building Museum are some of the largest indoor columns in the world, plus an indoor fountain, hundreds of busts and a clever cooling system, not to mention all the exhibits about, you guessed it, buildings. Scheduled tours are available and donations are appreciated.

National Law Enforcement Memorial.

Friendship Archway, Chinatown.

their pensions, once paid in cash.

To continue the walk to Chinatown, exit the museum, turn right to follow a brick walkway through lawns to 5th and G Sts. Cross both and saunter north on 5th St. to H St. Turn left to enter the heart of **Chinatown**.

At 6th St. there are a couple of short diversions to ponder. One could walk left a half-block to the **German-American Heritage Museum**, which highlights immigration and contributions to American education and conservation (*11:00-5:00, Tue-Fri*). Or a block right is the **Sixth and Eye** historic synagogue, a popular events venue in an intimate setting. On H St., walk to 7th St. and the elegant **Friendship Archway** (1986) in front of the Gallery Place–Chinatown Metro escalators [MILE 1.1].

From the Friendship Archway, cross 7th St. NW and continue west on H St. to 8th St. NW. Turn left, but notice to the right the looming **bell towers** of the Greater New Hope Baptist Church. (A good walk to Dupont Circle heads that way; *see p. 129.*) As you round the corner onto 8th St. (left), the towering red brick building above you is the Calvary Baptist Church (1862). Next, look for the **Edison Place Gallery** on the right before reaching G St. and the Smithsonian's **American Art Museum and Portrait Gallery** (since 1968).

Turn right on G St., cross 9th St. and pass by the **Martin Luther King, Jr. Library**. Continue west on G St. another block, then turn left on 10th St. St. Patrick's Catholic Church (1884) calls for a

Chinatown

Though much diminished from just 20 to 30 years ago, with many families forced out by rising rents, Chinatown retains just enough heritage, Chinese script and Oriental decor to affirm you're in a special cultural place. In some ways it feels like the center of the city, although with all the redevelopment in the downtown core in recent years, it's hard to say precisely where the city's center truly is. Clusters of new buildings have sprung up in almost every direction, luring people this way and that and tugging at the center. Yet the resilient, 30-year-old Friendship Archway seems to rise above it all, at least metaphorically.

Beauteous inside and out, the American Art Museum dates to 1867, as the former home of the U.S. Patent Office. Today's galleries of comtemporary art, American celebrities, sculptures and presidential portraits warrant extended browsing. Be sure to check out the upper floors. (11:30-7:00 daily, free; info: **si.edu/visit**.)

St. Patrick's Church.

You can still catch a play at Ford's Theatre—an excellent venue.

photo stop. Peasants to presidents have attended services here since 1794, just after the founding of the Federal City.

Walk down 10th St. to F St. and note the painted iron works in the building across F St. The loop turns left on F St. [MILE 1.7], but first stroll a half-block south on 10th St. to visit **Ford's Theatre** (1863), the place where President Lincoln was shot in 1865. The **Petersen House** (1849) where he took his last breath is right across the street. Free tickets are required and lines form in the busy season, but excellent exhibits and the view inside the lovely old theater are worth the wait. (*9:00-7:00, free or small fee to reserve; info*: **nps.gov/foth**).

Returning to F St. from the theater, turn right and walk east to 9th St., passing many historic buildings. Just beyond is the American Art Museum and Portrait Gallery's south entrance. Continue east to 7th St. and turn right. The Monaco Hotel at the corner was once the **General Post Office** (1839). Street performances often occur outside the Metro escalators nearby. Cross F St. and watch for a marker on the right commemorating **Samuel Morse** and the nation's **first telegraph office** (1845).

From afternoon to evening, the home stretch down **Penn Quarter's 7th St.** to Pennsylvania Ave becomes quite a lively scene in good weather, so allot some time to loiter and soak up the buzz. You'll find plenty of places to chow down or wet your whistle, although on Friday and Saturday nights many will fill up around the dinner hour.

After crossing E St., notice the **Shakespeare Theatre** on the right. March on to cross D St. (A left here would take you to the **Woolley Mammoth Theatre**, another local favorite.)

Your starting point at the **Navy Memorial** and Archives Metro Station is coming right up on the right [MILE 2.0]. If your timing is good, you can often catch a free summer concert in the plaza where the U.S. Navy Band frequently performs (*7:00 pm Tuesdays; see p. 43 for more about the Navy Memorial*).

11. Capitol Hill–Eastern Market Loop

- *Distance*: 2.8 mile-loop - *Allow 1.5 to 2 hours*
- *Start*: Pennsylvania Ave. SE at 2nd St. SE
- *Nearest Metro*: Capitol South (Walk north to Independence, east to 2nd St.)

Points of Interest: **Capitol Hill • John Phillip Sousa home • Market Park Eastern Market • Lincoln Park • Abraham Lincoln Emancipation Memorial Mary Bethune Memorial • Frederick Douglas Museum**

Architecture on E. Capitol St.

7th St. NE off Pennsylvania Ave.

Marion Park.

This 2.8-mile loop through the historic Capitol Hill neighborhood branches off the National Mall loop a couple of blocks east of the U.S. Capitol (*see p. 67*). The Capitol Hill trek leads a little deeper into the neighborhood and delivers a pleasing buffet of history, architecture, village hub-bub and relative quietude. Among the more noteworthy stops are Barracks Row, Eastern Market, Lincoln Park and an old church attended by late presidents. You'll find plenty of quaint and stylish eateries enroute.

Make your way to 2nd St. SE and Pennsylvania Ave. behind the **Library of Congress**, then cross to the southeast corner of the intersection [MILE 0.0]. Follow **Pennsylvania Ave.** east-ish (away from the Library of Congress) for a couple of blocks to 4th St. SE, passing several pubs and restaurants popular with Congressional staffers and local denizons. Turn right on 4th just before **Seward Square**. Walk south about three blocks, crossing North Carolina Ave. and D St. At E St. SE, cross to **Marion Park** and head left, working your way to the far southeast corner of the park at 6th and E Sts. [MILE 0.6]. Note that E St. spans both sides of park. From the park, continue south on 6th St. to G St. (there is no F St. here).

Turn left at G St. In a block, pass the old Christ Church on Capitol Hill (1807). John Quincy Adams, James Madison and James Monroe were among the presidential parishioners. The virtuous Adams attended services twice on Sundays. A few doors down on the left (636 G St.) is a private residence and boyhood home (1805) of the renowned and prolific march composer **John Phillip Sousa**—think *Stars and Stripes Forever* and *Semper Fidelis*. One can imagine the boy twirling his baton and leading imaginary marching bands around the neighborhood in the 1860s. This was serious stuff for young Sousa. By age 13, he was playing violin with the United States Marine Band headquartered just up the street.

Follow G St. east to 8th St. and turn left. Across 8th St. and to the right is the guarded entrance to the **Marine Barracks**. This is where Sousa, in his mid-twenties, would ultimately lead and transform the **U.S. Marine Band** into what is still the U.S. president's official ensemble. You can catch a free performance here on Friday evenings, May through August. (*Free, reservations*

Barracks Row

Businesses sprang up here two centuries ago to serve the Washington Navy Yard to the south, as well as the Marine Barracks. Riots in 1968, following the assassination of Martin Luther King, Jr., reduced some buildings to charred ruins, and things deteriorated from there. Beginning in the 1990s, however, new stars aligned and the area has since been charmingly restored.

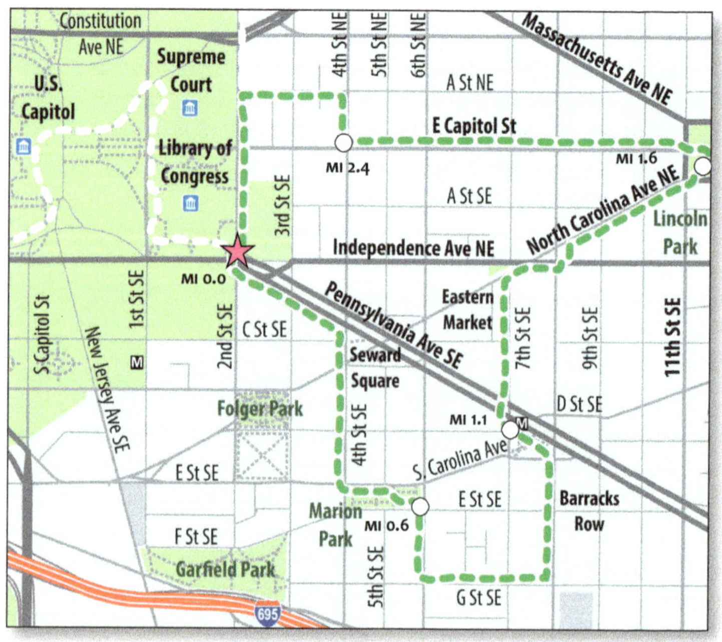

required; info: **barracks.marines.mil/ Parade-Information**).

Next, head north on 8th St. The commercial strip here is called **Barracks Row** and is one of DC's oldest historic business districts. Continue north to D St., cross and angle left into the **Market Park** square, ambling toward the obvious Eastern Market Metro escalators [MILE 1.1]. At the corner just beyond, cross both Pennsylvania Ave, and 7th St. Walk north on 7th St., passing more quaint cafes, shops and such, to reach the actual **Eastern Market** (1873) on the left. Be sure to walk on through. A popular street fair and flea market fill the street outside on weekends.

Browsing inside Eastern Market.

Just past the market, at North Carolina Ave., turn right, keeping to the sidewalk to cross 8th St. Hang a left here to cross Independence Ave. and jog right between a garden patch and an **extraordinary mosaic**. Continue right along North Carolina Ave. another three blocks to **Lincoln Park** [MILE 1.6].

Savor the sculptures near the center of the park, including one of the earliest memorials to Abraham Lincoln placed after his death, known as the **Emancipation Memorial** (1876). Frederick Douglass was the lead speaker at the dedication. Nearby is a memorial to **Mary McLeod Bethune**, a tireless teacher, friend of the Roosevelts and a leading advocate for African American causes. When the memorial to Ms. Bethune was dedicated in 1974, nearly 20,000 people came.

Circle back to the west end of Lincoln Park to East Capitol St. (in the direction Ms. Bethune is facing). Cross 11th St. and follow East Capitol St., a delectable DC residential avenue replete with stoic architecture and whimsical detail, for seven scenic blocks (11th St. to 4th St.). At 4th St. NE [MILE 2.4], turn right, then steal a left on A St. NE. Halfway down the block on the right is Frederick Douglass's first home in DC (next to the alley). The famed statesman, once enslaved, lived here with his family for a time in the 1870s before moving to the Cedar Hill estate in Anacostia where tours are available (*see page 181*).

In two blocks more, reach 2nd St. To complete the loop, head left (south) on 2nd St. to pass behind the U.S. Supreme Court and Library of Congress, reaching Pennsylvania Ave. in three blocks [MILE 2.8]. (Or turn right to find Massachusetts Ave. three blocks north. From there, Union Station is just a block to the left.)

Ms. Bethune's likeness was crafted by sculptor Robert Berks, whose creations also include the Einstein Memorial on Constitution Ave. and the JFK bust at the Kennedy Center.

12. Anacostia Riverwalk

- *Distance*: 1.0 to 3.2-mile loop - *Allow 1.0 to 3.0 hours*
- *Start*: Navy Yard/Ballpark Metro Station
- *Nearest Metro*: Navy Yard/Ballpark

Points of Interest: **Yards Park • Anacostia Riverwalk • Washington Navy Yard • 11th Street & Frederick Douglass Bridges • Nationals Park • Titanic Memorial • Washington Channel • The Wharf • Maine Avenue Fish Market Kenilworth Aquatic Gardens • Bladensburg Waterfront Park**

The Anacostia Riverwalk has developed nicely in recent years, with most of the 28 planned miles completed. A mostly paved trail system extends along both sides of the Anacostia River, with connections all the way to Bladensburg Waterfront Park, two miles northeast of the National Arboretum. Note that some areas can become deserted by nightfall, so try to complete your walk during the day.

Water play at Yards Park.

As described below, you can complete two out-and-back sections that are particularly inviting to footsters. or even a 3.2-mile loop. Some areas upriver, except Kenilworth Gardens (*p. 143*), tend to be of more interest to cyclists. Note also that the Riverwalk links to another 40 miles of mostly paved paths in the upper Anacostia watershed, with links to College Park and beyond (*see p. 169*). If you walk a few blocks of local streets, you can easily connect to the Southwest Waterfront and even the National Mall.

The tubular bridge, Yards Park.

Begin at the Navy Yard Metro Station [MILE 0.0]. Exit to New Jersey Ave. and M St., cross both streets and walk east along M St. for one block to a pedestrian corridor opposite 3rd St. SE; turn right. Walk this south to Tingey St. and turn left, then go right at 4th St. The old building with the smokestacks was part of a massive Naval Gun Factory, at one time the largest in the world.

Follow 4th St. to its end at beauteous **Yards Park** and the **Anacostia Riverwalk** [MILE 0.5]. The large attractive bridge downriver is the Frederick Douglass Bridge completed in 2021 (serves S. Capitol St.). An excellent waterfront walk leads that direction for nearly a half mile with connections to the bridge. (*More on that below.*)

For now, wander upriver (left) to explore the shore adjacent to the park and the historic **Washington Navy Yard** (1799), the oldest operating Navy installation in the U.S. The **National Museum of the U.S. Navy** is in the large white building inside the security fence, although access is complicated. A new Navy museum was planned nearby, but the Navy recently backed out of the deal after a building site had been located.

Keep walking along the river to the Vietnam-era **Swift Boat** on display outside the Navy's fence [MILE 0.8]. Continue around a couple of bends to access the **11th Street Bridge** over the Anacostia River. A major new elevated park spanning the river is proposed

The old Naval Gun Factory.

Navy Swift Boat.

here for the near future. In the meantime, a wide walkway on the bridge leads to an overlook in 200 yards [MILE 1.2]. If you've walked enough already, retrace your steps to Yards Park.

For the loop, continue across the bridge past a second overlook and watch for a paved path on the right that squiggles briefly to Marion Barry Ave. Turn right, then head left at the river on the south bank portion of the Anacostia Riverwalk [MILE 1.5]. In another half mile, just before the path makes a sweeping bend to the left, turn left to follow the right-hand sidewalk to access the big **Frederick Douglass Bridge** [MILE 2.3]. This leads directly across the river to Nationals Park. Head right along Potomac Ave. to reach the scenic riverfront promenade leading back to Yards Park [MILE 3.2].

If walking the opposite direction (downriver) from Yards Park, you'll cross a splendid **tubular bridge** near a kids' **water play area**, a popular cooling-off zone in the warmer months. Stay left to follow an over-water section of the Riverwalk that leads toward **Nationals Park** (2008), the first-ever LEED-certified major league

Titanic Memorial.

stadium. To catch an impromptu game, circle around to the north side of the stadium. (*Info*: **mlb.com/nationals**.) The Frederick Douglass Bridge is just beyond, as note above.

To carry on to the **Southwest Waterfront** from Nationals Park, turn right on S. Capitol St. and left on P St. In a half mile reach a treed walkway and the somber **Titanic Memorial**. Dedicated in 1931 at a site near the river at Foggy Bottom, the memorial was relocated here in 1968 to make way for the Kennedy Center. The Army's Fort McNair lies behind the memorial (*see inset below*).

Amble north along **Washington Channel** to the **Wharf**, a multi-billion-dollar redevelopment project completed in 2022. The design included much public space, piers, parks and an excellent waterfront promenade. There's much to explore here and plenty of places to linger, hit the river or catch a meal. Free outdoor music is common in the warmer months.

Keep on truckin' to reach the historic **Maine Avenue Fish Market** (1805). This is the oldest operating fish market in the

Fort McNair

Nestled at the confluence of the Anacostia and Potomac Rivers, this strategic site for defending against invaders was included in Pierre L'Enfant's 1791 plan for the city. It remains an active Army post today. It is also the place where the aiders and abetters of Lincoln's assassin were tried and hung in 1865. One Saturday each season, the courtroom could be viewed during an open house. At other times, a quick self-guided tour of the grounds was feasible with a photo ID (uncertain in 2026). Walk a block down 2nd St. to the gate to inquire.

U.S. You can keep walking up Maine Ave. beneath several overpasses to reach the **National Mall** in another 0.3 mile, near the east end of the Tidal Basin.

One other hot tip: the Smithsonian Metro Station is about a half mile north of the fish market. At the end of the boat harbor, just before passing under a railroad bridge across Maine Ave., take the steps on the left to a pedestrian overpass that leads to a large hotel. Follow the long walkway rightward around the building to some wide steps leading up to a circle at the end of Maryland Ave. Take Maryland Ave. one block and turn left on 12th St. In two blocks more, the Smithsonian Metro Station will be on the left.

For another good ramble farther upriver along the Anacostia Riverwalk, consider the scenic two-mile path from **Kenilworth Aquatic Gardens** to **Bladensburg Waterfront Park**. The trail opened in 2016, an excellent addition to DC's riverfront trail system. The gardens are also well worth a visit and offer a short saunter among multiple ponds and wetlands (*see also p. 169*). A gift shop and small visitor center can help you get oriented.

The gardens are famous for a rich variety of water lilies and lotus flowers. (*Open 8:00-4:00 Mon-Tues, till 8:00 Wed-Sun in summer.*) You can check on what's blooming and other details and directions at **nps.gov/keaq**. The gardens are located about five miles upriver from Yards Park, and perhaps better reached by car, bike or from the Deanwood Metro Station (a half mile walk or pedal from the gardens).

The Riverwalk here is highly recommended, by bike or on foot. It includes some elevated boardwalk and five bridges, thus the $22 million price tag.

Kenilworth Gardens boardwalk.

A new 400-foot-long trail bridge across the river to the National Arboretum close by is planned for the near future.

The Riverwalk also links to Maryland's portion of the upper watershed, reaching as far as Silver Spring, College Park and beyond. Given the miles, the more extensive trail system is perhaps best enjoyed by bike.

Some areas are a little isolated from the rest of DC, so if you're new to exploring remote sections of the trail system, go with a group or with someone who knows their way around. An added bonus is seasonal kayak rentals at Bladensburg Waterfront Park and also at the Wharf and near Yards Park.

Great blue heron at Kenilworth.

13. Potomac Heritage Trail

- *Distance*: 3.6 to 9.0 miles - *Allow 2 to 6 hours*
- *Start*: Theodore Roosevelt Island or Key Bridge
- *Nearest Metro*: Rosslyn

Points of Interest: **Potomac Heritage National Scenic Trail • Key Bridge • Mount Vernon Trail • Theodore Roosevelt Island • Potomac River • Windy Run Falls • Thrifton Hills Park • Custis Trail • Potomac Overlook Park & Nature Center • Gulf Branch Park & Nature Center • Fort Marcy**

While the C&O Canal Towpath gets much of the attention for a stroll up the Potomac River—it's wide, level and convenient to Georgetown—the Potomac Heritage Trail on the Virginia side of the river offers an actual hike on a boot-sized trail. If you're good with a more primitive path, you can enjoy a winding, scenic saunter for a couple of hours, or an eight-mile trudge (one way) to Turkey Run, or a loop back to Georgetown via Chain Bridge and the C&O Canal. Multiple access points offer a range of trip choices.

Crossing Spout Run.

Muddy spots, rough tread and rocky clambering in some areas may not be everyone's cup of tea, but that shouldn't be a big deal for most experienced hikers—if the river isn't running high. If it's been stormy, or about to be, consider postponing for drier weather. Improvements are ongoing and the trail seems destined to become a DC favorite.

On the Potomac Heritage Trail.

Locally, a good, carless hike starts at a trailhead near **Theodore Roosevelt Island**, where the Potomac Heritage Trail (PHT) splits off from the **Mount Vernon Trail** (a short walk from Key Bridge or the Rosslyn Metro Station; *see p. 101*). An out-and-back hike to the small, picturesque falls at Windy Run (when there's good flow) is an easy trek for most mortals, although traffic noise on G.W. Pkwy. detracts for the first mile. Figure

1.8 miles each way to the falls.

From the signed junction [MILE 0.0] on the Mount Vernon Trail just north of the Theodore Roosevelt Island parking area, head north. The PHT doesn't look like much at the beginning and can get a little muddy in damp weather, but things should quickly improve as you head upriver. The trail passes under **Key Bridge** [MILE 0.3] and hugs the **G.W. Parkway** in a few places before reaching a footbridge over **Spout Run** [MILE 1.0]. You'll pass good views of the **Potomac River** on the way to the falls at **Windy Run** [MILE 1.8]. Barely a trickle in drier times, the 30-foot **waterfall-cascade** can impress after a rain. In winter, following a few days of frigid weather, large icicles can form here (and elsewhere), so be cautious of slick surfaces and falling ice.

Left of the falls, an old trail steeply climbs a few stone steps and ledges into Windy Run's gradual valley above. Signs warn of the risk of a fall and advise visitors not to use the trail. I won't advise you to either, especially if it's snowy or icy. At other times, the stony steps are commonly hiked by those coming down to the river from **Windy Run Park** and vice-versa. Experienced hikers will likely find the steps easier to clamber up (if dry) than the short scramble at Gulf Branch Falls (described below) and perhaps wonder what the fuss is about. But don't chance it if you're unsure of your ability, or have younger kids in tow.

If you do head up, it's possible to complete a 4.4-mile loop back to Rosslyn and Key Bridge via neighborhood streets and the **Custis Trail**. The **Windy Run Trail** leads through the park, with some easy rock-hopping across the creek, to the end of Kenmore St. One could take the sidewalk up to Lorcom Ln., go left three blocks to Edgewood St., then cross to

Potomac Heritage Trail

The Potomac Heritage Trail is actually a part of the much larger Potomac Heritage National Scenic Trail, a major corridor running from the Allegheny Highlands of southwestern Pennsylvania to the mouth of the Potomac River at Chesapeake Bay. The system consists of more than 700 miles of existing trails, including, in the D.C. area, the C&O Canal Towpath, Mount Vernon Trail and this ten-mile chunk referred to simply as the Potomac Heritage Trail (PHT). Another 100 miles of planned new trails will help tie it all together. (*More info*: nps.gov/pohe).

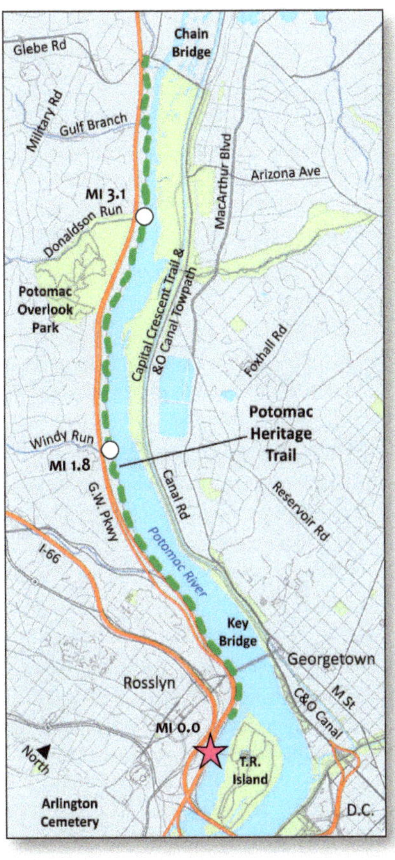

the paved path descending into **Thrifton Hills Park**. This path leads 200 yards to the I-66 overpass. Pass beneath it and immediately turn right to reach the Custis Trail, 1.1 miles from the PHT. A sharp right atop the ramp takes you to Key Bridge in another 1.5 miles. Custis makes a better bike ride than a walk, but will do for a hike in a pinch (just walk to the right so bikes can pass).

Back at Windy Run, if you continue up the PHT, you'll quickly reach the rusted relics of an **old steam boiler** that ran equipment associated with a rock quarry here over a century ago. Some of the stone was used in the construction of Healy Hall, the gothic building with the spiky towers at Georgetown University (prominent from near Key Bridge). If you keep on trucking upriver on the PHT 1.3 miles past Windy Run you'll come to **Donaldson Run**. About 0.1 mile farther is a nice rocky point good for a lunch break [MILE 3.2].

At Donaldson Run, you'll notice another steep path climbs an easy rocky ledge left of the creek, followed by a steep set of stone steps. If you head up, expect a few rock hops across the creek—generally easy unless the water is high. You'll pass the crumbling remains of an old dam on the left side. Then turn left at a signed junction to hike upslope into **Potomac Overlook Park**. The former overlook is long gone, but it's still a pretty nice park.

When you reach a junction just before the top of the ridge, turn right on the White Trail. This winds around the hillside to a small wood building just past a house. Aim for the little wood building for a fun **raptor surprise**. Then walk the paved park road right to the **nature center** for some excellent exhibits on the region's natural history (0.8 mile from the PHT).

Either return to the river the way you came, or keep following the park road for a two-mile neighborhood route back to Custis Trail (left on Military Rd., left on Nellie Custis Dr. and left on Lorcom Ln. to merge with the Windy Run loop above). The PHT-Donaldson-Custis loop is about 7.3 miles.

Back on the PHT, the trail beyond Donaldson Run becomes much more rugged, with a lot more clambering. Some sections may be very close to the river at higher flows, so due caution is in order. Strong currents and undertows should be adequate

Sadly, Abe, the beloved (and venomous) copperhead snake residing at the Potomac Overlook Nature Center for many years, passed away in 2025. They are shy critters and generally not aggressive. Nevertheless, it's good practice in the woods and rocks to always watch where you put your hands and feet. Bites are rarely fatal, but if you're bitten, call 911 or seek immediate medical attention.

Barred owl at Potomac Overlook Park.

Gulf Branch Falls.

warning for not getting too close to the water's edge.

Near **Gulf Branch**, the trail may be impassable if the river is running much above 30,000 cubic feet per second (to check the current flow, search online for "USGS Little Falls gage"). If the trail isn't clear, turn back. Mucking around the brush and rocks increases the risk of encountering poison ivy or even the occasional copperhead snake—the only venomous snake close to DC.

Across Gulf Branch, **steep stone steps** and generally easy scrambling (with a handrail) lead past the small, pretty **falls** to a choice between hiking along the creek for 0.7 mile to the **Gulf Branch Nature Center** (a local bus stops close by on weekdays), or switchbacking up the hillside on the PHT. If you choose the latter, the hike upriver is on much better tread and climbs high for great views, before descending to the **Chain Bridge** across the Potomac River. Head down a stone stairway to pass under the bridge [MILE 4.1]. Go left for the bridge walkway or right for **Fort Marcy**, about 0.6 mile up **Pimmit Run** (well signed). For points beyond, visit **nps.gov/pohe**. As you might have guessed, the PHT on the Virginia side doesn't connect all the way through to Great Falls, ending instead at Scott's Run (*see p. 184*).

If you walk across Chain Bridge to the Maryland side you'll find a ramp at the other end that links to the **C&O Canal Towpath** (*see p. 172*), where you can enjoy a more leisurely, four-mile walk back to **Georgetown** and Key Bridge. Figure a nine-mile loop back to your starting point, or 8.2 miles if you end your hike at Georgetown. If doing the PHT–C&O Canal loop, start with the PHT to get the more challenging part out of the way before the easy cruise back to Georgetown.

You could shorten the return by three miles by working up to MacArthur Blvd. to catch a bus back to Georgetown. Here's how: from Chain Bridge walk south on the C&O Canal Towpath 0.5 mile and climb the steps to the Capital Crescent Trail bridge at Arizona Ave. Cross the bridge to a path on the right which starts easy but steepens on the short haul up to Potomac Ave. Follow Potomac Ave. two blocks to Cathedral Ave., turn right and walk three pleasant blocks to MacArthur Blvd. The bus stop is a few yards to the right.

Great Falls, by the way, is still another ten miles upriver from Chain Bridge via the C&O towpath.

Trail signs help with wayfinding.

14. Bluemont–Four Mile–Lubber Run

- *Distance*: 4.6 to 8.0 miles - *Allow 2.0 to 4.0 hours*
- *Start*: Ballston or East Falls Church Metro Station
- *Nearest Metro*: Ballstone, East Falls Church

Points of Interest: **Ballston • Four Mile, W&OD, Bluemont & Lubber Run Trails • Bluemont Park • Glencarlyn Park • Lubber Run Amphitheater**

When the mood strikes to saunter some miles on easy paved paths, the trek from the Ballston or the East Falls Church Metro Station might satisfy the urge. The shorter 4.6-mile option from Ballston catches parts of the Bluemont Junction, Four Mile and Washington and Old Dominion (W&OD) Trails and some city streets. Or add another 3.4 miles to begin and end at East Falls Church. Both include a stroll along peaceful Lubber Run.

Bluemont Junction Trail. Expect similar paved trails along the Four Mile, W&OD and Lubber Run Trails.

Beginning at the Ballston Metro [MILE 0.0], head west along Fairfax Dr. about seven blocks to pick up the **Bluemont Junction Trail** behind a sound wall [MILE 0.4]. Turn left in 50 yards and follow the wide path a bit over a mile to the **W&OD Trail**. Cross it and the bridge ahead to meet the **Four Mile Trail** at the ballfields [MILE 1.6]. Turn left to carry on with the loop. (If you're doing a through hike or reached this point from the East Falls Church Metro and completed the loop described beiow, you would head right for the return via the W&OD and/or Four Mile Run Trails, which generally run parallel through this area.)

Sun going down at Lubber Run Park..

Now heading south from the **Four Mile/Bluemont Junction**, the loop passes through **Bluemont Park**. The trail might get a little confusing, but just stay on the paved path running between restrooms and a play area to continue along Four Mile Run. Soon after passing under Carlin Springs Rd., you'll be forced back onto the W&OD Trail.

Visit **walkarlington.com** for more good sauntering around greater Arlington.

Right after passing below Arlington Blvd., the Four Mile Trail rematerializes at a fork, but now stay left on the W&OD Trail through **Glencarlyn Park**.

Cross the creek on three bridges in the next quarter mile. Sixty yards past the third, turn left on a paved path* opposite a play area with restrooms, about a mile from Bluemont Junction. The path climbs briefly to the neighborhood above and the end of Park Dr.

Follow Park Dr. to Arlington Blvd. and cross the latter at the traffic light. Take an immediate left on another paved path and continue along the street ahead, crossing Columbus St. Walk a half-block more to the signed **Lubber Run Trail** on the right [MILE 3.2].

*The Four Mile Trail passes the play area and continues another five miles to the Mount Vernon Trai (see p. 161). From the play area, the next half mile is quite pleasant. Watch for a small, pretty waterfall-cascade just downstream of the first bridge.

Bluemont Junction caboose.

The attractive Lubber Run Trail leads along the creek to a quaint **amphitheater** in the forest, where you can often catch free live performances on summer nights. After a half mile, watch for an unpaved trail on the left just before a footbridge, an option that leads to 4th St. N and Edison St., continuing north about six blocks to rejoin the Bluemont Trail close to where you first reached it. Or skip this, cross the bridge and turn left at George Mason Dr., which also leads to the Bluemont. Walk right to return to the Ballston

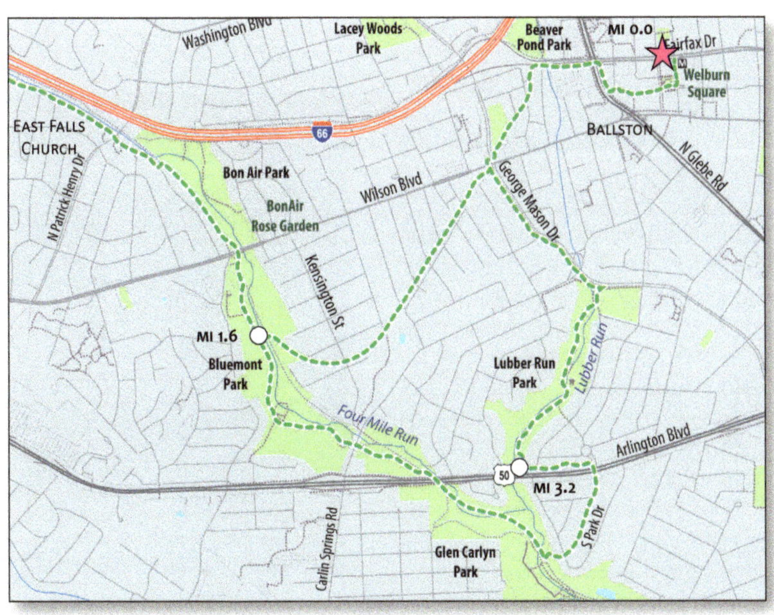

Metro [MILE 4.6].

If beginning at East Falls Church, exit the station beneath an overpass [MILE 0.0]; turn right on Sycamore St. and walk to the traffic light at 19th St. Cross both streets and in a couple steps more, turn left on the obvious paved path skirting the lawn. Cross a bridge and head left on a quiet street to find the W&OD Trail just ahead (well signed). Turn right to follow the W&OD along the I-66 sound wall.

At a fork [MILE 0.5], keep right on the Four Mile Trail (the fork is about 100 yards before a pedestrian overpass visible ahead). You could also stay on the W&OD all the way to Bluemont Junction, but the Four Mile is more interesting for footsters with less traffic noise.

The Four Mile Trail crosses a low bridge then continues 0.2 mile to Ohio St. Cross at a crosswalk (when safe) to a short, steep walkway leading down to a cul-de-sac. Follow this little street three short blocks to pick up the Four Mile Trail again at a bend [MILE 1.0]. Reach another cul-de-sac in 0.3 mile, but this time zag left then right to continue on the W&OD Trail.

Just before the next overpass (Wilson Blvd.), keep left at a fork to pass under the bridge. Beyond the bridge is another fork [MILE 1.7]. Keep left to continue on the W&OD Trail to a **caboose** above the creek at a place where steam trains met a century ago. Take the time to read the compelling history posted here. Then continue to the bridge and the Bluemont Junction Trail on the left [MILE 2.1].

Turn left for the direct route to Fairfax Dr. and Ballston, or cross the bridge to continue the loop from the junction as described above.

For a more interesting finish at Ballston, turn south (right) on Glebe Rd. to the end of the first building, then angle left to a trellis-covered walkway leading past a hotel to a plaza called **The Ellipse**. At the far end, cross Taylor St. and jog a little left to amble through **Welburn Square**. Then go left on Stuart St. a half block to the Metro station at Fairfax Dr.

Lots of modern buildings in Ballston.

Lubber Run Trail.

OLD TOWN ALEXANDRIA

Just across the river and a few heron flaps south of DC, lies Old Town Alexandria—close enough to make the cut for the National Nearby, but far enough away to feel like a new place. Or should we say, a new *old* place. Old Town is one of the oldest and largest historic districts in the U.S., with hundreds of historic buildings clustered around a highly walkable urban core.

The city traces its roots to 1749, shortly after Lawrence Washington, a colonial legislator, sent his little brother George out to survey the shore along Captain Alexander's estate on the Potomac River. It was eyed by some as a possible townsite and tobacco shipping port. The Captain wasn't too keen about having a new town amid his 500 acres of paradise, but negotiations ensued.

When the beer steins were empty and the politicking was over, the new town was declared. To smooth things over with the Captain, the town-makers promised to name the city after the Alexander family, an idea the captain apparently liked so much that he donated most of the land for the new town. The local citizenry, however, ignored all this and instead called their little town Bell Haven. It would take a few more years (and beers) before the official name finally stuck.

Today's Alexandria sprawls considerably beyond that early vision of a bustling tobacco port. Yet, amazingly, the city's historic core and renowned, authentic charm remain largely intact. With a clowder of land use tigers ever nipping at the shins of city planners, we can only hope the charm holds for another hundred years.

The old city is centered on a mile-long, quite walkable stretch of King St., between the Potomac River and the King Street Metro. Diverse shops, bookstores, posh and humble eateries, pubs and coffee shops, fine art and performance venues and the indispensible dispensaries of ice cream occupy dozens of quaint old buildings, some from the 1700s and early 1800s. City Hall, nearby churches and the 333-foot tall George Washington Masonic Memorial point their gables and spires to the clouds, while back down on Earth, brick walks, street trees, urban art and a few street musicians enrich the ambience.

Though King St. and the riverfront are main attractions, the Old Town Historic District extends across many more blocks. Historic sites abound, many of them pivotal in the stories of American Independence, the scurge of slavery, and the ensuing Civil War.

One could easily enjoy an aimless stroll along King St. without a map or a guide. But to add some depth and breadth to your adventure, consider one or both of the short loops suggested in the following pages.

The first begins at the King Street Metro Station in the "new" part of downtown and eases into the old city. The second begins at the riverfront in the heart of Old Town. From DC or Arlington, you can quickly reach King St. via the Metro. Or snag a foot ferry to or from DC or National Harbor (*see p. 174*).

15. Alexandria: New Town/Old Town

- *Distance*: 2.5-mile loop - *Allow 1.5 to 2 hours*
- *Start*: King Street Metro Station
- *Nearest Metro*: King Street

Points of Interest: **John Carlyle Square • U.S. Patent & Trade Office National Inventors Hall of Fame • African American Heritage Park Alexandria National Cemetery • Freedom House Museum • Friendship Firehouse • King Street • Washington Masonic Memorial**

The relatively new parts of Alexandria south of King St, also known as Carlyle, offer an interesting introduction to the modern city, although the loop outlined here quickly leaves the slicker parts behind in favor of the quaint old streets that lured most of us here to begin with. It's almost like visiting two cities in one walk. Allow an hour or more to complete this easy stroll.

Alexandria National Cemetery, established during the Civil War. Several of those who went after John Wilkes Boothe, Lincoln's assassin, are also buried here.

From the King Street Metro Station [MILE 0.0], exit near the station manager's kiosk and walk right (southwest) along the building past the bus shelters and continue on the walkway to a semi-hidden **pedestrian tunnel** under Duke St. Historical maps and artwork decorate the inside walls of the lighted tunnel (closed at night). When you emerge at the other end, walk across the small, brick plaza and continue rightward along Dulany St. to Jamieson Ave.

Cross Jamieson and stroll a half-block more to the next crosswalk. Cross to **Carlyle Square**, the plaza lined with glass-block pillars [MILE 0.3]. Head right toward a small geodesic globe for a nice photo op. The big daddy of glass pillars looms dead ahead, which, along with most of the surrounding buildings, comprise the **U.S. Patent and Trade Office** (2005). The big building also houses a small gift shop, several displays and a wall of inventors in the **National Inventors Hall of Fame** (*10:00-4:00 Mon-Fri,*

Geodesic globe near the U.S. Patent and Trade Office and Inventors Hall of Fame.

first Sat 11:00-3:00; free; info: **invent.org/museum**). To find it, enter the high atrium and hang a right just inside.

The walk turns left (east) at Ballenger Ave. near the globe, so explore the park and Hall of Fame as desired, then head east a block on Ballenger to John Carlyle St. Cross and turn right, but notice to the left another downtown park with an outdoor stage for summer events. After walking a block down John Carlyle St. and passing a few local eateries, turn left on Emerson Ave. Reach Holland Ln. in another block [MILE 0.6].

If safe, cross Holland Ln. here to the wheelchair ramp and red brick path on the opposite side, then head left into the city's **African American Heritage Park** You have a couple of options here. For the direct route, walk past a sculpture of bronze trees to the roofless **gazebo** at the corner. Or, for an extra 0.2-mile mosey (recommended), turn right down a set of stone steps and go right on the gravel path. Follow this short, scenic loop through forest and wetlands, then north along **Hooffs Run** (the creek). Major utility construction here may have altered this route.

African American Heritage Park.

East of Hooffs Run is the **Alexandria National Cemetery** (1862). Tragically filled to capacity just two years into the Civil War, it was the predecessor to Arlington National Cemetery. Access is from the east off Wilkes St.

The path soon reaches a walkway leading up to the gazebo noted above [MILE 1.0]. Ascend the easy ramp or steps and turn right on the curving brick path above. Go right a short block to a crosswalk that leads across Jamieson Ave. to a wide creekside path next to **Hooffs Run**. After a few steps, look back at the inconspicuous **stone bridge** (1856) you just crossed. Originally built

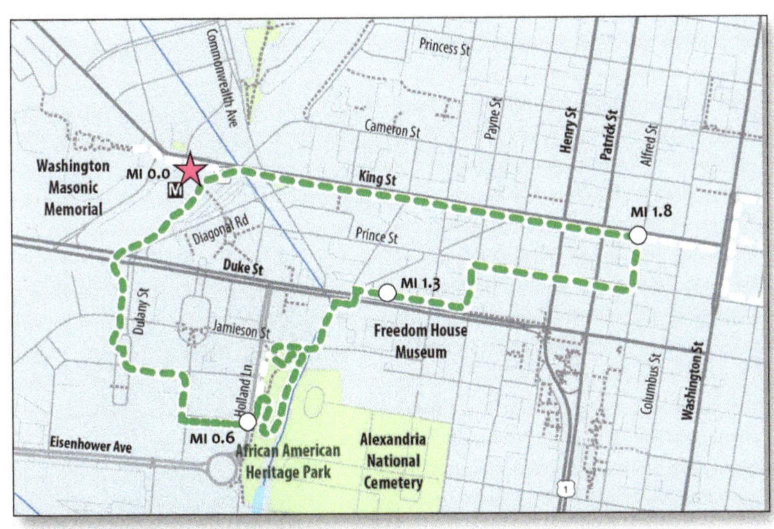

Historic Shiloh Baptist Church.

for Alexandria's first railroad, it's now the city's oldest surviving bridge.

When the path reaches Duke St., zag right (east) to the traffic light at S. Peyton St. Cross Duke St. here, but keep going east along Duke another block to the **Shiloh Baptist Church** (1893) [MILE 1.3], where you begin to leave newer Alexandria behind and enter the Old.

The Shiloh congregation was formed in the early 1860s by formerly enslaved people. The unassuming church stands adjacent to the notorious **slave pens** of what was, in the 1830s, one of the two largest slave trading operations in the U.S. (the other was in New Orleans). When Virginia seceded from the Union in 1861, Union troops took control of the city and those who were enslaved were granted relative freedom, despite continued horrid living conditions.

Duke St. can be a noisy-busy arterial, but tough it out just a tad more. On the next block, you'll find the building (1812) that housed in the 1830s the principal slave-trading company, **Franklin and Armfield**, and later, Price, Birch and Co., the last bastion of Alexandria's once-legal slave trade. Thousands of enslaved people were bought, sold and "penned" in and around this building.

James Birch sold into slavery Soloman Northup, the kidnapped free man from New York, whose heart-gripping story is told in the award-winning film, *12 Years a Slave*. The building now houses the excellent **Freedom House Museum** with moving exhibits about the slave trade and slave pens (*10:00-4:00 Thur-Fri, till 5:00 Sat-Sun, nominal admission fee; info:* **alexandriava.gov/FreedomHouse**).

At the next corner, turn left on Payne St. In a block, go right on Prince St. Follow this four blocks to Alfred St., passing the colorful, inviting facades of historic townhouses. At Alfred St., scoot left a half block to view some ancient firefighting equipment at the historic **Friendship Firehouse** (1855) Hours are limited (*nominal fee; info:* **alexandriava.gov/museums**). Continue a few steps more to King St. [MILE 1.8].

To further immerse yourself in lower **Old Town**, you can walk about nine blocks all the way down lovely old **King Street** to Union St. [MILE 2.3], just short of the river. The Old Town Lower Loop starts at the waterfront plaza fronting the boat harbor.

Or complete this UPPER LOOP by walking left (west) up King St. 0.7 mile to the Metro station. The **George Washington Masonic National Memorial** (1932) towers above and behind the station.

Friendship Firehouse.

City of Alexandria, with King St. (left), Amtrak station (center) and the Potomac River in the distance.

George Washington Masonic National Memorial

Built by the Masons in a decade and dedicated in 1932 to honor one of their own—our first U.S. president—this 333-foot tall monolith is perhaps Alexandria's most recognizable landmark. With its sheer scale, imposing front steps, fascinating interior and unique history, the Washington Masonic Memorial ranks among the grander monuments in the D.C. area. For a modest admission fee, a guide takes you up the elevator, with much to see on several floors, plus an awesome view from the observation deck. (Thur-Mon, by reservation; info: **gwmemorial.org**).

To reach the memorial from the King Street Metro, exit the station and walk left (northeast) along the front of the station to the King St. underpass below the trains. Turn left and pass through to the traffic light just ahead at the intersection with Callahan Dr. and Russel Rd.

Before making your way up to the memorial, look across King St. and a few yards up Russel Rd. On the right-hand side between the sidewalk and the street is a small fenced off block of stone. This is one of the original boundary markers (1791) for the District of Columbia (*see* p. 12). Then aim for the walkways and steps leading up to the main entrance to the memorial.

16. Alexandria: Old Town & Waterfront

- *Distance*: 1.6-mile loop - *Allow 1.0 to 2.0 hours*
- *Start*: Market Square, corner of King St. and Fairfax St.
- *Nearest Metro*: King Street

Points of Interest: **King Street • Torpedo Factory • Alexandria Seaport Foundation • Founders Park • Carlyle House & Garden • Alexandria City Hall Gadsby's Tavern • Ramsay House Stabler-Leadbeater Apothecary Museum Lyceum • Alexandria History Museum Athenaeum**

You'll find plenty of good walking along Old Town Alexandria's main drag, King St., as well as nearly every cross-street for blocks around. It's a treat to ramble along some of the same side streets George Washington, Thomas Jefferson and other presidents and statesmen trod over two centuries ago. One of their favorite watering holes, Gadsby's Tavern, is still there at the corner of Union and Cameron Sts., though minus the suds.

To add a little structure to your rambling, the following loop will take you to some of the more interesting sites and perhaps broaden your sense of what a great old town this truly is. The loop is also wheelchair-friendly, despite a few minor hills.

King Street is at the heart of what brings people to **Old Town** (locals and tourists alike), so be sure to hike a few blocks' worth before or after your more ambitious wandering. Stray at will when something catches your eye—a straight-up street grid makes it easy to find your way back to the start. Or just ask for directions. You'll find most Alexandrians to be a quite amicable bunch.

Begin the loop near City Hall and Market Square at the corner of King St. and Fairfax St. The Saturday morning farmer's market here is alleged to be the oldest, continuous market in the nation (since 1753) [MILE 0.0]. There are several ways to get here.

Alexandria City Hall.

Another sunny day at Market Square..

From the King Street Metro Station, you could saunter a mile down King St. allowing 30 minutes or so for leisurely walking. Or walk down from Alfred St. from where the previous walk, the New Town/Old Town upper loop, meets King St. Or save your feet for later and take the free trolley bus from the Metro station down to Market Square (between Royal and Fairfax Sts.), which is most of the way to waterfront. One could also bike here from the Mount Vernon Trail (MVT) (*see p. 161). Finally, foot ferries connect Old Town to Washington, DC, and National Harbor.

At Market Square next to Fairfax St., notice the yellow house on the corner with the big brick chimney. It's the **Ramsay House**, the oldest house in Alexandria. Built in 1724 at another location, it was barged up the river in 1749 and placed here by the city's first mayor, William Ramsay. Two centuries later, the town renovated the old house and in 1956 made it a visitor center, as it remains today (*open daily 10:00-6:00*).

Across King St. you'll find the **Stabler-Leadbeater Apothecary Museum** (1805), a remarkably intact historic pharmacy, a few doors down on Fairfax St.

Riverfront plaza, Old Town Alexandria.

Stroll down King St. to Union St. and angle left up the steps and into the covered pedestrian walk that leads past an impressive timeline summing up the history of Alexandria. Continue ahead to the riverfront plaza and Torpedo Factory to the left. (For wheelchair access, stay on King St. a half block.) Street musicians and artists often perform in and around the plaza or along the street.

Check out the **Torpedo Factory** (1918) now or later (restrooms inside). Yes, the Navy once made torpedoes here, though production stopped soon after WWII. The building has housed an elaborate complex of art studios for more than 50 years. You can easily burn an hour or more browsing three floors of working

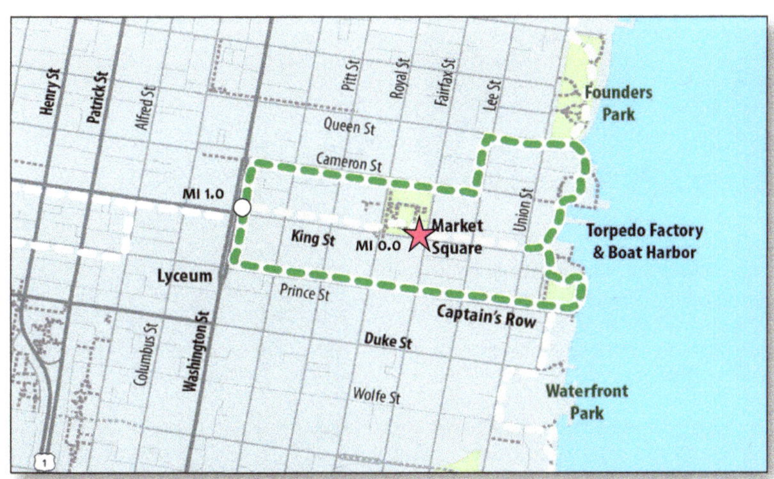

artists and their eye-catching bounty.

Now, looking at the river, head left on the boardwalk along the marina and out around a restaurant. You'll soon reach a small boatbuilding workshop operated by the **Alexandria Seaport Foundation**, which helps young people learn the art of traditional boatbuilding. **Founders Park** is just beyond. If you have a hankering, explore the park and points farther upriver via Alexandria's Waterfront Walk (*see also the MVT on p. 161*). Otherwise, go straight and hop on over to the corner of Union St. and Queen St. [MILE 0.2].

Cross Union St. to follow Queen St. west one block to Lee St.; turn left. Take Lee St. to Cameron St. and cross both streets to the fenced **Carlyle Garden** on the corner. You may be able to access the garden from a small parking lot on Cameron St. imediately uphill. From the garden (if open), take a narrow red-brick path uphill to another gate and the main entrance to **Carlyle House** (1753), one of the oldest buildings in Alexandria [MILE 0.6]. If the gate is closed, take the sidewalk up to Fairfax St. and turn left.

From Carlyle House, return to Cameron St. On the corner next to Carlyle House is the original **Bank of Alexandria** (1792). The cream yellow building on the corner to the north (across Cameron) is the **Wise Tavern** (1788), which has a rather special place in American history, as explained on a plaque near the corner. Do check it out. Continue up Cameron adjacent to **Alexandria City Hall** (1871). When you're half-way up the block, you might duck inside for a display of historic photos.

Continuing along Cameron St., cross Royal St. to the famed **Gadsby's Tavern** (1785). Well preserved though no longer a pub, it was one of George Washington's favored hangouts in Alexandria. A small museum here is open most days with variable hours (*nominal admission fee, or more for a tour; info*: **alexandriava.gov/museums/location/visit-gadsbys-tavern-museum**). Outside on the corner is the old underground ice house.

Keep chugging up the left side of Cameron and cross Pitt St. On the next

Carlyle House, on Fairfax St., is open for tours (10:00-4:00 most days, closed Wednesday; Info: **novaparks.com/parks/carlyle-house-historic-park**). The original owner, Scotsman John Carlyle, was a founder of Alexandria. Calling on the Carlyles at their posh Georgian abode were some of the nation's Founding Fathers: George Mason and Benjamin Franklin, to name a couple.

The Marquis de Lafayette, George and at least three other presidents dined and savored the suds at Gadsby's Tavern: Thomas Jefferson, John Adams and James Madison. The brief tour, for a modest fee, is highly recommended. The City Hotel (1790) next door still hosts a classy restaurant and period events in the ballroom.

block, keep an eye out for a plaque on the left identifying the location of George Washington's townhouse (white with two dormers). The house is a 1960 replica of the original and remains a private residence with no public access.

Continue to Washington St., Alexandria's chunk of the George Washington Memorial Parkway. The walk turns left here, but note the church and grounds across Washington St. This is Christ Church (1773), another major Old Town landmark—George Washington and Robert E. Lee were regular patrons, Washington with his own family pew. In 1942, Franklin Roosevelt brought Winston Churchill here for a service.

Follow Washington St. left a block to reach King St. [MILE 1.0]. The loop continues straight on Washington St. (recommended, see the next paragraph). Or bail out here and head left down King St. for the easy 0.4-mile stroll back to the Market Square or Torpedo Factory. Halfway to the river.

To continue the Lower Loop (just two blocks longer), cross King St. and walk south on Washington St. another block to Prince St. Notice the columned building on the corner. This is the Lyceum (1839), once a science and lecture hall, then a hospital during the Civil War, and now Alexandria's History Museum and worth browsing (generally *11:00-4:00 Thur-Sun, nominal admission fee, info:* **alexandriava.gov/Museums**).

Heading left on Prince St., follow it six blocks to Union St. On the way, at Pitt St., look to the right a half-block for the St. Paul's Episcopal Church (1817). The church was designed by the prolific British architect, Benjamin Latrobe, one of the principal architects of the U.S. Capitol. Just after crossing Royal St., keep an eye peeled for the old Elks Lodge (1909), with a distinguished bronze elk hanging outside a second-story window.

The Lyceum (Alexandria History Museum).

At Lee St., on the left is the Greek neo-classical Athenaeum (1852) [MILE 1.4]. Originally a bank, then a church, the building now houses an art gallery and venue for special events. The large white house next door (uphill) dates to the 1780s. Ahead, you'll enter an area known as Captains Row with beautiful old brick townhomes also dating to the 1780s. The cobblestone street preserves the original sense of place here for posterity—notwithstanding the late model cars lining the curbstones. You might need more than a boatman's salary to snag one of these places today.

At Union St., walk left a block to King St. [MILE 1.6], and the Fitzgerald Warehouse (1797) on the southeast corner, built to withstand frequent flooding of the river. As an alternative, you could continue to the end of Prince St. at Waterfront Park and wander left or right along the water's edge for a good look at the mighty Potomac and the almost as mighty Woodrow Wilson Bridge (Capital Beltway). National Harbor is just beyond it.

To explore more of Alexandria's pedestrian-friendly, historically rich waterfront, consider the next two walks in this guide They follow the Mount Vernon Trail and also offer enjoyable, family-friendly bike rides.

Mount Vernon Trail

On the Virginia side of the Potomac River, the Mount Vernon Trail (MVT) is one of the more popular trails inside the Beltway. Joggers and cyclists especially gravitate here all year long. But the trail's 18-mile length is plenty walkable too, and easily completed over several outings. The MVT is paved throughout, except for a few pleasant boardwalk sections. And despite some short hills, it's generally wheelchair-friendly.

Due to the high volume of bikes on nice weekends, you may find things more relaxed early or late in the day, on weekdays, or when the weather is less than perfect. A few areas also tend to be more congested than others, like the MVT's north end at Rosslyn, the Theodore Roosevelt Island parking lot, Gravelly Point Park near the airport, the Old Town Alexandria waterfront and at the Mount Vernon estate where the trail technically begins at Mile Zero. Traffic noise can be annoying at times, and some sections are certainly more interesting than others, as noted in the descriptions below. But don't let all that deter you from enjoying a good walk along the Potomac.

Always walk to the right so bikes can squirt past. Cyclists are supposed to yield to pedestrians, but keep an eye out for the less courteous rider. To enhance the experience for hikers within such an exceptional greenway corridor, the National Park Service really ought to add some skinnier foot trails in strategic locations to provide at least an occasional reprieve from heavier bike traffic. Volunteers could help make it happen.

There are many places to access the trail from DC and Northern Virginia, and several segments are convenient to Metro stations (Rosslyn, Arlington Cemetery, Crystal City and King Street). The River Loop (*p. 97*) travels the north 1.5 miles of the MVT, from Key Bridge to Memorial Bridge.

One of several bridges along the Mount Vernon Trail, this one near Reagan National Airport.

What follows are a brief accounts of the three-mile section from Memorial Bridge downriver to Crystal City, and the four-mile section from Crystal City to King St. in Old Town. Through most of Old Town, the MVT bike route follows Union St. However, there's a great pedestrian-only route along much of the Alexandria riverfront known as the Waterfront Walk. It rejoins the MVT 0.4 mile north of Jones Point (a mile south of King St.). This is followed by a 1.8-mile section from the lighthouse to the Dyke Marsh Trail near Bellhaven Marina.

To hike the rest of the trail to Mount Vernon, it may be more practical to drive, bike or bus to a closer starting point (*as noted on p. 167*).

17. MVT: DC to Old Town

- *Distance*: 3.3 to 6.7 miles one way - *Allow 1.5 to 3.5 hours*
- *Start*: Arlington National Cemetery Metro or Memorial Bridge, *Map p. 164*
- *Nearest Metro*: Arlington National Cemetery, Crystal City

Points of Interest: **Arlington National Cemetery • George Washington Memorial Parkway • Lady Bird Johnson Park • Merchant Marine Memorial Lyndon Johnson Memorial • Gravelly Point Park • Four Mile Run Trail Orinoco Bay Park • Founders Park • Torpedo Factory • Old Town**

On the MVT near the Navy–Merchant Marine Memorial, crossing over Boundary Channel and the trail to the Lyndon Johnson Memorial. Washington Monument is conspicuous across the Potomac River.

Navy-Merchant Marine Memorial.

The 6.7-mile trek along the Mount Vernon Trail (MVT) from Memorial Bridge or Arlington National Cemetery to Old Town Alexandria can easily be split into two shorter walks by starting or ending at Crystal City, roughly halfway to Old Town. Some parts are more appealing than others, but both segments have enough interesting stuff to make them worth putting up with a few dull minutes here or there. The recommended start is at the Arlington Cemetery Metro Station [MILE 0.0]. Scroll down a few paragraphs if you prefer to start at Crystal City. (*To visit the cemetery, see p. 180.*)

For the northerly segment (3.3 miles), the easiest access to the MVT near Memorial Bridge is to either walk there from Lincoln Memorial (*see River Loop, p. 97*), or exit the Arlington National Cemetery Metro Station (south side), turn right at the top of the escalator, and follow the sidewalk and paved path to the far side of a large traffic circle. Cross two lanes of traffic at a crosswalk (generally not difficult) and turn right at the signed trail junction just beyond (left leads to the bridge).

Cross a one-lane ramp, then stay left at a fork. Finally, cross the two north-bound lanes of **George Washington Memorial Pkwy** at a crosswalk (usually just a brief wait for a break in traffic). Immediately ahead is a T-intersection with the MVT [MILE 0.5]; turn right (left would take you to Theodore Roosevelt Island and Rosslyn).

The trail is well signed to Alexandria. The first bit of greenspace is called **Lady Bird Johnson Park**, a great place for tulips and daffodils in spring. A memorial to her husband and our 36th President, **Lyndon Johnson**, is reached by staying left at the next fork [MILE 1.1], near the curiously captivating **Navy-Merchant Marine Memorial**; however, the MVT stays right here to cross the bridge over **Boundary Channel**, as in the boundary between Virginia and Washington, D.C.

Continuing south on the MVT, you'll pass beneath I-395, U.S. 1, a railroad overpass and Metrorail bridge, before reaching **Gravelly Point Park** [MILE 2.2], a popular place to watch airliners take off and land at **Reagan National Airport**.

As the MVT passes the airport (this is the dull part), you'll cross three more trail bridges. Just after the second is a junction [MILE 3.0]. The right fork circles around to Crystal City, passing through a tunnel to Crystal Dr. and a recently revamped water park and kiosks on the right (0.3 mile from the junction). Live music and other events are often held here on summer evenings. For the Crystal City Metro Station, walk left a few yards, then up 18th St. a longish block. If starting your walk at Crystal City, the same route in reverse, of course, will take you to the MVT, where you would turn right for Old Town Alexandria.

Back at the Crystal City fork, continue south on the MVT across the next bridge and soon find a path to the airport on the left [MILE 3.3]. This optional side trip provides access to the terminal, the **Abingdon Plantation** historic site and the airport Metro. Getting to the Metro from here is somewhat circuitous (*see inset next page*).

LBJ Memorial

For the LBJ Memorial, follow the left fork near the Navy-Merchant Marine Memorial and stroll beneath the bridge to a parking lot and boat harbor. Walk to the shore of Boundary Channel and head right on a lumpy path. The Pentagon is across the channel, which also marks the D.C.-Virginia boundary. Walk to the north end of the parking lot where signs point to the memorial, 0.5 mile from the MVT. Explore the loop, small plaza and a monolithic stone marker. A scenic footbridge crosses the channel to another parking lot. Retrace your steps to the MVT.

At Gravelly Point watching planes land.

Abingdon Plantation

For the ruins of this 18th century tobacco plantation, preserved in a surreal setting between airport parking garages, take the short airport path off the MVT, a little south of Crystal City. The path rounds a curve and leads down a concrete ramp to a short tunnel and back up another ramp that spits you out on the other side of a road. Aim for the obvious entrance to the parking garage and climb the steps one level up. Then jog right and walk east across the garage to a black and white painted walkway; turn right. Follow this to its end near a sidewalk and a grassy hill. (A door to the left will get you to a sky bridge and the airport Metro station.) Another pathway leads up the grassy hill to the Abingdon ruins. Excellent interpretive signs will fill you in on the story of this intriguing and historically important place. Return to the MVT by the same route.

Continuing on the MVT to the south end of the airport, you'll find a junction with the Four Mile Run Trail on the left [MILE 4.1]. This portion of the Four Mile Run Trail is generally of more interest to cyclists (a better chunk to walk is north of Columbia Pike; *see p. 148*). Staying right, you'll pass **Dangerfield Island** and sailboat marina [MILE 4.9], where you can chow down or rent a bike or boat in season. In a quarter-mile more, reach a slithering **boardwalk** section through a large wetland. Just beyond this, keep left to find another boardwalk and the river's edge at the start of the Alexandria waterfront [MILE 5.5].

Walk through a caged boardwalk to find a junction at **Tidelock Park**. Go left (bikes stay right) and follow the squiggly path to the waterfront. This begins Alexandria's **Waterfront Walk**, which leads to Old Town. You'll swing around a couple of office buildings to a large plaza with steps and curious **sculptures**, including a miniature version of the Washington Monument [MILE 5.8].

Walk along the river through **Rivergate** and **Orinoco Bay Parks**, before running out of trail at Pendleton St. Walk left and around the corner to follow Union St. one block to pick up the waterfront trail again at **Founders Park** [MILE 6.3]. Again, just follow the river to the main **plaza** and **Torpedo Factory** on the **Old Town** waterfront. A covered walkway leads to **King St**, the main drag in Old Town [MILE 6.7]. If you started at the Crystal City Metro, it's a four-mile walk to this point.

MVT, a slithering boardwalk north of Old Town Alexandria.

Potomac River from the MVT.

MVT: Memorial Bridge to Crystal City & Old Town Alexandria

18. MVT: Old Town to Dyke Marsh

- *Distance*: 2.8 to 7.8 miles round trip - *Allow 1.5 to 4 hours*
- *Start*: Old Town riverfront plaza (Torpedo Factory)
- *Nearest Metro*: King Street

Points of Interest: **Torpedo Factory • King Street • Waterfront Park Captains Row • Shipyard Park • Jones Point Lighthouse Woodrow Wilson Bridge • George Washington Memorial Parkway • Dyke Marsh**

Waterfront Walk, Shipyard Park.

Torpedo Factory, Alexandria.

Alexandria's foot-friendly waterfront offers some enjoyable urban carousing along the Potomac River, with good views, much history, almost no hills (wheelchair-friendly) and something new around every bend. An interconnecting pedestrian route, called the Waterfront Walk, snakes around developed areas to link nine riverfront parks. The Mount Vernon Trail (MVT) follows Union St. through Old Town (the cycling route). The Waterfront Walk rejoins the MVT near Jones Point.

The previous trail description covers the area north of King St. as part of a longer hike from Crystal City and beyond. Heading south from **King Street** is just as entertaining, and quieter traffic-wise. Figure three miles round trip to the Jones Point Lighthouse, or a longish 7.8 miles to the Dyke Marsh overlook and back. For King St. and greater **Old Town** see p. 156.

Begin at the **riverfront plaza** in front of the **Torpedo Factory** (*see p. 156 for directions*) [MILE 0.0]. Walk south to the bottom of King St. and follow the obvious paths along the waterfront. Notice the cannon and a modest monument to shipbuilders in the park, and the tall ship Providence usually docked nearby. A major boardwalk leads to more pathway beyond. While the multi-story development here is fairly new, just a block or two away from the water you'll still find cobblestone streets and city blocks filled

MVT: Old Town Alexandria to Jones Point & Dyke Marsh

with charming homes dating to the late 1700s and early 1800s.

Round a bend to the right to enter **Shipyard Park** [MILE 0.5]. A good path leads around more condominiums to **Fords Landing** named for a Ford car parts assembly plant that once jutted into the river here. Note that railings are absent, so keep the kids close. Interpretive signs share some of the area's history. Rest benches and, if you're lucky, an onshore summer breeze make this a good place to sit and imagine how things might have looked a century or two ago. Once around this development, you'll intersect the **MVT** at a sharp bend [MILE 1.0]; turn left.

The route now enters **Jones Point Park**. At the end of a black metal fence, jog a little left to read an interpretive sign about the old shipyard that once occupied the riverfront here. Continue on the gravel path along the river's edge to where it meets pavement again. But rather than rejoining the MVT there, continue straight ahead, walking along the water and under the massive **Woodrow Wilson Bridge**, a part of I-495, the Capital Beltway. Stay left on another gravel path in trees along the river. Follow this around a bend to the **Jones Point Lighthouse** (1855) [MILE 1.4]. The first **cornerstone** of the District of Columbia was laid here in 1791. Stone markers line the old boundaries (*see also p. 166*).

When you leave the lighthouse, generally stay left to walk past more interpretive signs to the MVT, which runs left along the base of the big bridge. Head left when you reach it and continue up the hill to the **G.W. Pkwy** [MILE 2.0]. The MVT turns left here and leaves Alexandria behind.

For a short side trip to a nice view of the river and Alexandria waterfront,

Jones Point Lighthouse..

turn right instead, then right again in a few yards on the wide path adjacent to the west-bound lanes of the Woodrow Wilson Bridge. Reach the first of two signed **overlooks** about 0.6 mile from the point you left the MVT, making this a 1.2-mile side trip—or more. You could also walk (or bike) another two miles to National Harbor, perhaps returning to Old Town by foot ferry.

MVT below Woodrow Wilson Bridge.

Back on the MVT heading south, the next pleasant section crosses **Cameron Run**, once known as Great Hunting Creek, on an attractive stone-faced bridge. The path runs close to the river before reaching a picnic area with prime spots along the water, plus restrooms. Just ahead is the road into **Belle Haven Marina** [MILE 3.1], an optional stroll to the left (kayak and sailboat rentals available). Close by is the trailhead for **Dyke Marsh** (recommended). A large sign tells you about the marsh and its wildlife. A 0.8-mile trail follows an old road bed and boardwalk to a scenic **overlook** on the river. Return to Alexandria by the same route. (Or walk another half mile south on the MVT to a lengthy boardwalk across more of Dyke Marsh.)

Prothonotary Warbler. Dyke Marsh is a local favorite for birding.

From the Belle Haven access road, the MVT continues another seven miles to **Mount Vernon**. Busses run from there back to the Huntington Metro Station (40-minute ride), but not via G.W. Pkwy. So bus access in between Alexandria and Mount Vernon is not terribly convenient to the MVT. That makes for a long one-way hike if you choose to continue on. It's a scenic slog nonetheless. Diehards might prefer to catch the Huntington bus to Mount Vernon and begin a northward trek more ceremoniously at **Mile Zero**. (*Search online for Fairfax Connector 151.*)

Dyke Marsh and MVT, south of Belle Haven Marina.

Major kudos if you hike the entire MVT. Something worth celebrating!

Other Sights & Walks Around DC

For more good walks and sights to see around greater Washington, DC, check out the suggestions below. Space doesn't allow for detailed maps and descriptions, but the routes are typically straight-forward. Basic navigation skills and a good DC map should suffice, or research details online.

Most of the following are located inside the Capital Beltway and often accessible by Metro, bus or bike:

Parks & Natural Areas

- National Arboretum
- Kenilworth Aquatic Gardens
- College Park & Lake Artemesia
- Greenbelt Park
- Sligo Creek
- Capital Crescent
- C&O Canal Towpath
- Glover Archbold Trail
- Tregaron Conservancy
- Hains Point
- Oxon Hill Farm & National Harbor
- Fort Circle & Fort Dupont

Urban Saunters

- Union Station to Chinatown
- Chinatown to Foggy Bottom
- Simón Bolívar to Albert Einstein
- Southwest Waterfront & Wharf
- DC Heritage Neighborhood Trails
- Downtown Bethesda, MD
- Downtown Silver Spring, MD

More DC Sights on Foot

- U.S. Marines/Iwo Jima Memorial
- Arlington National Cemetery
- 9/11 Pentagon Memorial & Air Force Memorial
- Cedar Hill & Anacostia Museum
- National Cathedral & Garden
- Basilica of Immaculate Conception

Beyond the Beltway

- Great Falls
- Along the Potomac River
- Chesapeake Bay & Delmarva
- Shenandoah National Park
- Other Regional Favorites

▶ Parks & Natural Areas

A number of larger parks and natural areas inside the Beltway offer good hiking and easy sauntering. Check out the following gems in DC's big outside.

National Arboretum

Expect miles of paths and much to ogle at the **National Arboretum** (1927), a little east of downtown Washington. Highlights include Fern Valley, the Asian Gardens, Dwarf Conifer Forest, Capitol Columns, flowering tree and shrub collections, and botanical research facilities on nearly 500 acres of rolling meadow and forest managed by the U.S. Department of Agriculture.

There's no Metro station nearby, but it's easy enough to drive or take a Metrobus to the entrance off Bladensburg Rd. NE, a mile north of H St. A bus runs often. (The handy streetcar along H St. was discontinued in early 2026.) Step off the bus near R St. and follow it two blocks east to the big parking lot and arboretum's main entrance (well signed).

Walk up the short hill to the nearby visitor center where you can find a map and the latest info. Something is always blooming from early spring through fall, though winter walks can be pretty nice too. (*Open 8:00-5:00 every day but Christmas; free admission; info:* **usna.usda.gov**.)

A planned trail bridge across the Anacostia River will eventually connect the arboretum to **Kenilworth Aquatic Gardens** and the **Anacostia Riverwalk** (p. 140), which will enhance bike and foot access immensely.

Kenilworth Aquatic Gardens

Soft paths meander through a cluster of historic, excavated ponds at Kenilworth Gardens, harboring waterfowl, lilies and other plants from around the world. More trails and boardwalks explore native woods and wetlands, and a small national park visitor center helps explain the goings on.

A major link in the **Anacostia Riverwalk** opened in the fall of 2016 and passes by the gardens, including over-water sections. That and a planned new trail bridge to the National Arboretum should give communities on both sides of the river all the more reason to don our walking or biking shoes to explore the Anacostia River corridor (*see p. 143*). The parking lot and main entrance to the gardens are off Anacostia Ave., a half-mile northwest of the Deanwood Metro Station. Browse the website for further details and directions, **nps.gov/keaq**.

College Park & Lake Artemesia

An extensive system of paved trails offers good walking in and around the city of College Park and the University of Maryland, about eight miles northeast of DC. The College Park Metro Station serves the area and provides potential access for hikers and bikers to **Lake Artemesia**. The lake is good for a family friendly, two to three-mile stroll (as well as picnicking and birding).

You can fill out the adventure with

a visit to the university grounds or the historic College Park Aviation Museum located at the world's oldest operating airport (10-minute walk from the Metro station). Wilbur Wright was a flight instructor here. The museum is open most days of the year (9:00-5:00, nominal admission fee). To reach it by Metro, walk out the east side of the Metro station (not the tunnel), amble left of the bus stop to Campus Dr. The museum is to the right (well signed).

Trail-wise, one could reach Lake Artemesia from the Metro by exiting via the tunnel to Calvert Rd. and walking west to Rhode Island Ave. Turn right and walk several blocks to the crosswalk at Campus Dr. (a 10-minute walk to here). Cross when safe to the obvious paved path and in a quarter mile more (after a bridge) turn right. Then keep right to reach the pleasant loops around Lake Artemesia. If a longer bike ride beckons, the Northeast Branch Anacostia Trail leads south toward Bladensburg and beyond as part of the Anacostia River trail system (see also p. 143). Maps are recommended and easy to come by online.

Greenbelt Park

This lesser known national park, located seven miles northeast of DC, spans more than 1,000 acres of rolling forest and includes a large, pleasant campground (over 170 sites), showers and nine miles of nature trails.

Find the entrance at the north end of the park off Greenbelt Rd, a little west of the junction of the Capital Beltway and Baltimore-Washington Pkwy. Budget travelers could feasibly walk or bike to the park and campground from the College Park Metro Station via Campus Dr. and Good Luck Rd (under two miles). Open year round. A ranger station and park brochure can get you oriented. (See also **nps.gov/gree**.)

Sligo Creek

This pleasant, mostly paved, 10-mile hiker-biker trail runs between Wheaton and Hyattsville, generally along the relatively quiet Sligo Creek Pkwy. It's a well used branch of the greater Anacostia Tributary Trail system. With a meandering creekside greenway and more than two dozen bridges along the way, any part of the trail makes an interesting walk, particularly in the more extensive natural areas. Multiple parks and picnic areas offer access and parking, with potential Metro access immediately southwest of the West Hyattsville station (more appealing to cyclists). There's also reasonable access from the Silver Spring and Forest Glen stations if you have a good map or GPS.

For a decent, Metro-to-Metro, five-mile hiking loop (not quite a loop), exit the Forest Glen station and cross to

Sligo Creek.

the east side of Georgia Ave. Walk the north side of Forest Glen Rd. one block to Woodland Dr. and turn left. In a few blocks, turn right on Belvedere Blvd. at General Getty Park, or first make a quick tour of the loop around the park. Follow Belvedere to its end at Dameron Dr. and turn right. In two blocks head left through a small park area (opposite Sanford Rd.) to finally reach the Sligo Creek Trail, a mile from the Forest Glen Metro. There's a very nice one-mile stretch to the left, or for a longer trek continue walking north to Wheaton Regional Park in 2.6 miles (see p. 187).

For the trek to Silver Spring head right (south) when you first reach the Sligo Creek Trail. Stay on the main path as it wanders back and forth across the creek, beneath the Capital Beltway and across several roads. At Wayne Ave. (3.0 miles), continue along Sligo Creek Pkwy. past a small parking area and over a bridge. At the next small parking area, a quarter-mile past Wayne Ave., turn right to leave the trail. it's about five miles from here to the West Hyattsville Metro Station.

A new Green Trail connection to Silver Spring is planned for the near future, in conjunction with construction of the new Purple Line light rail system. For now, you can cross Dale Dr. (a quarter mile south of Wayne Ave.) and walk up Hartford Ave. Take the first right on Denver Rd., which leads to Nolte Park. Follow the path around the ballfields and descend a few steps to Easley St.; turn left. Follow Easley around the bend to the Bullis Park ballfield and take the paved path on the right. It leads past a play area to Houston St. Jog right, then go left on Hankin St. and left on Bonifant St. In two blocks more, turn right on Fenton St. and follow that three blocks through downtown Silver Spring to Colesville Rd. Turn left to reach the Metro station in another three blocks (see also p. 179).

Capital Crescent

A kind of bicycle beltway, the Capital Crescent Trail, a/k/a Georgetown Branch Trail, links communities, parks and other major trails on the north side of the metro area. Note that construction of the new Purple Line light rail system may create some obstacles and detours, especially between Bethesda and Silver Spring, until it's finished in 2027 or 2028. Search the trail and Purple Line online for the latest routes and closures.

If not blocked off somewhere, one could enjoy an ambitious three-hour trek along the 7.5-mile chunk from Bethesda to Georgetown, which passes through Little Falls Park and an impressive tunnel under MacArthur Blvd. Or walk from Georgetown as far as Fletcher's Cove (2.3 miles) and return via the C&O Canal Towpath, where the two trails run parallel. Bethesda to the Rock Creek Hiker-Biker Trail (2.3 miles) may be another possibility.

A two-mile paved loop at Little Falls (and a shortcut midway) makes a nice family outing on foot or by bike. Navigate to Westmoreland Park by car for easiest access. Whatever your choice, expect some company on this popular trail almost any day of the year. (*See also* **cctrail.org**.)

For the longer hike to Georgetown, exit the Bethesda Metro Station to the west side of Wisconsin Ave. and walk south about three blocks to Bethesda Ave; turn right. The Capital Crescent Trail is just ahead cutting diagonally through the intersection with Woodmont Ave. Turn left for Little Falls (2.2 miles from Bethesda Metro), the tunnel (3.3 miles) and Georgetown. Or go right (if open) for

Rock Creek or just check out Bethesda's people-friendly downtown (*see p. 179*).

From Georgetown, you might start at the fountain in **Waterfront Park**. Walk upriver past the **Labyrinth** to the end of the park, keep under the viaduct and **Key Bridge** to a little beyond the kayak and wake board rental place to pick up the paved path. Just past the **Arizona Ave Bridge** (3.2 miles), it may be possible to cut right through the neighborhood and catch a bus on MacArthur Blvd. for a lift back to Georgetown.

C&O Canal Towpath

The **Georgetown** and **River Loops** (*pp. 97 and 105*) touch on the C&O Canal's story and include short sections of the **Towpath** running parallel to M St. Upriver from Georgetown's **Key Bridge,** the trail takes you to **Fletcher's Landing** (picnicking, boat rentals) in 2.3 miles. The **Capital Crescent Trail** (*p. 171*) runs parallel to the C&O and offers a slight change of scenery for the return walk. See the **Potomac Heritage Trail** for a longer loop via **Chain Bridge** (*p. 144*).

Another popular, scenic stretch is at **Great Falls** on the Maryland side of the Potomac River (*see p. 183*), between the museum/visitor center and Widewater/Old Angler's Inn, two miles to the south. Watch for turtles. Canal barge rides are sometimes available on weekends, April-October, although restoration work in 2026 might delay things.

Find the main entrance to the national park off MacArthur Blvd. about four miles northwest of the Beltway. Scenic hikes lead to and along the river, while a museum and visitor center share some compelling history of the area.

If you're headed to Great Falls, maybe also check out the beauteous, historic carousel (May-September) at **Glen Echo**, adjacent to the **Clara Barton House** and one-time headquarters of the American Red Cross. Above Great Falls, the possibilities are boundless for the next 170 miles of the C&O, including historic Harpers Ferry (*p. 189*). For maps and details, visit **nps.gov/choh**.

Glover Archbold Trail

Like a mini Rock Creek Park (not all that mini), this 220-acre NPS greenway reaches almost from **Tenleytown** to **Georgetown**, a four-mile trek overall. A good three-mile trail (unpaved) runs the length of the park and is often used by nearby residents, maybe less so by other DC denizens. It was named for its two principal 1924 land donors, and fortunately escaped being turned into a four-lane highway in the late-1940s.

To walk it all, exit the Tenleytown Met-

ro Station to the west side of Wisconsin Ave. and walk south about two blocks to the traffic circle. Continue several more blocks to Van Ness St, or nab a bus to this point. Turn right here to find the unpaved trail on the left just ahead, where it cuts through a big lawn area a half-mile from the Metro station (well signed).

Stay on the main path throughout, often close to the creek, Foundry Run, or explore various spur trails to neighborhoods. Signs are usually posted at major junctions and street crossings. You might need to walk a little left or right from crosswalks to locate the continuing path (at Reservoir Rd., a grassy slope leads down to the path).

The **Glover Archbold Trail** ends at Canal Rd., not far from **Georgetown University**. Walk left about 70 yards along the sidewalk, then at the end of a guardrail, hang a left on a steep walkway leading down to a curious **tunnel** beneath Canal Rd. At its other end you'll find the **Capital Crescent Trail** (*p. 171*) and some steps on the left leading up to the **C&O Canal Towpath**. Either of those will take you a half-mile downriver to **Key Bridge** in Georgetown.

Tregaron Conservancy

Gardiner Greene Hubbard, co-founder and first president of the National Geographic Society, purchased a prime parcel in Cleveland Park in the 1880s and built a mansion there called **Twin Oaks**. It must have impressed inventor Alexander Graham Bell, who'd already married Hubbard's daughter. But time does fly and years later, half the estate, including the mansion, would be acquired by Taiwan for its embassy, while the other half was purchased by Joseph Davies, a former ambassador to Russia, and his wife Marjorie Merriweather Post, the heir to Post cereals and, for a time, the richest woman in America. They named

Tregaron Conservancy.

their little paradise **Tregaron**, after a Davies family town in Wales.

Three decades ago, the estate was nearly lost to a housing development. But thanks to the work of the **Tregaron Conservancy**, another kind of wealth—Tregaron's natural and human history—was ultimately preserved across 13 acres for all to enjoy.

For a two-mile loop, you can walk to the estate from the Cleveland Park Metro Station. Exit to the east side of Connecticut Ave. and walk south past a good selection of neighborhood shops and eateries. Immediately after crossing a bridge, turn right at a crosswalk and head west along Devonshire Pl. Keep left at the fork on Cortland Pl. and follow this to its end at Klingle Rd. The entrance to Tregaron's trails is directly across the street (0.7 mile to here). There is street parking here also.

The soft-surface path bends left to a small pond with rest benches. If desired, walk around the left side and climb a few stone steps. At the landing above, turn right and descend another set of steps back to the pond. Before a little arched bridge, turn left to walk downstream under a stone arch bridge; stay left at the fork. You can choose between several routes, including the **Grand Staircase Trail**, to complete a loop. Notice the paved Klingle Valley Trail below (lit at night). Eventually work your way there via several short footbridges for an uphill return to the start.

You can also work north to the gate at Macomb St., then either carry on with briefly west to the National Cathedral, or make an easy return to the Cleveland Park Metro Station by turning right on Macomb St. and left on Connecticut Ave.

Hains Point

A four-mile spin around Hains Point and the public golf course is an easy escape from the crowds on the Mall. The less traveled road is popular with bikes and joggers, who generally go clockwise with the traffic. The loop is also a good, family-friendly bike ride. On foot, either direction works.

You can get there from the National Mall at the George Mason Memorial (*see p. 80*). If you were standing at the entrance to the memorial looking at pensive George, head right on the sidewalk adjacent to Ohio Dr. SW. Pass beneath the I-395 overpass, take the crosswalk over to the west walkway next to the Potomac River and go left. Note that portions of the walkway have subsided and may be under water during higher tides, forcing you to walk along the road or lawn, generally no big deal.

For a much shorter loop, watch for Buckeye Dr. which crosses to the east side of the peninsula north of the golf course and meets the loop road and walkway 1.5 miles north of Hains Point. Tennis courts are close by. A nice miniature golf course is a short putt south.

The peninsula was named for Army General Peter Hains, a veteran of the Civil War, Spanish-American War and WWI. Across Washington Channel is DC's Southwest Waterfront, also known as the Wharf. Farther south is historic Fort McNair. From the tennis courts, Ohio Dr. leads north to the Tidal Basin.

On the way, you can extend the walk to the Southwest Waterfront (*see p. 178*) by turning left on a walkway adjacent to the I-395 bridge, just past the tennis courts. Atop the ramp, go right to cross over the channel. Traffic noise is annoying, but there are good views of the harbor and historic fish market. Follow a zigzag wheelchair ramp to Benjamin Banneker Overlook (left goes to the Mall and Smithsonian Castle). Circle right and take the obvious path down to Maine Ave. Cross and turn right for the fish market. Then continue along Maine Ave. to reach the Tidal Basin. This option adds a mile to the Hains Point walk.

Oxon Hill Farm & National Harbor

It's most efficient to drive to Oxon Hill Farm, on the east side of the Potomac River, just north of the Beltway. You'll find about two miles of kid-friendly walking trails to mosey, among farm animals, historic outbuildings, a small visitor center, veggie gardens, native woods and the riverfront at Oxon Cove (*9:00-4:00 daily*).

National Harbor is nearby, but on the south side of the Beltway (no Metro stations). Good paths lead along the river north and south (wheelchair and stroller-friendly). The Harbor is basically a resort area with an interesting beach and some unexpected quirkiness, like the half-buried sculpture called The Awakening. Also bike and kayak rentals, the Capital Wheel, a Chesapeake Bay mosaic and plenty of eats and shops.

You can make a bit more of an adventure of it by taking the foot ferry from Old Town or biking over the noisy, but scenic, Woodrow Wilson Memorial Bridge from Jones Point Park in Alexandria (*see p. 165*). The trek to National Harbor is

National Harbor beach.

3.2 miles each way (or 4.6 from King St). The path from the bridge to the Harbor is nicely designed and a pleasant walk. Midway, a tunnel leads to a pond and a semi-dull hiking or biking route to Oxon Hill Farm, 1.4 miles from the tunnel. This paved path climbs a long hill past the new casino to Oxon Hill Rd (go left) and Bald Eagle Rd (left again) to reach the farm.

Fort Circle & Fort Dupont

Fort Marcy.

Almost since its inception, Washington, DC has been defended by military forts along the Potomac and Anacostia Rivers and elsewhere.

A "circle of forts" nearly enclosed the city during the Civil War and many are now parks with maintained trails. At Fort Dupont, south of the Anacostia River, you can learn about other old forts, summer concerts and the Fort Circle Hiker-Biker Trail (*some isolated areas, so go with a group; info*: **nps.gov/cwdw**).

Farther south, the sprawling lawns, munching deer herds, visitor center and massive brick and stone works at Fort Washington overlook the Potomac River, inviting another foray. Cannons, big doors and a drawbridge at Washington's oldest fort have kept the bad guys at bay for decades. The waterfront path is mildly interesting. (*Info:* **nps.gov/fowa**).

Urban Saunters

This guide describes many miles of worthwhile urban rambles around the greater metro area. If you're hungry for more, here are some candidates for further exploration. Some are short, pleasant walks between Metro stations. Others you might need to do a little homework to set your own course.

Union Station to Chinatown

For a fine stroll a little off the beaten path, try this route from Union Station to the National Building Museum and Chinatown. Or add a mile or two by continuing on to Farragut Square, the White House, Foggy Bottom (next page) or Dupont Circle (*p. 129*).

From Union Station, head west toward the National Postal Museum, worth a stop even if you're not a seasoned philatelist (stamp collector). The Postal Museum (1993) shares a building with DC's old city post office (1914). Expanded to two floors in 2013, the museum contains excellent displays on stamps, printing, the history of the mail and collecting.

Jog around the corner at 1st St. NE and take the Massachusetts Ave. sidewalk down to the next traffic light. Cross North Capitol St. to the National Guard Memorial and Museum. The museum offers galleries, artifacts, exhibits, video and compelling stories detailing the history of the Guard, including the colonial and U.S. militias that preceded it. Press the intercom button for access (*9:00-4:00*) and check in briefly at the desk.

Cross Massachusetts Ave. to view the

Holodomor Memorial (2015) honoring the Ukrainian victims of that horrific 1930s genocide. Just behind the memorial, turn right on F St.

After a long block away from some of the noisier downtown hubbub, cross New Jersey Ave. and a sliver of 1st St. NW. On your lef is an unusual glass tower shaped like a vertical wing. Keep walking straight ahead, passing through the trim greenspace of Georgetown University's Law Center to 2nd and 3rd Sts. NW.

Pass the Holy Rosary Catholic Church (1923) on the right, adjacent to the Casa Italiana (1981), an Italian language school adorned with statues of four greats from Italian society and the arts. On the opposite corner is the oldest synagogue in DC (1876), now the Lillian and Albert Small Jewish Museum. Remarkably, the brick building was moved here several years ago from its original site just up the street.

At G St. find the elaborate red brick National Building Museum commanding the entire block. The building's decorative bas-relief is prominent. The main F St. entrance is on the left (south) side, across from the Judiciary Square Metro and the National Law Enforcement Officers Memorial. Take a peek inside the museum then continue to 5th St., turn right to H St., then left to Chinatown and the Friendship Archway at 7th and H Sts. (*see also p. 129*).

Floor tile, National Building Museum.

Chinatown to Foggy Bottom

This slice of downtown Washington picks up a few more sites of interest among blocks of mostly modern architecture, as well as the White House, Renwick Gallery, the Museum of Women in the Arts, the Textile Museum, other historic buildings, plazas and park-like squares. It's an easy two-mile stroll to get better acquainted with the heart of the city. To add some distance, start at Union Station (above) or continue on to Georgetown.

Begin at the Friendship Archway at H and 7th Sts. NW in front of the Chinatown-Gallery Place Metro Station. Cross 7th St. and continue west on H St. to a little past 9th St. Look for a passageway on the right called *The Gateway*. Pass through to a broad plaza, then hang a quick left on Palmer Alley to amble a stretch of upscale retail. When the pedestrian way ends at 11th St., turn right, then go left at the next corner (another plaza) to follow New York Ave. Just before 13th St., find the entrance to the 1987 National Museum of Women in the Arts on the left (*10:00-5:00 Tuesday through Sunday, modest admission fee*).

Next, head right on 13th St. to I St. and cross to Franklin Square, a beautifully restored, kid-friendly park presumably named for the illustrious Benjamin.

Walk through the square to the far corner at 14th St. NW and K St. Continue west a block on K St. to **McPherson Square**, then make a diagonal through this square past **Union Army General James McPherson's** proud statue (1876), before heading right on I St. A Metro station and the U.S. Department of **Veterans Affairs** are close by.

As you cross 16th St. NW, notice the White House in plain view to the south. At 17th St., turn right to saunter through **Farragut Square**, popular with the lunch crowd. Civil War **Admiral David Farragut** (1881) in the center is remembered for the line, "Damn the torpedoes, full speed ahead!" Metro stations are at both ends of the square.

You may have noticed that much of the old architecture in downtown Washington is still intact, though in many cases just a few walls or facades above the street are original, with modern structures nestled behind. Uniquely absent are the 40-storey skyscrapers common to other major American cities. To maintain a somewhat European feel to a city juxtaposed with so much grandeur, building heights have been restricted in downtown DC since 1899. Rarely does a building exceed twelve stories, a reality that contributes much to the city's human scale of development. There are no dark canyons of overwhelming hotel and office towers impeding the flow of light and air. While the mega-developers would love to cash in on greater height and density, the city has so far resisted.

From the center of Farragut Square (1881), angle slightly right to reach the corner of 17th and I Sts. (there is no J St.) and cross the latter. Follow 17th St. two blocks south to Pennsylvania Ave. The **Renwick Gallery** and **White House** are to the left (*see also p. 50*).

Walk west along Pennsylvania Ave. to just past 18th St. and make a soft left on H St. The **World Bank** is on your left and unassuming **Edward R. Murrow Park** is that patch of green on the north side of Pennsylvania. Staying on H St., cross 19th, swagger past the **IMF** (while pondering the age-old question, *What could I do with a billion dollars?*), then cross 20th St. to the campus of **George Washington University**.

Washington's bust at G.W. University.

The next two blocks invite some meandering to check out the grounds and buildings, including the **Textile Museum** with much to see at 21st and G Sts. (*Tue-Sat, 10:00-5:00, modest donation suggested; info:* **museum.gwu.edu**). Or just continue west on H St. to 22nd and turn right. In a block, turn left on I St. to find the Foggy Bottom Metro in one block more. To continue to **Georgetown**, turn right (north) on 23rd St., cross **Washington Circle** and look to the left for Pennsylvania Ave., which will take you over the nearby Rock Creek bridge and into Georgetown at M St.

Simón Bolívar to Albert Einstein

This short jaunt snags a few sights of interest that are a little off the beaten track, but still fairly close to the Mall. Begin at the corner of 17th St. NW and Constitution Ave. and follow the Americas Mini-Loop described on p. 92 When you reach the statue of **Simón Bolívar**, opposite the **Art Museum of**

the Americas, continue past the small reflecting pond to cross Virginia Ave. Immediately cross 19th St. NW to a walkway cutting through a lawn area, then turn left on 20th St. (notice the fountain to the right). Note that if you continued west on C St. for another block, you would reach the U.S. State Department (1941), where a worthwhile tour of the Diplomatic Reception Rooms may available (reserve in advance).

At Constitution Ave., head right to pass the stout Federal Reserve building (1937). Cross 21st St. and keep slogging past the National Academy of Sciences (1924), where occasional tours may be offered to view the ornate ceilings, interior decor, exhibits, portraits and science-based artwork. (*Info:* **cpnas.org**.)

Fittingly, outside the National Academy of Sciences, near the corner at 22nd St. NW, sits a larger-than-life bronze statue of the renowned physicist Albert Einstein, pondering his equations. The memorial was dedicated in 1979 to honor his 100th birthday. The sculptor, Robert Berks, also crafted the famed JFK bust at the Kennedy Center.

Perhaps stroll over to the Lincoln Memorial from there. To reach Einstein from the Lincoln Memorial or Vietnam Veterans Memorial on the Mall, walk north along Henry Bacon Dr. to Constitution Ave. and cross both streets. The nearest Metro station, Foggy Bottom, is a slog up the hill on 23rd St. NW, 0.6 mile from Dr. Einstein.

Southwest Waterfront/Wharf

A massive redevelopment project known as the Wharf (2022) reinvented the Southwest Waterfront, creating something of a resort atmosphere that also includes substantial walkways, piers and other public space. A wide promenade leads along the broad Washington Channel between the Tidal Basin and Potomac River. A lazy waterfront stroll extends from the highrises northwest to

Wharf on DC's Southwest Waterfront.

the Municipal Fish Market and National Mall, and southeasterly along a quiet park to the Titanic Memorial and Fort McNair. Determined footsters can carry on to the Navy Yard neighborhood, Anacostia and beyond.

One can easily walk to the Wharf from the National Mall via Maine Ave., or from the Waterfront Metro Station. From the latter, walk two blocks west on M St. to 6th St. SW. Turn left, round a bend and make your way toward the waterfront close by. Walk left (south) 0.3 mile to the rather sobering Titanic Memorial.

To connect to the Navy Yard and Anacostia Riverwalk, head east from the Titanic to P St. and follow it a few blocks more to S. Capitol St. Turn right, then go left on Potomac Ave. to find the Riverwalk on the other side of Nationals Park (baseball stadium). *See p. 140 for more on the Riverwalk.*

DC Neighborhood Heritage Trails

This guide highlights quite a number of historical sites, though in a magnificent old city like Washington, there are, of course, far more stories and places worth visiting than could possibly be listed here. Various guidebooks, and even guided walking tours, are available to help you sleuth them out.

Thanks also to the good work of Cultural Tourism DC, there are at least 18 Neighborhood Heritage Trails around the city. You may have noticed a few of the eye-catching signs on various street corners. They not only identify and describe countless historical sites and structures, but also share some of the great stories of people and communities that have made a difference here over the last thee centuries. Each walk can be easily completed in an hour or two and are highly recommended. For maps and details, an app and more, check out the website at **eventsdc.com/dc-neighborhood-heritage-trails**.

Downtown Bethesda, MD

Downtown Bethesda offers enjoyable rambling, easily accessed from the Bethesda Metro Station or Capital Crescent Trail. Shops and eateries abound. Exit the Metro station to the west side of Wisconsin Ave., walk around a cascading water feature and past the big yellow sculpture and up a few steps to a circular fountain beyond. The plaza narrows, but amble ahead and leftward to pass another waterfall, before descending a herd of short stairways to Montgomery Lane. Turn right, then left at the traffic light at Woodmont Ave.

In two blocks, go right on Elm St. Then just before reaching the next corner (a long block), follow an inviting pedestrian thoroughfare to the left called Bethesda Lane. Caroline Freeland Park and the Bethesda Library are close by. Walk through the archways of Bethesda Lane, a nice place to linger, to Bethesda Ave.; turn left.

Near Woodmont Ave, notice the Capital Crescent Trail (CCT) on the right (*see also p. 171*). Follow the paved path 100 yards to a wide, curvy walkway on the left. A few yards beyond is a sitting area with an information sign and map of the CCT. Take the curvy walkway to Woodmont Ave. Turn left to meet Bethesda Ave. at the next corner; turn right. At Wisconsin Ave. find the Bethesda Metro Station three blocks to the left.

Downtown Silver Spring, MD

Silver Spring's contemporary downtown is worth a spin around the block, or several, really. A classy old theater, a plaza that converts to a winter ice rink, tons of shops and eateries and interesting urban design are entertaining enough for casual footsters.

From the Silver Spring Metro Station, one idea is to exit the station to Colesville Rd. and make a quick right on Wayne Ave. (left side may be nicer). Pass a plaza and follow a passage way under a modern building to Georgia Ave. Cross to Ellsworth Dr. and walk that a block to Fenton St. and Veterans Plaza. You can wander from here. Or once the Green Trail is finished, head east to Sligo Creek (see *p. 170*).

Another work in progress is the eight-mile Metropolitan Branch Trail that will eventually connect the Silver Spring Metro Station to DC's Union Station, passing several other Metro stations and many points of interest to hikers and bikers. (*Info*: **metbranchtrail.com**.)

Downtown Silver Spring.

▶ More DC Sights on Foot

Here's another handful of major DC area sights to visit on foot, mostly as easy saunters.

U.S. Marines/Iwo Jima Memorial

North of **Arlington National Cemetery** near Rosslyn is the larger-than-life sculpture of U.S. Marines raising the American flag at **Iwo Jima** near the end of WWII, based on the famous photo from that event. Perhaps the best way to reach it on foot is via the Arlington Cemetery Metro Station. Walk west on Memorial Ave. toward the **Memorial to Women in Military Service** (1997) and turn right (north) on Schley Dr. In 100 yards turn right on the **Custis Walk** and continue 0.3 mile.

Where the Custis Walk leaves the Cemetery grounds head left, but notice a paved path on the right—it will take you the half mile back to the Metro if the Cemetery is closed when you return. Check out the towering **Carillon** donated to the U.S. by The Netherlands in 1954 and restored in 2022. The bells toll at noon and 6:00 pm daily. Follow the path north and stay right at the fork for **Iwo Jima** (1954), a mile from the Metro.

Arlington National Cemetery

This renowned resting place for American veterans and leaders, dating back to the Civil War, is a humbling place to explore—a stunning reality check on the real cost of war. For additional background on the **Arlington National Cemetery** (1864), see the **River Loop** on p. 97, or visit **arlingtoncemetery.mil** for details on where and when to go and what to see. (*Open 8:00 am-7:00 pm, till 5:00 pm October-March.*)

You can get there easily from the Arlington Cemetery Metro Station. (*The station closes at 10:00 pm April-September, 7:00 pm October-March.*) Or walk across **Memorial Bridge** from Lincoln Memorial and the Mall, a 20-minute hike.

If you need a tip for a good walking tour of the Cemetery, follow the winding path away from the visitor center (pick up a map there) to Roosevelt Dr. Follow it up the hill to the **Tomb of the Unknown Soldier** (1921) and **Memorial Amphitheater** (1920). At the Tomb, pause to observe the frequent **Changing of the Guard**. Stroll to several memorials close by, then pick up the **Crook Walk** just north of the Amphitheater. It leads down then up many steps to **Arlington House** (1803) and an excellent view of Washington, D.C. The **Kennedy Gravesite** is just below, but you'll need to make a wide turn on roads to reach the access point (well signed). Then follow **Custis Walk** to Schley Dr. and turn right to return to the visitor center. Or continue north on the Custis Walk to visit the **U.S. Marines/Iwo Jima Memorial** (*left*).

9/11 Pentagon Memorial & Air Force Memorial

This humbling reminder of the tragic events of September 11, 2001, is best reached from the Pentagon Metro Station, less than a half mile away. As you exit the station, conspicuous signs point the way. Sidewalks lead around the south side of the **Pentagon**, passing between parking lots and entering the **9/11 Memorial** on the southwest side. A new visitor center is planned here. In the meantime, you can try to make sense of it all by looking for a sign noting a phone number you can dial for a recorded audio tour. The **Air Force Memorial**, described below, is close by. Pentagon tours may be available, but must be reserved in advance.

The sky-high Air Force Memorial (2006) is a 15-minute walk from the 9/11 Pentagon Memorial and definitely worth a visit. The shining, curved blades reach 270 feet in height—far more impressive than one might imagine from afar.

Air Force Memorial.

As you exit the Pentagon's 9/11 Memorial, turn right at the corner and walk through the underpass just ahead. Stay on the sidewalk to a traffic light. Cross here and continue leftward and upward along Columbia Pike, below the grassy hill, to a hidden entrance gate left (south) of the memorial. (Note that major construction in 2026 may alter access somewhat, as the memorial is integrated into an expansion of the burial grounds at the adjacent Arlington National Cemetery.)

Cedar Hill & Anacostia Museum

Douglass house at Cedar Hill..

Cedar Hill and the Anacostia Museum are both worthy of a visit, and though doable on foot, going by car or bus isn't such a bad idea, at least for now. Trails and connectivity across the river are improving (see the **Anacostia Riverwalk** on p. 140). Ongoing bridge improvements for crossing the river have enhanced bike and pedestrian access considerably. After a period of economic stress, those investments, plus a rich history and growing arts focus foretell better days ahead for this 160-year-old DC community.

Cedar Hill is where the formerly enslaved statesman Frederick Douglass spent the waning years of his life. Scheduled tours of the house are available, along with a small visitor center and short film about his remarkable life. Either drive there (recommended) or bike, bus or walk the 0.7 mile from the Anacostia Metro Station. (*Details and directions*: **nps.gov/frdo**).

The **Smithsonian Anacostia Community Museum** is a crossroads of art, history and culture established over a half century ago. Exhibits and collections reflect diverse American stories of urban living, with an emphasis on communities "east of the river." View a broad assortment of artwork, crafts, artifacts, documents and films (*from 10:00-5:00*). The research library contains hundreds of local books and tens of thousands of photographs, plus Wi-Fi. Artists, speakers and performers often make free public appearances. (*Info*: **anacostia.si.edu**).

From the Anacostia Metro it's a quick bus ride or a hilly, not-too-interesting 1.3-mile walk (or pedal). A free Smithsonian shuttle from the Mall runs on summer weekends. The **Fort Circle Trail** is also close by (*see p. 175*).

National Cathedral & Garden

This impressive, dare we say, monumental DC landmark, at 301 feet tall, is visible from many areas of the city. The world's sixth largest **cathedral** is really something to marvel at up close. Completed in 1990, the English-inspired Gothic structure took 83 years to construct. An earthquake in August 2011 busted things up some and expensive repairs were still underway in 2026.

For a look inside America's best known cathedral, you could attend mass (Episcopalian) or spring for a guided tour, including a view from the heights (*10:00 am or later, modest fee; Info:* **cathedral.org/visit-tour**). Or amble around the inspired **Bishop's Garden** across the drive to the south, via the stone archway opposite the cathedral.

The nearest Metro station is at Tenleytown. Snag a bus or walk south on Wisconsin Ave. 1.3 miles to Woodley Rd. Or from Georgetown, head north on Wisconsin Ave. to just beyond Cathedral Ave. (under two miles). A parking garage is also available. For a more interesting trek, hike through the **Tregaron Conservancy** from the Cleveland Park Metro Station, then from the north gate go west on Macomb (*see p. 173*). Turn left on 34th St., right on Lowell St. and left on 36th St. The cathedral looms—you can't miss it.

Basilica of Immaculate Conception

Many may not realize it, but this enormous **Catholic basilica** ranks among the largest churches in the world, with 70 chapels, great arched halls and a sublime crypt, all fantastically finished in a multitude of colored tiles, stonework, glass and voluminous artwork—enough to rattle even the most ardent agnostic. The basilica (1961) and adjacent campus of **Catholic University** are easily reached from the Brookland Metro Station. Exit to the wide path curving up the hill above a lawn area. Jog right at the street, then take the next left and follow this up the hill through campus to the obvious domed basilica and 329-foot high tower. (*Open 6:00 am-6:00 pm daily, tours available.*)

Basilica of Immaculate Conception.

Beyond the Beltway

- **Great Falls**
- **Along the Potomac River**
- **Chesapeake & Delmarva**
- **Shenandoah National Park**
- **Other Regional Favorites**

If you're angling to get out of town, there are plenty of good hikes and walks within a one to three-hour drive of the DC metro area. A few are highlighted here. Pick up a regional hiking guide at a bookstore or outdoor shop for the full scoop on these and many more. From the mountains to the coast, you'll find ridge rambles to rocky overlooks, treks to scenic waterfalls and wildlife areas, lakeside and seaside walks, and easy strolls among small towns and historic sites.

Some of the best semi-local hikes can be found at Great Falls Park, along the Potomac River, on Sugarloaf Mountain, Sky Meadows, Bull Run Mountains, Harpers Ferry and Shenandoah National Park, among others. There are a number of regional parks and natural areas with countless miles of trails to trod, including lesser known parks and historic areas managed by the National Park Service.

When hiking in more remote areas, prepare accordingly, be nice to your feet and don't lose the trail. Remember there may be a few venomous snakes around—rattlesnakes and copperheads. Rattlesnakes seem to prefer rocky areas in the mountains, while copperheads are more likely in wooded areas. Though the slithering critters are rarely encountered, it's good practice to stay on the trail and watch where you step or put your hands. (*If bitten, seek medical attention immediately.*) Poison ivy (hairy vines and leaves of three) is very common in the forest—another good reason to stick to the trail.

▶ Great Falls

While the Potomac River's famous falls are, indeed, great and are a main attraction near DC, the rocky gorge below the falls is also impressive and worth some extra wandering. Expect good trails and multiple overlooks on both the Virginia and Maryland sides of the Potomac. If you had to pick one, the Maryland side may be a slight favorite, since you have to earn the wider view of the falls with a short hike on the boardwalk across **Olmsted Island**. That said, **Great Falls** and **Mather Gorge** are stunning from either side.

The Virginia side is officially **Great Falls (National) Park**, which offers quicker access to view the falls. Expert kayakers occasionally thread their way through the torrent. A good hiking loop leads south past more overlooks where you might also see rock climbers jamming the cracks below. But take care near the edges (kids especially). You can access this side of Great Falls from Georgetown Pike about 4.3 miles northwest of the Capital Beltway (Exit 44).

The Maryland side is within the **C&O Canal National Historical Park**, where a

Mather Gorge below the falls.

Billy Goat Trail near Great Falls, best for experienced hikers (not as hard as it looks).

half-mile stroll on an excellent trail and boardwalk leads to the main viewpoint. (With a setting so dramatic, the Park Service really ought to extend the boardwalk into a loop with some additional vistas.)

The walk south from the C&O Visitor Center along the Towpath is also quite scenic. One could feasibly bike here from Georgetown via the Towpath (15 miles each way; *see p. 102*). If traveling by car, take MacArthur Blvd. and/or Clara Barton Pkwy. (they run parallel) 3.9 miles west from the Beltway (Exit 41) and follow signs.

If a scenic, rocky scramble sounds tantalizing, the Billy Goat Trail south of the C&O Visitor Center and Olmsted Island is a local favorite. Some exposure to heights means it may not be everyone's cup of tea, but most experienced hikers will have no difficulty clambering along. Follow the beaten path and paint marks on the rocks, and turn back if it becomes too much. For details, pick up a regional hiking guide or check at the info desk or the park's websites (**nps.gov/grfa** *and* **www.nps.gov/choh**). By all means, stay out of the river, even where it looks calm and inviting—strong currents and undertows have claimed many lives.

▶ Along the Potomac River

Parks and preserves along the Potomac River are quite extensive both upstream and downstream of DC. Below are a few sites that are just a short drive from the city.

Difficult Run

The Difficult Run Trail (not that difficult) is a lengthy trail accounting for 10+ miles of Fairfax County's Cross County Trail (40+ miles), which leads across northern Virginia from the Occuquan River to Great Falls (*Info*: **fairfaxcounty.gov/parks/trails/cross-county-trail**). The most popular section of Difficult Run may be the scenic 1.3-mile finish near Great Falls. It's often done as a loop with the Ridge Trail and other connecting routes within the national park.

Most folks start at the Georgetown Pike signed parking lot on the left just under four miles west of the Beltway. Follow the big creek downstream and under the Pike for great views of slabby cascades and a rocky gorge. At the signed junction for the Ridge Trail, it's worth making the short descent to the wide confluence with the Potomac River, before returning to the Ridge Trail for further exploring (carry a trail map or GPS app). You can also wander upstream from the parking lot for many not-difficult miles of supplemental adventuring.

Scott's Run & Turkey Run

A popular maze of trails (6+ miles) lead through the hilly terrain above Scott's Run to the Potomac River and a scenic waterfall at the confluence. The Potomac Heritage Trail also passes through the area (*see p. 144.*) Trail maps are

posted at various locations and at **fairfaxcounty.gov/parks/scotts-run**.

The Scotts Run nature area is on the Virginia side of the river, with two parking lots off Georgetown Pike, just west of the Beltway. Go on a weekday or early on the weekend for less company on the trails. Though rare, a bear was spotted in the park not so long ago.

Three miles downriver is Turkey Run, just off the G.W. Pkwy north of Arlington. You'll find short trails, woodsy picnicking and a link down to the Potomac Heritage Trail. (The route to Scott's Run includes a 0.8-mile section of Live Oak Dr.) Or, hike three miles south to Fort Marcy, one of the "circle of forts" that safeguarded DC during the Civil War. Cannons are perched in a grassy glen and interpretive signs tell the story.

Mount Vernon Estate

George Washington's family estate, Mount Vernon, has a long and illustrious history, manifested in well maintained grounds, gardens and historic buildings. The main house has stood since the 1700s. A network of walking paths leads to all the interesting features, so it's easy to knock out a couple of miles of leisurely walking here, albeit for a modest fee. Tours are available and recommended.

The 500-acre estate is located adjacent to the Potomac River at the south end of the G.W. Pkwy. and at Mile Zero of the Mount Vernon Trail (about 15 miles from DC; *see p. 167*). You can drive, bike or bus from the Huntington Metro Station. (*Open daily 9:00-5:00, 4:00 November-March, modest admission fee;* **mountvernon.org**).

Pohick Bay & Mason Neck

A few miles south of Mount Vernon are two more sizeable parks with hike-worthy trails, camping, cabins, kayak rentals and the rest. Pohick Bay Regional Park also has a water play area and golf course. Mason Neck State Park is a little wilder and adjacent to the Elizabeth Hartwell Mason Neck National Wildlife Refuge. Watch for bald eagles. Park details and trail info are at **novaparks.com/parks/pohick-bay-regional-park** and **fws.gov/refuge/elizabeth-hartwell-mason-neck**.

▶ Chesapeake & Delmarva

When a trip to the beach calls, Chesapeake Bay and the Atlantic coast are the logical destinations, and reasonably close enough to be considered for either a day or overnight trip. The 150-mile-long peninsula that forms the Chesapeake is known as Delmarva, for the three states (Delaware, Maryland and Virginia) that span its landmass. The area is also commonly referred to as the Eastern Shore. Many small towns are spread

Cape Henlopen State Park, Delaware.

across the peninsula and worth exploring while checking out nearby parks, trails, beaches and historic sites.

James Michener researched and wrote his epic historic novel *Chesapeake* while living in St. Michaels. Rehoboth Beach is a fun town with a seaside boardwalk not to be missed. Delaware's sandy beaches to the north and south are very popular in the warmer months. The Assateague National Seashore is another fabulous destination.

If you're new to the area, Maryland's capital of Annapolis offers a perfect jumping off point for this alluring region. Explore the old city on foot, including the excellent Maritime Museum before crossing the massive Bay Bridge to Delmarva.

Shenandoah National Park

One of the great national parks of the eastern U.S., Shenandoah is the go-to mountain park for much of the greater DC region. The 105-mile Skyline Dr. runs the length of the park, mostly near the crest of the Blue Ridge Mountains. Campgrounds, visitor centers, ranger talks, overlooks, waterfalls and over 500 miles of trails ensure plenty of adventures to choose from almost any time of the year. The park is just a 90-minute drive (70 miles) from DC and can be reached via I-66 or from scenic roads through Sperryville and the Virginia countryside. Park pass or entrance fee required.

Summer offers a welcome reprieve from the lowland heat and humidity, but also more traffic and fuller campgrounds on the weekends. (Campsites can fill up, so reserve in advance if possible via **recreation.gov**.) Fall means color, milder days and cooler nights around the campfire. Winter can get cold and snowy, with frozen waterfalls and lonely trails. Parts of Skyline Dr. close in winter.

A few favorite hikes include Stony Man, Hawksbill, Whiteoak Falls, Marys Rock and Old Rag Mountain. The Appalachian Trail also runs the length of the park. For maps and details, stop by a visitor center or access the park website at **nps.gov/shen**.

Other Regional Favorites

Across the Mid-Atlantic region are many more parklands, natural areas and historic sites with good trails for rambling. Here are a few more within easy reach of DC.

Cabin John

On the Maryland side of the Potomac River, a nine-mile trail in pleasant forest follows Cabin John Creek from MacArthur Blvd near Glen Echo to Cabin John Regional Park and beyond. This major park has other trails, an excellent nature center, walk-in campsites, picnic and play areas, and even a two-mile miniature train ride (April-October).

For park access from the I-270 Spur (Exit 1), follow Democracy Blvd. west less than a mile to the Locust Grove Nature Center parking lot on the right. For a trail map, camping and hours for the nature center, visit **montgomeryparks.org/parks-and-trails/cabin-john-regional-park**.

Rock Creek Regional Park (Rockville, MD)

This isn't the same park as the famous one in DC, though it is the same creek in a similar landscape good for hiking. It's almost two parks in one, one each at Frank and Needwood Lakes. Find picnic and play areas, a nature center and 13 miles of trails, including lakeside loops. The paved, 14.5-mile Rock Creek Hiker-Biker Trail now connects all the way to Rock Creek Park in DC, starting at the visitor center at the south end of Needwood Lake.

Either bike there from DC's Rock Creek Park, or access one of the park entrances off Avery Rd., one and two miles north of Norbeck Rd., or off Muncaster Mill Rd. at the nature center north of Frank Lake. (*See* **montgomeryparks.org/parks-trails/trails** *for maps and details*.) One could feasibly reach the area via paved paths and sidewalks from either the Rockville or Shady Grove Metro Stations (each are two miles from the trail). Montgomery County's Ride On buses will get you there too, but you'll need to sort out the options.

Wheaton Park/ Brookside Gardens

Wheaton Regional Park, a few miles north of Silver Spring, has a lot going for it, including the usual amenities for a large park, plus a nature center, horse stables, 11 miles of trails and even a carousel and miniature train ride if your dogs are tired. And there's Brookside Gardens, to boot, a 50-acre spread of landscaped walkways, terraces, picturesque ponds, horticultural displays and formal gardens, plus a **conservatory** full of tropical plants. The park and gardens are good for both lazy and ambitious walking. Dogs are okay, but not in the gardens.

Access via Glenallen Ave. a mile east of Georgia Ave. and the Glenmont Metro Station. To walk to the park and gardens from the Metro station, exit to the east side of Georgia Ave. and go north briefly to Glenallen Ave.; turn right. Follow Glenallen via sidewalks and paved path to the gardens entrance at Heurich Rd.

Patuxent Research Refuge

This major wildlife refuge spreads across 20 square miles of diverse habitats supporting dozens of species of mammals, amphibians and reptiles, and nearly 250 bird species. The refuge is located midway between Washington and Baltimore, just east of the Baltimore-Washington Pkwy. At least 30 miles of trails and boardwalks access forest, meadows, lakes and wetlands near the Patuxent and Little Patuxent Rivers.

A large National Wildlife Visitor Center is open Wednesday through Saturday 10:00-4:00. A free tram runs seasonally. Hunting occurs in fall and winter, though many trails remain open to hiking. Begin at the South Tract by taking the Powder Mill Rd. exit from the parkway and driving 1.8 miles east to the signed refuge entrance on the right. For trail maps, directions and details, visit **fws.gov/refuge/patuxent-research**.

HUNTLEY MEADOWS

One of the larger wetland conservation areas near DC is **Huntley Meadows**, a few miles south of Alexandria. Broad, level trails, boardwalks and a view tower bring you up close and personal with a wide variety of birds and other wildlife, including turtles, snakes, rodents, deer, otter and fox. Birders love this place in spring and early summer. A nature center will help you identify what you see, while keeping the kids entertained as well. Easiest access (by car or Fairfax Connector bus from Huntington Metro) is at the corner of Lockheed Blvd. and Harrison Lane, west of Richmond Hwy.

OCCOQUAN RIVER

About 20 miles southwest of DC, near the quaint, historic town of **Occoquan**, you'll find a major corridor of parks and preserves all along the Occoquan River. Where it joins the Potomac River, the **Occoquan Bay National Wildlife Refuge** has miles of walking paths. Above the town are 20 miles of river, reservoir and woodlands spread among several regional parks (**Sandy Run**, **Fountainhead**, **Hemlock Overlook** and **Bull Run**). Hiking and mountain biking trails abound, including the 17-mile **Bull Run Occoquan Trail** and the 40+ mile **Cross County Trail** running north to Great Falls. Maybe try the Fountainhead or Bull Run parks to get acquainted with the area. Access is from the north side of the river. (*Details at:* **novaparks.com**).

BULL RUN, LEOPOLD'S & SKY MEADOWS

Ruins near a 1700s grist mill.

For high-quality mountain hiking less than an hour's drive from DC, the privately run **Bull Run Mountains Conservancy** protects a 2,500-acre forest with several nice loop trails and pre-Civil War ruins, including the **Chapman's Gristmill** and **cemetery**. From I-66 Exit 40, head briefly south then west on the John Marshall Hwy. In 2.7 miles turn right, then make a quick left. (*Info:* **brmconservancy.org**.)

The nearby **Leopold's Preserve**, just west of Haymarket, is also privately owned but open to the public, including overlooks, historic sites and seven miles of trails. (*Info*: **leopoldspreserve.com**)

Farther west (off Hwy. 17, seven miles north of I-66) is the historic 1,860-acre **Sky Meadows State Park**. This exceptional park has high rolling hills with forest and open meadows, 20+ miles of trails, hike-in campsites, historic buildings and some of the best views near DC. (*Info*: **dcr.virginia.gov/state-parks/sky-meadows**.)

MEADOWLARK BOTANICAL GARDENS

For a pleasant stroll among ornamental and native gardens and ponds, **Meadowlark's** 95 acres and several miles of paths might be calling. Begin at the visitor center off Beulah Rd., south of the Dulles Access Rd. and a few miles west of Tysons Corner. Plan on spending at least a couple of hours here. (*Open 10:00am daily, except some major holidays, till 7:00-8:00pm April-September, earlier October-March; nominal fee. Info*: **novaparks.com/parks/meadowlark-botanical-gardens**.)

Sugarloaf Mountain

Sugarloaf is the nearest actual mountain to DC. You'll find a scenic, one-lane mountain loop road and about 15 miles of hiking trails traversing 3,000 acres of privately protected forest land open to the public (donations welcome). The trail network connects picnic areas to rocky overlooks and impressive views from the 1,282-foot summit. In the past, the area was considered a potential location for the presidential retreat of Camp David. Drive there via Comus Rd., west off I-270 about 20 miles north of the Beltway. *Open daily 8:00-4:00; info*: **sugarloafmd.com**.

Harpers Ferry

Wander the beautiful, historic town of Harpers Ferry at the confluence of the Shenandoah and Potomac Rivers while you eat ice cream or visualize John Brown's brash war against slavery via intepretive signs, exhibits and museums. *Info*: **nps.gov/hafe**.

Or float the Shenandoah river in summer, with good tubing at lower water levels. Or take a hike nearby. The C&O Canal Towpath passes through here, as does the Appalachian Trail, where you can ponder a 1,000+ mile jaunt to Georgia or Maine. For something a little less ambitious, Maryland Heights is worth the steep trudge (four miles round trip). Or stroll to Jefferson Rock or across the old railroad bridge. Harpers Ferry is about 65 miles northwest of DC.

Appalachian Trail

The famed Appalachian Trail, or A.T. as it's usually called, extends for 2,198 miles across 14 states, almost entirely within the Appalachian Mountains. Millions of people hike some part of this National Scenic Trail every year, while thousands of dedicated hikers have spent months on end trekking from Georgia to Maine, an epic experience never to be forgotten.

Near DC, four states account for more than a third of the total distance: Maryland (41 miles), Virginia (557 miles), West Virginia (just 2.4 miles) and Pennsylvania (230 miles). Just over 100 miles pass through Shenandoah National Park alone.

But you don't have to be devoted backpacker to enjoy the many scenic rewards along the trail. To check out the trail in bite-sized chunks, Shenandoah and Harpers Ferry, of course, are great choices, along with South Mountain's Annapolis Rock near Frederick, Maryland, and along the Blue Ridge Parkway in southern Virginia and into North Carolina.

For all the best info on the A.T., visit the website of the Appalachian Trail Conservancy at **appalachiantrail.org**.

McAfee Knob near the A.T., Roanoke, VA.

Online Resources

Parks & Trails info

Federal

National Park Service, National Capital Region (*many sites*): **nps.gov/orgs/1465**
National Mall: **nps.gov/nama**
Rock Creek Park: **nps.gov/rocr**
Great Falls Park: **nps.gov/grfa**
Greenbelt Park: nps.gov/gree
C&O Canal National Historical Park: **nps.gov/choh**
Potomac Heritage Trail: **nps.gov/pohe**
Shenandoah National Park: **nps.gov/shen**
Patuxent Research Refuge: **fws.gov/refuge/patuxent-research**

Local & Regional

DC trails/bikeways info & maps: **trails.ddot.dc.gov**
Northern Virginia park & trail info: **novaparks.com**
Arlington park & trail info: **parks.arlingtonva.us/off-street-trails**
Arlington Walks (brochure with maps): **walkarlington.com**
Alexandria park & trail info: **alexandriava.gov/parks**
Fairfax County park & trail info: **fairfaxcounty.gov/parks**
Prince George's County park & trail info: **pgparks.com**
Montgomery County park & trail info: **montgomeryparks.org/parks-trails/trails**
Capital Crescent Trail: **cctrail.org**

Monuments, Memorials & Federal Buildings

National parks smartphone app: **nps.gov/locations/dc/get-the-app.htm**
Washington Monument: **nps.gov/wamo**
Lincoln/Thomas Jefferson Memorials: **nps.gov/linc**, **nps.gov/thje**
Martin Luther King, Jr. Memorial: **nps.gov/mlkm**
U.S. Capitol tours & info: **visitthecapitol.gov**
White House tours & info: **whitehouse.gov/visit**
National Archives: **archives.gov/museum**
U.S. Supreme Court tours & info: **supremecourt.gov**
Library of Congress tours & info: **loc.gov/visit**
Arlington National Cemetery: **arlingtoncemetery.mil**
Belmont-Paul Women's Equality National Monument: **nps.gov/bepa**

Museums, Galleries & Gardens

Smithsonian Institution (museums, galleries & National Zoo): **si.edu**
National Gallery of Art & Sculpture Garden: **nga.gov**
National Building Museum: **nbm.org**
U.S. Botanic Garden: **usbg.gov**
National Arboretum: **usna.usda.gov**
National Museum of Women in the Arts: **nmwa.org**
U.S. Holocaust Museum: **ushmm.org**

General Travel Info

DC Metro - Metrorail (subway) & Metrobus: **wmata.com**
Amtrak for DC & Union Station: **amtrak.com/stations/was**
MARC Train: **mta.maryland.gov**
Capital Bikeshare: **capitalbikeshare.com**
Foot ferry/water taxi (Mar-Dec): **cityexperiences.com/washington-dc/city-cruises/water-taxi/washington-dc-water-taxi**
Destination DC: **washington.org**

Search online for guided tours on foot or by bike, Segway, amphibious "Duck," or hop-on/hop-off bus—all great ways to get introduced to the city.

Hiking & Volunteer Groups

Appalachian Trail Conservancy: **appalachiantrail.org**
Potomac Appalachian Trail Club: **patc.net**
Sierra Club/DC & Potomac Region: **dc.sierraclub.org**
Capital Hiking Club: **capitalhikingclub.org**
Wanderbirds Hiking Club: **wanderbirds.org**
American Volkssport Association: **ava.org**
Rock Creek Conservancy: **rockcreekconservancy.org**
Tregaron Conservancy: **tregaron.org**
Washington Area Bicyclist Association: **waba.org**
Rails to Trails Conservancy: **railstotrails.org/state/dc**

Many park agencies & conservation groups also support volunteer programs

Miscellaneous

DC Statehood; **dcvote.org**, **statehood.dc.gov**, **lwvdc.org/statehood**,
NPS Cherry Blossoms/Bloom Watch: **nps.gov/cherry**
Kennedy Center & Millennium Stage: **kennedy-center.org**
Bureau of Engraving & Printing: **bep.gov**
Historical Society of Washington, D.C.: **dchistory.org**
Cultural Tourism DC & Neighborhood Heritage Trails: **eventsdc.com/dc-neighborhood-heritage-trails**
DC Metropolitan Police: **mpdc.dc.gov** - Emergencies: **call 911**
Trust for the National Mall: **nationalmall.org**
National Mall Coalition: **www.nationalmallcoalition.org**
Mount Vernon Estate: **mountvernon.org**
George Washington Masonic National Memorial: **gwmemorial.org**
Foreign Embassies: **washington.org/visit-dc/international-embassies-in-washington-dc**
Ford's Theater: **fords.org**
Torpedo Factory (Alexandria): **torpedofactory.org**

D.C. Bucket List

Ultimate DC Encounters all of the following sites around the National Mall and National Nearby, more or less in the order listed on these two pages, followed by sites visited on other walks. To keep track of your progress, check the boxes as you visit each site or complete each walk or hike.

National Mall

- ☐ U.S. Navy Memorial
- ☐ Naval Heritage Center
- ☐ National Archives
- ☐ FBI Building
- ☐ Old Post Office
- ☐ Federal Triangle
- ☐ Environmental Protection Agency
- ☐ Woodrow Wilson Plaza
- ☐ Freedom Plaza
- ☐ General Pulaski Monument
- ☐ WWI Memorial
- ☐ General Pershing statue
- ☐ Bald Eagle Memorial
- ☐ White House Visitor Center
- ☐ William T. Sherman Monument
- ☐ U.S. Treasury
- ☐ Alexander Hamilton statue
- ☐ The Extra Mile
- ☐ Marquis de Lafayette statue
- ☐ White House–North Portico
- ☐ Lafayette Square
- ☐ President Andrew Jackson Memorial
- ☐ St. John's Episcopal Church
- ☐ General Von Steuben statue
- ☐ Decatur House
- ☐ General Jean de Rochambeau statue
- ☐ Blair House
- ☐ Renwick Gallery
- ☐ Eisenhower Executive Office Bldg
- ☐ Corcoran School of the Arts
- ☐ First Division Monument
- ☐ President's Park
- ☐ White House–South Lawn
- ☐ National Christmas Tree
- ☐ Zero Milestone
- ☐ The Ellipse
- ☐ Ellipse Visitor Pavilion
- ☐ Boy Scout Memorial
- ☐ Enid Haupt Fountains
- ☐ German-American Friendship Garden
- ☐ Washington Monument
- ☐ Enid A. Haupt Garden
- ☐ Smithsonian Castle
- ☐ Smithsonian Arts & Industries Bldg
- ☐ Voyage Model Solar System
- ☐ Smithsonian Carousel
- ☐ Mary Livingston Ripley Garden
- ☐ Hirshhorn Museum
- ☐ Hirshhorn Sculpture Garden
- ☐ National Air & Space Museum
- ☐ Phoebe Waterman Haas Public Observatory
- ☐ Dwight D. Eisenhower Memorial
- ☐ National Museum of American Indian
- ☐ Capitol Reflecting Pool
- ☐ Mid-Atlantic Regional Garden
- ☐ U.S. Botanic Garden & Conservatory
- ☐ Bartholdi Park & Fountain
- ☐ James Garfield Memorial
- ☐ Ulysses S. Grant Memorial
- ☐ Peace Monument
- ☐ Summerhouse
- ☐ U.S. Capitol–West Lawn & West Steps

- ☐ U.S. Capitol–East Plaza
- ☐ Capitol Visitor Center
- ☐ U.S. Supreme Court
- ☐ Court of Neptune Fountain
- ☐ Library of Congress
- ☐ Folger Shakespeare Theatre & Library
- ☐ Belmont-Paul Women's Equality National Monument
- ☐ VFW
- ☐ Stanton Park
- ☐ General Nathanael Greene statue
- ☐ Federal Judicial Center
- ☐ Union Station
- ☐ Postal Museum
- ☐ National Guard Memorial Museum
- ☐ Holodomor Memorial
- ☐ Freedom Bell
- ☐ Christopher Columbus Fountain
- ☐ Senate Park & Fountain
- ☐ Japanese-American Memorial
- ☐ Robert A. Taft Memorial & Carillon
- ☐ U.S Department of Labor
- ☐ William Blackstone Statue
- ☐ General George Meade Monument
- ☐ John Marshall Park
- ☐ Canadian Embassy
- ☐ Andrew W. Mellon Memorial Fountain
- ☐ Federal Trade Commission
- ☐ National Gallery of Art East
- ☐ National Gallery of Art West
- ☐ Sculpture Garden & Ice Rink
- ☐ Smithsonian Museum of Natural History
- ☐ Grand Army of the Republic Memorial
- ☐ Temperance Fountain
- ☐ General Winfield Scott Hancock Memorial
- ☐ Sylvan Theater
- ☐ Museum of African American History & Culture
- ☐ Museum of American History
- ☐ Tidal Basin
- ☐ Bureau of Engraving & Printing
- ☐ U.S. Holocaust Museum
- ☐ Survey Lodge
- ☐ Floral Library
- ☐ Thomas Jefferson Memorial
- ☐ George Mason Memorial
- ☐ West Potomac Park
- ☐ Franklin Delano Roosevelt Memorial
- ☐ Martin Luther King, Jr. Memorial
- ☐ Ash Woods
- ☐ District of Columbia War Memorial
- ☐ U.S. Park Police Horse Stables
- ☐ Korean War Veterans Memorial
- ☐ John Ericsson Memorial
- ☐ Lincoln Memorial & Reflecting Pool
- ☐ Vietnam Veterans Memorial
- ☐ Vietnam Women's Memorial
- ☐ Constitution Gardens
- ☐ Memorial to the Signers of the Declaration of Independence
- ☐ WWII Memorial
- ☐ John Paul Jones Memorial
- ☐ U.S. Department of Agriculture
- ☐ Freer Gallery of Art
- ☐ S. Dillon Ripley Center
- ☐ Arthur M. Sackler Gallery
- ☐ Second Division Memorial
- ☐ Lockkeeper's House
- ☐ Organization of American States
- ☐ Daughters of American Revolution
- ☐ American Red Cross
- ☐ Amerigo Vespucci sculpture
- ☐ U.S. Department of Interior Museum
- ☐ Art Museum of the Americas
- ☐ Simón Bolívar Monument
- ☐ José Artigas statue
- ☐ Memorial Bridge

National Nearby

- ☐ Arlington National Cemetery
- ☐ Theodore Roosevelt Memorial
- ☐ Key Bridge
- ☐ Francis Scott Key Park
- ☐ Old Stone House
- ☐ C&O Canal & Towpath
- ☐ Justice William O. Douglas bust
- ☐ Georgetown Waterfront Park
- ☐ Kennedy Center
- ☐ Peter's Point
- ☐ Car Barn
- ☐ Exorcist Stairs
- ☐ Georgetown University
- ☐ Volta Laboratory
- ☐ Volta Park
- ☐ Book Hill
- ☐ Georgetown Library
- ☐ Duke Ellington School of the Arts
- ☐ Dumbarton Oaks Park
- ☐ Montrose Park
- ☐ Dumbarton Oaks Garden & Museum
- ☐ Oak Hill Cemetery
- ☐ Evermay
- ☐ Dumbarton House
- ☐ Rose Park
- ☐ Dupont Circle
- ☐ Gandhi statue
- ☐ Anderson House
- ☐ Cosmos Club
- ☐ General Philip Sheridan Memorial
- ☐ Dumbarton Bridge
- ☐ Winston Churchill statue
- ☐ Nelson Mandela statue
- ☐ Woodrow Wilson House
- ☐ Mitchell Park
- ☐ Spanish Steps
- ☐ Phillips Collection Gallery
- ☐ Duke Ellington Memorial Bridge
- ☐ National Zoo & Olmsted Walk
- ☐ Peirce Mill
- ☐ Boulder Bridge
- ☐ Rock Creek Nature Center
- ☐ Miller Cabin
- ☐ Milkhouse Ford
- ☐ Fort DeRussy
- ☐ Rabaut Park
- ☐ Meridian Hill/Malcolm X Park
- ☐ Joan of Arc statue
- ☐ Dante statue
- ☐ James Buchanan statue
- ☐ African American Civil War Memorial & Museum
- ☐ House of the Temple
- ☐ Friendship Archway
- ☐ Mount Vernon Square
- ☐ Carnegie Library
- ☐ Kiplinger Gallery
- ☐ Samuel Gompers Memorial Park
- ☐ Mary McLeod Bethune Museum
- ☐ General George Henry Thomas statue
- ☐ Samuel Hahnemann Monument
- ☐ General Winfield Scott Memorial
- ☐ Daniel Webster statue
- ☐ John Witherspoon statue
- ☐ Abraham Lincoln Statue
- ☐ Darlington Memorial
- ☐ National Law Enforcement Officers Memorial & Museum
- ☐ National Building Museum
- ☐ German-American Heritage Museum
- ☐ Pepco Edison Place Gallery
- ☐ Smithsonian American Art Museum & National Portrait Gallery
- ☐ Martin Luther King, Jr. Memorial Library
- ☐ St. Patrick's Church
- ☐ Ford's Theater
- ☐ Petersen House

- ☐ Seward Square
- ☐ Marion Park
- ☐ John Phillip Sousa home
- ☐ Marine Barracks
- ☐ Barracks Row
- ☐ Market Park
- ☐ Eastern Market
- ☐ Abraham Lincoln Emancipation Memorial
- ☐ Mary McLeod Bethune Memorial
- ☐ Yards Park
- ☐ National Museum of the U.S. Navy
- ☐ Nationals Park
- ☐ Fort McNair
- ☐ Titanic Memorial
- ☐ Wharf/Southwest Waterfront
- ☐ Maine Avenue Fish Market
- ☐ Kenilworth Aquatic Gardens
- ☐ Bladensburg Waterfront Park
- ☐ Windy Run Falls
- ☐ Thrifton Hills Park
- ☐ Potomac Overlook Park/Nature Center
- ☐ Gulf Branch Park/Nature Center
- ☐ Chain Bridge
- ☐ Fort Marcy
- ☐ The Ellipse (Ballston)
- ☐ Welburn Square
- ☐ Bluemont Park
- ☐ Glencarlyn Park
- ☐ Lubber Run Amphitheater
- ☐ John Carlyle Square (Alexandria)
- ☐ U.S. Patent & Trade Office
- ☐ National Inventors Hall of Fame
- ☐ African American Heritage Park
- ☐ Alexandria National Cemetery
- ☐ Shiloh Baptist Church
- ☐ Freedom House Museum
- ☐ Friendship Firehouse
- ☐ King Street
- ☐ Washington Masonic Memorial
- ☐ D.C. boundary markers
- ☐ Torpedo Factory
- ☐ Alexandria Seaport Foundation
- ☐ Founders Park
- ☐ Carlyle House & Garden
- ☐ Wise Tavern
- ☐ Alexandria City Hall
- ☐ Gadsby's Tavern
- ☐ Market Square
- ☐ Ramsay House
- ☐ Stabler-Leadbeater Apothecary Museum
- ☐ Lyceum & Alexandria History Museum
- ☐ Athenaeum
- ☐ Captains Row
- ☐ Waterfront Park
- ☐ Lady Bird Johnson Park
- ☐ Merchant Marine Memorial
- ☐ Lyndon Johnson Memorial
- ☐ Gravelly Point Park
- ☐ Abingdon Plantation
- ☐ Dangerfield Island
- ☐ Tidelock Park
- ☐ Rivergate Park
- ☐ Orinoco Bay Park
- ☐ Shipyard Park
- ☐ Fords Landing
- ☐ Jones Point Park & Lighthouse
- ☐ Woodrow Wilson Bridge
- ☐ Belle Haven Marina
- ☐ Dyke Marsh
- ☐ U.S. Marines/Iwo Jima Memorial
- ☐ 9/11 Pentagon Memorial
- ☐ Air Force Memorial
- ☐ National Arbortetum
- ☐ Cedar Hill
- ☐ Anacostia Community Museum
- ☐ National Cathedral & Bishops Garden
- ☐ Basilica of Immaculate Conception

Index

About the Author

When he's not kicking up dust in the mountains or visiting a national park, or some hidden gem or quaint little town somewhere, Ken Wilcox loves hoofing it up the trail or up the street. This guide is a result of many hundreds of miles of traipsing around Washington D.C. and the greater metro area, collecting notes and photos over several years.

Ken has worked as an outdoor recreation planner in Washington, D.C. and in the Pacific Northwest, with a specialty in trail planning and design. He is also an experienced tour guide and the author of four guidebooks to trails in Washington State, and a new memoir of mountain adventures across North America titled *Boots on Fire* (2026). Since 2011, Ken and his wife Kris have enjoyed dipping their toes in both oceans (and both Washingtons) and hope to keep it up for some time to come.

www.ingramcontent.com/pod-product-compliance
Ingram Content Group UK Ltd.
Pitfield, Milton Keynes, MK11 3LW, UK
UKHW062257290726
14090UKWH00017B/735